THE NATION
OR THE UMMAH

THE NATION OR THE UMMAH

ISLAMISM AND TURKISH FOREIGN POLICY

BIROL BAŞKAN AND
ÖMER TAŞPINAR

SUNY
PRESS

Published by State University of New York Press, Albany

Printed in the United States of America

For information, contact State University of New York Press, Albany, NY
www.sunypress.edu

Library of Congress Cataloging-in-Publication Data

Names: Başkan, Birol, author | Taşpınar, Ömer, author.
Title: The nation or the Ummah / by Birol Başkan and Ömer Taşpınar.
Description: Albany : State University of New York Press, [2021] | Includes
   bibliographical references and index.
Identifiers: ISBN 9781438486475 (hardcover : alk. paper) | ISBN 9781438486499
   (ebook) | ISBN 9781438486482 (pbk. : alk. paper)
Further information is available at the Library of Congress.

10 9 8 7 6 5 4 3 2 1

to our moms,

Nezaket Başkan and Nuran Taşpınar

CONTENTS

ACKNOWLEDGMENTS

Books are sometimes born in coffee houses. The idea of undertaking a collaborative project was born in numerous conversations we had at Saxbys Georgetown in the fall of 2019. The topic just came out naturally as we tried to understand how we, citizens of Turkey, reached a deep sense of malaise in both domestic and foreign affairs. Our conversations often reached the same conclusion: the Arab Spring repeatedly appeared as a truly watershed event, a real turning point not just for the Middle East but also for Turkey. And not just for Turkish foreign policy but also for the domestic predicament. This is how we embarked on the intellectual journey ending with this book. In many ways, more than a book, this was also a quest to understand our own fate.

From the beginning to the end we were fortunate to have the moral and intellectual support of Feyza Gümüşlüoğlu and Gönül Tol, without whom this book would not come to fruition. We were also fortunate to receive academic and intellectual support from a number of friends and colleagues. We would like to cite in particular Adam Oler, Afyare Elmi, Burak Bilgehan Özpek, Bülent Aras, Cengiz Çandar, Doğan Gürpınar, Gencer Özcan, Karim Sadjadpour, Mark Farha, Paul Salem, Philip Gordon, Suat Kınıklıoğlu, Yaşar Yakış, and Yusuf el Şerif.

We thank Uluslararası İlişkiler dergisi and Routledge Taylor and Francis Group for allowing us to reprint certain parts of our earlier publications: Birol Başkan, "Turkey between Qatar and Saudi Arabia: Changing Regional and Bilateral Relations," *Uluslararası İlişkiler* 16, no. 62 (2019): 85–99; Birol Başkan, "Islamism and Turkey's Foreign Policy during the Arab Spring," in *Islamism, Populism and Turkish Foreign Policy*, ed. Burak Bilgehan Özpek and Bill Park (New York: Routledge, 2019); Ömer Taşpınar, *Kurdish Nationalism and Political Islam in Turkey: Kemalist Identity in Transition* (New York: Routledge, 2005).

And finally, we are grateful to Michael Rinella, his editorial team, and two anonymous reviewers at State University of New York Press for their interest, encouragement, suggestions, and criticisms.

INTRODUCTION

"I want to give a very sincere advice, a very genuine warning to Egypt's President Mr. Hosni Mubarak; . . . listen to the people's callings and their most humane demands. Respond without any hesitation to the desire of change coming from the people . . . Freedoms cannot be delayed and ignored in today's world."

—Recep Tayyip Erdoğan, Turkey's Then
Prime Minister, February 1, 2011

Turkey enthusiastically welcomed the Arab Spring[1] even though this watershed event targeted those very regimes with which it had built cordial relations. Ankara eagerly developed strong relations with the post–Arab Spring regimes that came to power in Tunisia, Egypt, and Libya, helping them diplomatically, financially, and even in the latter case militarily so that they could stay in power. Turkey's support to the anti-regime forces in Syria went beyond mere diplomacy and came to include logistics, finance, and weapons.

Turkey paid a heavy price for its stance. A military coup in Egypt overthrew the new regime Ankara had diplomatically and economically supported. Under the leadership of Recep Tayyip Erdoğan, the Turkish government reacted so harshly to the coup that a total collapse in its diplomatic relations with this most populous Arab country became inevitable. And by supporting the anti-regime forces in Syria, Turkey directly contributed to this country's plunge into a bloody civil war and as a result came to bear the brunt of the ensuing massive refuge crisis.

This warm embrace of the Arab Spring clearly put at risk Ankara's interests with the pro–status quo powers of the region, namely Saudi

Arabia and the United Arab Emirates, the two Arab countries that had always been Turkey's largest trading partners in the Middle East. Turkey's actions and reactions during the Arab Spring eventually led to its isolation and badly tarnished its image in the region.[2]

Why did Turkey embrace the Arab Spring with such hubris? This book seeks to explain the logic behind Turkish foreign policy during and after the Arab Spring to shed light on what constituted a sea change in Ankara's traditional approach toward the region. In an attempt to see the connections between domestic political change and foreign policy reformulation, the study closely examines how Turkey's internal evolution under the ruling Adalet ve Kalkınma Partisi (Justice and Development Party—the JDP) impacted its strategic logic during this tumultuous era. The core assertion of our study is that Islamism as both ideology and vision goes a long way in explaining the prism through which the JDP approached the Arab Spring and implemented its strategy. As the analysis will illustrate, such an ideological approach constitutes a sharp departure from the conventional foreign policy ideology of Turkey known as Kemalism—named after the founding father of the republic Mustafa Kemal Atatürk.

This rather radical shift from Kemalism to Islamism has not been sudden. It took almost a decade for the JDP to consolidate its political power at home. Only after he subdued political resistance and monopolized decision making, the country's hegemonic leader, then Prime Minister, now President Erdoğan, ventured into an Islamist direction in his foreign policy.[3] Even then, it remains questionable if such a turn would have been feasible without exceptionally tempting regional opportunities, such as the collapse of the deeply entrenched political autocratic systems in Tunisia, Egypt and Libya. In that sense, the domestic political context of Turkey and the regional context of the Middle East had to serendipitously converge for an Islamist foreign policy to emerge.

When the regional upheaval began, JDP's reemerging Islamist ideology quickly adopted a theory that saw what was happening in the region in line with its assumptions, ideals, vision, and expectations.[4] According to this ideological interpretation, the Arab Spring was a unique historic opportunity that was sweeping away the culturally alienated ruling establishments in the Arab world and bringing to power the "true voice" of the people, the Islamists. Acting on such an ideological interpretation of the events, foreign policy makers in Ankara welcomed the Arab Spring with the calculation that Turkey could better work with the new post-

Arab Spring regimes in the Middle East and thus improve its own sphere influence in the region and standing in the world.

For about two and half years—from late 2010 when the first signs of unrest emerged until the summer of 2013, when the military coup in Egypt toppled the Muslim Brotherhood government—the Arab Spring provided great hope and expectations to Turkey's Islamist decision makers. In such a regional context foreign policy makers in Ankara needed to make strategic sense of what was unfolding in region. Islamism provided the most convenient explanatory prism. It could simply be not a coincidence that just when Turkey was getting rid of its secularist shackles and returning to a sense of "Muslim greatness" the Arab Spring was also toppling deeply rooted secularist autocrats. In the eyes of the JDP special providence was at play. The time was finally ripe both at home and in the region for the peaceful and democratic rise of Islam. The Kemalists within the Turkish Ministry of Foreign Affairs or in the Turkish General Staff no longer had the power, the political will, and the strategic vision to resist what seemed like divine justice.

This is not to suggest, however, that Islamism single handedly determined every twist and turn of Turkish foreign policy during the Arab Spring. Pragmatism, mercantilism, and opportunism were never fully out the door. For instance, while Turkey very quickly called on the leader of Egypt to step down, it decided to wait for months before doing the same with the leader of Syria. Similarly, because of financial interests with the Qaddafi regime, Ankara opposed military intervention in Libya, but later changed its position when it saw the tide turning and Western powers mobilizing. In Syria, after burning bridges with the Assad regime and mobilizing the opposition against Damascus, Ankara itself began to call for a Western military intervention. The JDP's selectivity became even more obvious in Yemen and Bahrain, where it left the direction of developments in the hands of the Gulf States while elsewhere it saw its historical responsibility to become involved. Turkey's Islamism during this era was never fully divorced from geopolitical considerations and economic interests.

In short, this book claims and illustrates the influential role ideology played in shaping the general direction of Turkey's foreign policy during the Arab Spring. Yet, given the role of pragmatic considerations in driving some specific actions and reactions, our discussion also recognizes that Islamism never provided an all-encompassing "road map" for Turkey's actions during this period. In many ways, Islamism, especially in the Turkish case, is what can be called a "thin" ideology, which provides broad objectives without a detailed course of action or blueprint. And even these broad objectives are subject to interpretation and evaluation.

Ideology is an often overlooked factor in scholarly analyses of foreign policy and international politics. This is not without good reason. The concept ideology is highly elusive, often confused with others, hotly contested, and often employed pejoratively. As David McLellan declares, ideology might indeed be "the most elusive concept in the whole of social science."[5] To elaborate on the book's argument, therefore, it might be useful to clarify the concept first and then discuss what major international relations theories say about it.

Ideology and International Relations Theories

Ideology is at its core a set of ideas and beliefs, some of which are unconsciously held, more often than not unquestioned, and passionately defended to be true.[6] Beyond this core, ideology consists of derivative ideas and beliefs, which fall in two broad categories: one category consists of political, economic, social, or cultural policy recommendations. The other is an interpretive framework, which enables ideology's adherents to make sense of historical and contemporary events and actors.

Ideologies should be viewed as competing traditions of thinking. They are not products of single individuals, but rather constructed and reconstructed over a long period of time with contributions from many different individuals sharing the same core ideas and beliefs and upholding the similar derivative ideas and beliefs. It is because they are traditions ideologies have their own existence independently of political individuals, groups, movements, or parties. As such, they are part of the structure within which the agency makes choices. It is often the case that ideologies are not overly descriptive. They set forth ideals, but do not specify in detail method(s) or mechanism(s) to realize them. Hence ideology's adherents are left free to pick the best method(s) or mechanism(s) to pursue their desired ideals. If it helps the ultimate ideals, ideology can even condone and encourage the pursuit of a strategy that will facilitate acquisition of more power and wealth. However paradoxical it might seem, ideology's adherents can therefore be pragmatic and realistic as well. All in all, it might prove elusive to see ideology at work and study it as a cause.

Not only this elusiveness of both defining the term ideology and proving its existence, but also the term's heavily negative connotations affected its treatment in the field of international relations. The term in fact has a rather long history. It was in the aftermath of the French Revolution that Antoine Destutt de Tracy coined the concept ideology in reference to a new science—the science of ideas. This new science, de Tracy envisioned, was to investigate the sensual origins of ideas. Yet the project failed to evolve into a separate science, as it happened in the case of sociology or psychology. Instead, soon after its conceptualization, ideology acquired a very pejorative connotation, thanks to Napoleon Bonaparte.[7] This negative perception of ideology has continued unabated until modern times, at the intellectual, popular, and academic levels.

Alvin W. Gouldner vividly captures the state of scholarship by the 1970s: "in the ordinary language of everyday life, as in the extraordinary language of sociology (be it academic sociology or Marxist), 'ideology' is stigmatized as a pathological object. It is seen as irrational cognition; as defective discourse; as false consciousness; as bad sociology."[8] Ideology serves such functions, or better "dysfunctions," Gouldner argues, "that might just as well be realized by numerous other 'adaptive' responses to 'cultural strain': alcoholism, psychosomatic symptoms, and nail-chewing . . . as cognition." Gouldner goes on to add, "ideology is cast in the role of the force of darkness, the nonrational," and adds, "When speaking of ideology, sociology loses its hushed voice and opaque language; its technical language suddenly joins forces with blunt and lively common parlance. It characterizes ideology as the mind-inflaming realm of the doctrinaire, the dogmatic, the impassioned, the dehumanizing, the false, the irrational and, of course, the 'extremist' consciousness."[9]

Then newly developing, the discipline of international relations escaped from this unfolding conceptual mess simply by declaring ideology as unnecessary to its subject area. "International politics," declares Hans Morgenthau, "like all politics, is a struggle for power." Whatever statesmen ultimately hope to realize in international politics, Morgenthau holds, they have to pursue power first to realize them. "Power is," declares Morgenthau, "always the immediate aim."[10] This has always been the feature of international politics. "The struggle for power," Morgenthau states, "is universal in time and space and is an undeniable fact of experience . . . Throughout historical time, regardless of social, economic, and political conditions, states have met each other in contests for power."[11] Having defined states' first and foremost objective as the pursuit of power, realism holds that studying their ultimate objectives becomes unnecessary for the broader study of international politics or international relations.

If studying ideology is unnecessary for the doyen of the realist school of international relations, Hans Morgenthau, it becomes irrelevant for the founder of the neorealist school, Kenneth Waltz. As a matter of fact, for Kenneth Waltz, any subsystemic feature, be it economy, social, or ideology, will "lead to the infinite proliferation of variables" and thus unnecessarily complicate any study of world politics.[12] What really critically matters in international relations is the distribution of material capabilities or, more specifically, economic and military power, across the states. In the anarchic international state environment, "the pressures of competition," Waltz declares, "weigh more heavily than ideological preferences or internal political pressures."[13] Ideology, like any other substate feature for that matter, inescapably becomes subordinate to state interest. International movements, whether inspired by cosmopolitan liberalism in the mid-nineteenth century, international socialism in the early twentieth century, or international communism post-1917 Revolution, for example, were all, Waltz claims, "captured by individual nations, adherents of the creed were harnessed to the nation's interest, international programs were manipulated by national governments, and ideology became a prop to national policy."[14]

For the sake of clarification, neither Morgenthau nor Waltz explicitly suggests that ideology plays no role in driving states' foreign policies. Morgenthau acknowledges that ideology might inform states' ultimate objectives, for the realization of which, though, they will need power. Waltz, on the other hand, suggests that states might pay a heavy price in the survival of the fittest environment of international relations if they ideologically pursue their foreign policies.[15]

Three other prominent neorealists, Stephen Krasner, Stephen Walt, and John Mearsheimer, also argue that ideology might play a role in driving state foreign policies. Krasner, for example, argues that the United States pursued openly ideological objectives in waging a bloody war in Vietnam and paid a heavy price for that.[16] Walt, on the other hand, argues that states with similar ideologies are more likely to forge alliances.[17] In his later book, Walt argues that ideologies lead states into conflicts, especially in post-revolutionary contexts.[18] Mearsheimer likewise acknowledges especially nationalism's role in generating a number of interstate conflicts in the past as well as great powers' pursuit of their ideologies abroad.[19] Despite these acknowledgements, however, it is fair to say that the realist/

neorealist school treats ideology as a residual category and prioritizes power or economic interest or more materialistic factors. Ideology either plays no role or, if it does, a limited role under extraordinary circumstances.

Neorealism's rival, Neoliberalism, is no different. Neoliberalism argues that international institutions and norms alleviate the so-called security dilemma, which realism/neorealism claims states face in the anarchic international system, and promote interstate cooperation. When it comes to ideology, however, neoliberalism has many parallels with neorealism. Robert Keohane, the most prominent member of this school, argues that states pursue "wealth and power" and, he almost reluctantly adds, "perhaps other values as well."[20] Keohane even empties "ideology" out of an otherwise Marxist concept, hegemony, when he claims that hegemony is not "false consciousness."[21] Keohane argues that non-hegemonic states also pursue their self-interests when they abide by the hegemonic world order.[22]

Constructivism, the third major school in international relations, emerges as a critique of both realism/neorealism and neoliberalism on the grounds that they are overly materialistic and argues that ideational factors, such as norms, beliefs, culture, and ideology, are also critical in shaping state interests.[23] Yet ideology does not receive an exclusive treatment even in the hands of constructivists:[24] this is in large part because influential constructivists either adhere to systemic level of analysis and hence ignore state- or substate-level factors, including ideology,[25] or focus their attentions on other, more general categories of ideational factors, such as norms and culture.[26]

Foreign policy analysis, a subfield that distinguished itself from international relations in the late 1950s and early 1960s,[27] is much more open to ideology's role in international relations as it focuses on the actual processes of foreign policy decision-making. Such a focus necessitates taking into account factors that guide actual individuals or groups of individuals. These factors are multisourced internally as well as externally: "The mind of a foreign policymaker," declare Valerie M. Hudson and Benjamin S. Day, "is not a tabula rasa: it contains complex and intricately related information and patterns, such as beliefs, attitudes, values, experiences, emotions, traits, style, memory, and national and self-conceptions." Furthermore, Hudson and Day add, "Each decision maker's mind is a microcosm of the variety possible in a given society. Culture, history, geography, economics, political institutions, ideology, demographics, and innumerable other factors shape the societal context in which the decision maker operates."[28]

As Kenneth Waltz rightly predicts, foreign policy analysis uncovers a wide variety of factors from all levels of analysis that affect foreign policy making. Ideology is one of these factors and influences foreign policy making through multiple channels.[29] Scholarly analyses of Turkey's foreign policy illustrate these channels.[30] Ideology, for example, sets goals to be realized and principles to be adopted for foreign policy. According to Mustafa Aydın, Kemalism, the official state ideology since the foundation of the Republic, set three major goals and principles for governments: the first is the protection of complete independence of the Turkish nation-state; the second is the pursuit of a realistic and peaceful foreign policy; and the third is the attainment of a status on par with the most advanced (civilized) nations in world.[31] As Aydın also alludes, these goals and principles not only guide and inspire foreign policy makers, but also serve as parameters or red lines of foreign policy that governments should not or cannot cross over.[32]

For Kemalism, the most advanced and civilized nations in the world are from/in the West, and therefore the third goal/principle, for a number of studies, imposes a pro-Western orientation in foreign policy making. "The strong ideological orientation," Philip Robins claims, "contained an umbilical link between the Western value system of the Kemalist elite and the external orientation of the state." This orientation was best typified by Turkey's "Westpolitik," in other words, Turkey's membership in the North Atlantic Treaty Organization or NATO and its relations with the United States and its pursuit of membership in the EU [the European Union].[33] Bozdağlıoğlu also argues that it is because of Kemalist ideology that "Turkey, throughout its modern history, fully identified itself with the West, especially with Europe, and established close relations with the United States, while she maintained a very low profile in her relations with the Muslim Middle East, from which she derived much of her cultural heritage."[34]

Bozdağlıoğlu's study stands as an example of how the constructivist turn in international relations influenced scholarly analyses of Turkey's foreign policy: ideology is primarily treated as a marker or constituent of identity. A number of studies follows this line of inquiry. Hasan Kösebalaban, for example, distinguishes four ideology-identity groups in Turkey and attaches to each foreign policy positions. For example, secularist nationalists (Kemalists) oppose "integrationist policies that compromise national sovereignty" and "close relations with the Arab world and Islamic Republic of Iran"; Islamic nationalists support "close cooperative relations and integration with the Muslim world" and "competitive relations with Iran" and oppose "close relations with Israel"; secular liberals support "close cooperative relations and integration with the West (thus in favor of solving problems with Greece)" and are not enthusiastic about integration with the non-Western countries; finally, Islamic liberals support "close cooperative relations and integration with the West as well as with the Muslim world" and "competitive relations with Iran and Greece" and are not enthusiastic about "close relations with Israel."[35]

In this book we depart from the existing studies by describing in detail the content of ideology under consideration and seeking to pin it down as an explanation for an observed change in Turkey's foreign policy. First we delink the ideology-identity axis so frequently observed in constructivist studies. This is not to suggest that ideologies singly or in combination do not contribute to the formation of a particular identity. It is rather to argue that ideology should not strictly be equated with any specific, unidimensional, identity-related, or unrelated foreign policy as the existing studies tend to do. Ideology prescribes ultimate goals or ideals, say, the unity of all Muslims, but generally is not specific enough to list specific policies to realize those goals or ideals.

The existing studies tend to derive their ideology-identity categorizations from the policies pursued by actors while they are in power and therefore provide almost tautological explanations based on the assumption that there is a seamless connection between actual policies and ideological-identity configurations. As we explore, what is followed as policy may not always reflect ideological convictions. By the same token, ideological inclinations before coming to power are perhaps more important, because they reflect with more fidelity the ideals and aspirations without the limits imposed by what is politically feasible.

What is needed in a foreign policy analysis is a more detailed description of the content of the ideology under consideration.[36] As will be seen, ideology provides quite general political goals and ideals to be realized. It is equally critical and even more pertinent that ideology provide an interpretive framework with which its adherents interpret the world. Ideology-guided interpretive framework is what helps its adherents make sense of their environments, especially in times of high uncertainty. Ideology then influences foreign policy through two channels: first, by setting ideals and aspirations for realization; and second, by establishing a prism to interpret international/regional events.[37]

Our work is an attempt to focus more exclusively on ideology as an independent driver of policy.[38] This book claims that it is because of ideology that its adherents pursue a particular course of action or adopt a particular foreign policy. To prove this claim, the book shows the fit between the ideology under consideration, Islamism, and the particular course of action or foreign policy under consideration, embracing the Arab Spring. Furthermore, to add more persuasion to the argument, the book discusses what course of action or foreign policy adherents of an alternative, preferably opposing, ideology would follow. Fortunately, one ideology, Kemalism, has been hegemonic in driving foreign policy in our case, and thus the past gives us plenty of material to think counterfactually.

Sources, Transliteration, and Outline of the Book

Turkish foreign policy has attracted considerable scholarly attention. In Turkey itself is a vibrant community of international relations scholars and foreign policy analysts who have produced high-quality analyses in both English and Turkish.[39] This scholarly output is too voluminous to provide any fair review or even bibliography of it in the limited space available here.[40] For the most part, our narrative greatly benefits from this literature. Citations provided throughout the book, however, are in no way exhaustive of all available studies in English and Turkish.

We focus in this book mostly on recent developments in Turkish foreign policy. The pre–Arab Spring history of Turkey and Turkish foreign policy is well studied, and we do not claim any empirical or theoretical novelty in our analysis of that period.[41] The more recent post–Arab Spring history and Turkish foreign policy is less studied and thus constitutes the main concentration in our analysis.[42] In our narrative of events from 2010 to 2013, we rely on, in addition to print and online media, Siyaset, Ekonomi ve Toplum Araştırmaları Vakfı's, popularly known as SETA, yearbooks of Turkish foreign policy, which are detailed annual accounts of foreign policy actions Turkey had taken in the years under consideration.[43]

The literature on Turkish Islamism is growing, but not sizable in English. However, it is overly sociological in nature,[44] generally focusing on (Islamist) movement(s), not on (Islamist) ideas.[45] As we repeatedly stated, this book is more interested and hence focused on the content of Islamism than on the history of the movement(s) Islamism has generated. To construct the core ideal of Islamism and the interpretive framework Islamism has developed, we heavily relied on primary sources, journalistic pieces, and books penned by prominent Islamist figures. Citations are provided throughout our discussion on Islamism. But we would like to acknowledge that İslamcı Dergiler Projesi (Islamist Journals Project) of an Istanbul-based research center, İlmi Etüdler Derneği (Organization of Scientific Studies), runs a website that provides invaluable access to all critical Islamist magazines we needed.[46]

Modern Turkish has many words borrowed from Arabic and Persian. Furthermore, Turkey had used Arabic script before 1928 and adopted Latin in that year. In our transliterations we use the current Turkish orthography of all non-English words of Turkish or Arabic or Persian origin: hence, Necip, not Najeeb; Said, not Sa'id; Cemal, not Jamal.

We do not adhere to this method, however, when an Arabic or Persian or Turkish word has already become familiar in English: hence, Quran, not Kuran, Istanbul, not İstanbul.

The modern Turkish alphabet has some letters that either do not exist in English or are pronounced differently: for example, "a" is pronounced as "u" in "shut," c as "j" in Jack, ç as "ch" in church, "g" as "g" in game, ı as "e" in open, "j" as s in "leisure," "ö" as "u" in "turn," ş as "sh" in "shine," "ü" as "u" in cube, and finally ğ is not pronounced at all.

The book's narrative is laid out in four major chapters. Chapter 1 discusses the broad contours of Turkey's "traditional" foreign policy, the parameters of which were formed during the early decades of the Republic and had been preserved by its once all powerful military. This chapter serves to illustrate the Islamist departure of the JDP's foreign policy during the Arab Spring, suggesting that if Turkey had pursued its traditionally cautious foreign policy, it would not have reacted to the Arab Spring in the way it did. The reason behind Turkey's embracing of the Arab Spring should be sought in the ideology of the ruling party in Turkey, which happened to be Islamism. Yet the JDP could not pursue an Islamist foreign policy in the 2010s for the peculiar features of the domestic context within which the party came to power.

Chapter 2 discusses the domestic hurdles the JDP faced in the pre–Arab Spring period and argue that the domestic context the party faced tempered its Islamist orientations. The chapter takes a look at Turkish foreign policy in this period, describing it as "neo-Ottomanism," and discusses how neo-Ottomanism is different from Kemalism and Islamism yet still shares similarities with them in some other ways. By 2010, the JDP could pacify the powerful Kemalist forces in Turkey and had an almost free hand in steering Turkish foreign policy. As fate would have it, the Arab Spring erupted around the same time, providing an ideological foreign policy platform for the domestic Islamist turn in Turkey.

Chapter 3 first discusses how the JDP pacified the military, once the bastion of Kemalism in Turkey, and thus came to dominate Turkish politics. With its hands untied, the JDP now came to pursue an Islamist foreign policy, and the Arab Spring provided that opportunity. The chapter describes how Turkey reacted to the unfolding of the Arab Spring and by doing so put at risk its relations with the broader Arab world.

Chapter 4 constructs the Islamist interpretative framework. The chapter first details how Ahmet Davutoğlu, who is generally viewed as the chief architect of Turkey's foreign policy under the JDP well until the mid-2010s, interpreted the Arab Spring and argues that Davutoğlu's own interpretation heavily borrows from the historical Islamist interpretive framework. The chapter then traces Islamism's origin, discusses its core ideal that concerns international relations, and constructs the interpretive framework Islamism has developed from its origin in the late nineteenth century to the late twentieth century. We argue that without taking into account Islamism's core ideal and interpretive framework, it is hard to explain Turkey's enthusiastic embrace of the Arab Spring. Yet Islamism did not have its impact on Turkish foreign policy in the 2000s, for in that period the JDP still had to consolidate its hold on power in Turkey.

The book concludes by discussing a question that resurfaces from time to time: can Turkey serve as a model for the Arab World? We argue in short that the political, economic, and cultural elements that define the Turkish model are not easily "transferable" to the Arab world.

Chapter 1

TURKEY'S TRADITIONAL KEMALIST FOREIGN POLICY

Turkey's pursuit of an Islamist foreign policy during the Arab Spring came under very opportune domestic conditions. By 2011, after almost 8 years in power and having won a new election, Turkey's ruling Justice and Development Party (JDP) had consolidated power. Other powerful actors, such as the military and civilian bureaucracy with secularist leanings were marginalized and emasculated. Coming to that point required caution and patience. Between 2002 and 2010, the JDP had to carefully navigate around skeptical secularist legal institutions, suspicious of a secret Islamist agenda. Such distrust was often motivated by Kemalist instincts that defined the official ideology of the Republic. The departure from Kemalism became all the more obvious during the Arab Spring, as the JDP embarked on a journey that clearly challenged the "traditional" norms of Turkish foreign policy. To better understand this significant shift, it will be instructive to first understand what Kemalist foreign policy entailed. The secularist fundamentals of this Kemalist policy, formed under Mustafa Kemal Atatürk, can be traced back to the founding decades of the republic.

In addition to these formative decades of the Turkish republic, the 1990s also requires special focus. It was during this decade that Turkey's two critical identity problems, namely political Islam and Kurdish nationalism, forcefully reemerged and caused considerable tension in civil-military relations. In 1995, for the first time in modern Turkish history, an Islamist party managed to form a coalition government. The JDP's Islamist predecessor, Refah Partisi (The Welfare Party—the WP), had a rapid rise and abrupt fall before its extinction under Kemalist civilian and military duress.

It was also during the 1990s, often called a "lost decade," that Turkey's military confrontation with violent Kurdish nationalism reached a climax.[1]

Lessons learned from the trials and tribulations of this Islamist experiment between 1995 and 1997 loomed large in the minds of Recep Tayyip Erdoğan and Abdullah Gül when they formed the JDP in August 2001. They were quick to qualify themselves as "conservative democrats" in a discernible rejection of Islamism.[2] Such restraint lasted until the Arab Spring. By 2011, after its third electoral victory, the JDP was finally in full control of the state and confident enough to throw caution to the wind.

As fate would have it, the Arab Spring came at a time when Erdoğan was no longer confined by Kemalist norms of caution and prudence in foreign policy. The JDP had Islamist roots, but its foreign policy of "zero problems with neighbors" until the Arab Spring had echoes of Atatürk's famous, nationally memorized slogan: "peace at home, peace in the world."[3] Zero problems with neighbors, in that sense, was a pragmatic slogan both Kemalists and the JDP could embrace. It was void of any ideological presumption and had no Islamist inclination. With the premium it put on maintaining good relations with all regional actors, including Israel, Armenia, Greece, and Russia, "zero problem with neighbors" embraced realism and rationalism. Based on diplomatic and economic engagement with all countries in its neighborhood, it was a product of willful acceptance of the status quo. Today this first decade of JDP foreign policy is often remembered with nostalgia as an era of constructive engagement and prudence.[4]

As the JDP was finally able to throw caution to the wind, drastic developments in the region combined with a much stronger position at home enabled Erdoğan and his influential foreign minister, Ahmet Davutoğlu, to set sail toward Islamist waters. As a political party with roots in Turkey's own version of the Muslim Brotherhood, there was nothing more normal than the JDP's support of Muslim Brotherhood–oriented parties in the Arab world. In the eyes of the JDP, the Arab Spring was a journey from autocracy to democracy, and it echoed to some extent Turkey's own democratization from 2002 to 2011 under a moderately Islamist party. In what Erdoğan probably saw as divine justice, Turkey was now truly emerging as a model for the region.[5] Regional dynamics of democratization in the Middle East were now converging with Turkey's own political transformation under the JDP.

The divine part of such justice was that Islamist parties in the Middle East now had a real chance to become the vanguard of political change and were ready to assume power with democratic elections. For Erdoğan, this meant he could safely claim that his political support for the Muslim Brotherhood in Tunisia, Egypt, Libya, and Syria was support for democracy, not political Islam. Such dynamics offered plausible deniability and a legitimate cover against accusations that Turkey was pursuing an Islamist agenda. What should not be contested, however, is the fact that the JDP's activism stood in sharp contrast to conventional norms of a Kemalist foreign policy.[6]

Before we analyze the JDP's Islamic idealism during the Arab Spring, it is important to analyze how a Kemalist policy would have differed from the path followed during this turbulent time. Kemalist foreign policy probably would have opted for realism in lieu of idealism. Traditional Kemalist norms of Turkish foreign policy were status quo oriented with a sense of benign neglect for the Middle East. A deeper understanding of why Kemalist policies would reject the audacity displayed by Erdoğan and Davutoğlu's Islamism during and after the Arab Spring requires a clear understanding of what Kemalist strategic thinking stood for during most of Republican history vis à vis the Middle East.

As we will see shortly, prudence and caution were the trademarks of such policies that came to be challenged first by Turgut Özal in the 1990–1991 US-led Gulf War against Iraq. Yet Özal did not have a free hand in pursuing what even then was seen as an activist "neo-Ottoman" policy.[7] He had to contend with the powerful Kemalist national security establishment. His strategic vision of both Turkey and Turkish foreign policy triggered accusations of being soft on the Kurdish question. In a pattern that would become familiar during the 1990s, the Kurdish question, then aggravated by the emergence of the Partiya Karkeren Kurdistan (Workers of Kurdistan Party) or the PKK, in the previous decade, loomed large in the conceptualization of Kemalist prudence toward the region.

The interplay between identity and ideology was therefore highly evident in Kemalist policy making.[8] The military was particularly adamant in its rejection of any foreign policy adventure that would jeopardize Turkey's already vulnerable position on the Kurdish front.[9] In an interesting irony with the Özal era, when the JDP adopted an activist foreign policy in the Middle East, it was also pursuing a peace process with the PKK, an organization that had waged numerous terrorist attacks against both military and civilian populations across Turkey. Unlike during Özal's time, the Kemalist establishment was much weaker in the 2010s. Yet there was still no doubt that in the eyes of realist Kemalists and certainly the emasculated military, the peace process with Kurds was ill-advised. In their eyes, Kurdish separatism and terrorism remained an existential threat and the Achilles' heel of the republic. As a result, Ankara had to first mind its own business before venturing into the stormy waters of the Middle East.

In other words, an activist policy in the Arab world was dangerous because it transcended the nationalist, security-first Kemalist norms imposed by the Kurdish question.[10] Atatürk's slogan of "Peace at home and peace in the world" was in that sense emblematic of this mindset. Yet analyzing what Kemalism and its foreign policy vision stands for requires going beyond aspirational sloganeering. To illustrate the JDP's departure from Kemalist norm, one has to start with defining the Kemalist norm. In the Turkish context, this means first analyzing what Kemalism as a political project is about and proceeding with an assessment of what it envisions in foreign policy. These are the main questions we are turning to this next section.

The Domestic Context of Kemalism

Mustafa Kemal Atatürk was a military man who fought in the Trablusgarb (Libya) war (1911–1912), the Balkan wars (1912–1913), and the First World War (1914–1918). After the Ottoman Empire collapsed and its territories were divided among the Allied powers with a small piece of territory left for the Turks in Anatolia, he successfully led an independence war and cleared all foreign forces from what is now Turkey. Mustafa Kemal was also the main driver and force behind subsequent reforms, first and foremost abolishing the sultanate in 1922 and the caliphate in 1924 and founding the republic in 1923. The set of norms that came to symbolize the reforms undertaken in the 1920s and the 1930s can therefore be aptly named as Kemalism after Mustafa Kemal Atatürk, the founder and the first president of the republic.[11]

It should be noted from the outset, however, that defining Kemalism as an ideology is a problematic issue. There is little agreement among Kemalists themselves about what Kemalism exactly means as a contemporary political project. That Kemalism in the context of the 1930s represented a progressive political agenda based on establishing a secular Turkish nation-state is not contested. The modernization and westernization dimension of the original project, put forward by Mustafa Kemal himself, is also widely accepted.

What is more problematic, however, is what Kemalism represents in the Turkish political context of the twenty-first century. This difficulty in explaining what Kemalism truly stands for in the modern Turkish political context is understandable. In many ways, Kemalism is already a success story. Despite imperfections, modern Turkey is a secular nation-state and a notionally democratic republic. There is of course major room for improvement in terms of establishing a "liberal" democracy in Turkey. However, liberalism was never on the Kemalist political agenda, and it would be unfair to blame Kemalism for this. After all, liberalism was not on the global agenda of the 1930s. It is therefore possible to argue that Kemalism, as a secularist-nationalist political project aimed at nation building, modernization, and westernization, achieved, to a large degree, its goal. In modern Turkey, it is this very success of Kemalism that transformed it into a conservative ideology in the last few decades. Kemalism, in other words, displays an urge to protect what has been achieved. Especially for Turkey's once politically powerful military, which saw in itself the duty to protect the achievements of the republic, Kemalism represents a defensive political reaction against the "enemies" of the secular Turkish republic: Kurdish nationalism and political Islam.[12] More than a coherent ideology, Kemalism has therefore turned into a secularist and nationalist reflex.

In the 1920s and 1930s, the founding fathers of the Turkish republic had envisioned for Turkey a linear process of modernization at the end of which an ethnically homogenous and unambiguously secular state would emerge. Such linear progress naturally proved elusive. But what emerged in the 1990s proved particularly disturbing for Kemalists; both political Islam and Kurdish nationalism were on the rise after being relatively dormant during the Cold War. Facing the twin threats considered to be existential challenges to the republic Atatürk founded, the military marshaled its secularist and nationalist Kemalist reflex and once again engaged in political engineering to protect the foundational principles of the system. This Kemalist reflex in the 1990s proved highly detrimental for Turkish democracy. It not only exacerbated Kurdish dissent and criminalized Islamism after the soft coup of 1997 but also alienated Turkey from the West. At the Luxembourg Summit in December 1997, the European Union (EU) no longer referred to Turkey as a candidate for the enlargement process. A special strategy was to be adopted for Turkey instead of including it in the group of countries that would start accession negotiations. Ankara seemed increasingly isolated in the West because of its nationalist, autocratic, illiberal, and ultra-secularist predicament. A Kemalist sense of frustration and rupture with the West was imminent.

It is important to remember in this context that the Kemalist reaction to Kurdish dissent and political Islam goes back to the inception of the republic. During its formative decades, the strongest reaction to Kemalism's secularist nation building came in the form of Kurdish and Islamist rebellions. Between 1925 and 1938, a total of eighteen uprisings had to be forcefully suppressed in eastern provinces of Anatolia.[13] As a result, Kurdish nationalism and political Islam have been identified from the outset as "existential threats" to the Kemalist modernization project. These major rebellions traumatized the young republic's Kemalist leaders and created their suspicion of all things Kurdish and Islamic in the years to come. The power of religion was not a surprise for Atatürk's one-party regime. Having himself mobilized Anatolian masses with a call to Jihad during the war of independence (1919–22), Atatürk was a military commander who had firsthand experience with the galvanizing power of Islam as a rallying force.[14] He was determined to deny his opponents such an opportunity.

Despite the bold decision to end the caliphate—an institution that still had social and political meaning in the eyes of pious masses at home and in the Muslim world—the fledgling Kemalist republic developed a highly patriarchal understanding of secularism in remarkable continuity with the Ottoman tradition of state supremacy over religious affairs. Instead of separating religious affairs from politics, Turkish laicism incorporated the Islamic establishment in the state bureaucracy. This was designed to not only facilitate the administration of religion by the state but also to better control and shape the Islamic realm. More than a constitutional principal separating state and mosque, laicism in its Turkish context became a major instrument for social engineering in pursuit of westernization.[15] Control over the Islamic establishment was crucial because religion, in the wrong hands, could easily turn into a counterrevolutionary force against westernization. More fundamentally, the Kemalist revolution saw in Islam the causes of Ottoman social, cultural, political, and economic stagnation. In that sense, Islam was an impediment to modernization.

Another distinctive and highly problematic aspect of Kemalist secularism is the reluctance to maintain equal distance to all faiths. As a result, non-Muslim citizens of the modern secular Turkish republic face systemic discrimination. In fact, the secular republic's discrimination against its non-Muslim citizens in some cases went even deeper than under Ottoman times. While the Islamic empire had non-Muslim ambassadors, the secular Turkish republic decided to fire non-Muslims from the bureaucracy.[16] For instance, it is remarkable that to this day the secular Turkish republic does not have a single non-Muslim diplomat. In practice, Sunni Islam remains the religion of the Turkish republic despite the official façade of secularism. The incorporation of Sunni religious personnel into the state bureaucracy clearly shows that secularism in its Turkish context is about political control rather than legal separation.

The place where we see such control most visibly is in the public administration of religion in modern Turkey. The government-controlled Diyanet İşleri Başkanlığı (Directorate of Religious Affairs—DRA) super-vises and regulates Islam throughout the country. It appoints and pays the salaries of the country's imams and issues standardized sermons at the service of good citizenship and civic duties to be read out in thousands of mosques each Friday. With hundreds of offices (müftülük) at the prov-ince and sub-province levels, this governmental institution is in charge of administrating and supervising all religious institutions and services.[17]

The instrumentalization of religion was particularly apparent in textbooks used in the education of Islam. For instance, as early as in the late 1920s, a certain number of clerics were commissioned to compose new books of religious teaching adapted to the requests of the Kemalist authorities. The career of Ahmet Hamdi Akseki is clearly illustrative of this trend. A prolific author and president of the DRA, in the numerous pedagogical works he composed for the education of religion, Akseki pre-scribed the love of the fatherland, obedience to orders, zealous work, strict compliance with military rules, respect for the Turkish flag, submission to the laws and to the state requirements, sacrifice of one's life for the safety of the nation, and so on.[18] Other textbooks published during that period aired identical prescriptions: a Muslim truly worthy of that name had to love his country, pay his taxes regularly, respect the laws of the republic, submit to the progressive guidance of the state officials, do his utmost to learn modern techniques, apply scrupulously the principles of good hygiene, consult a doctor in case of illness to avoid being the cause of epidemics, and work energetically for the development of the country. In short, the main responsibility of a Muslim was to become a model citizen.

Such a conceptualization of secularism turned a reformed Islamic identity into a political weapon highly adaptable to what the state considered its main strategic objectives, ranging from citizenship building to fighting communism during the Cold War. Even the staunchly secularist Turkish military did not hesitate to use Islam after the 1980 military takeover to eradicate the leftist tendencies in Turkish society. In doing so, neither the political parties nor the military faced a secularist dilemma because the state had at its disposition the institutional apparatus of official Islam, with hundreds of religious high schools and thousands of mosques, imams, and schools that teach Quran, Islam's Holy Book.[19]

Once the Cold War started and Turkey joined NATO, the threat perception of the Kemalist military shifted from the Kurdish and Islamic challenge to the communist domestic and international threat. This was also reflected in the domestic dynamics as right-wing and left-wing ideological divides during the 1960s and 1970s polarized the country more than Kurdish and Islamic identity. Ideological politics shaped and preoccupied Kemalist instincts as long as the Cold War lasted. The fact that right-wing and left-wing rivalries rather than Kurdish and Islamist cleavages polarized the Turkish nation clearly reflected the fault lines of the international bipolar system. The ideological positions were delineated with considerable clarity and consistency: the left maintained a relative distance from the United States, while the right saw Washington as the indispensable ally in the national and global anticommunist struggle.

Even Kemalist generals showed signs of ideological division along center-right and center-left lines. The fact that Cyprus-centered problems with the United States often occurred under center-left governments associated with Kemalism—namely Cumhuriyetçi Halk Partisi (the Republican People's Party—the RPP)—contributed to an already existing Kemalist and nationalist suspicion of the West. Overall, however, the military apparatus remained by and large pro-American. As a NATO ally, sharing borders with the Soviet Union, the Turkish military bureaucracy had clear anticommunist proclivities. In the global diplomatic context of the Cold War, the state needed the United States' military and political support, especially if it hoped to deter the next-door Soviet Union and its dangerous ideology.[20]

It is important to note that while Cold War ideological polarization eclipsed Turkey's ethnic and religious identity problems, neither political Islam nor Kurdish nationalism fully disappeared. In reality, they were just overshadowed by right-wing and left-wing politics. Kurdish dissent found its place within the socialist left, while Islamic dissent became part of the anticommunist struggle. Once the Cold War ended, the context rapidly changed, and Kemalist Turkey once again found herself struggling to come to terms with political Islam and Kurdish nationalism.

By the 1990s, it was as if Turkey had suddenly returned to its formative decades of the 1920s and 1930s, during which Ankara faced Kurdish-Islamic rebellions challenging the secularist and nationalist precepts of Kemalism. Back in the 1930s, the fledgling Turkish republic had crushed the twin threats of Kurdish and Islamic dissent. Now, in the much different domestic and international context of the 1990s, the same Kemalist nationalist and secularist reflex appeared determined to follow a similar path of repression. Such Kemalist action, as we will see, led to disastrous results on the Kurdish front and had unintended consequences in the fight against political Islam. And not surprisingly, the renewed problems of Kurdish nationalism and Islamism had a strong impact on foreign policy.

Kemalist Foreign Policy

The most important issue that shaped the parameters of Kemalist foreign policy was the Kurdish question. The spatial distribution of Kurds, stretching across five states in the region, has had important implications for Turkish foreign policy.[21] Once again, the roots of the impact of the Kurdish question on Turkish foreign policy goes back to the foundational years. Immediately after the War of Independence and the proclamation of a Turkish republic, the domestic Kurdish challenge shaped the future of Kemalist strategies. In 1925, the Sheikh Said rebellion—the first in a series of Kurdish uprisings between 1925 and 1938—tempered the territorial ambitions of the fledgling republic and set a cautious tone in foreign policy. Prudence, caution, realism, and a security-first approach have therefore set the tone for the foreign policy associated with Atatürk in the 1930s and 1940s. The trauma created by these Kurdish rebellions played a critical role in shaping Kemalist foreign policy.

The Sheikh Said rebellion, which was eventually decisively suppressed, convinced the founding fathers not to pursue territorial claims over the oil-rich Mosul province that the British Foreign Office had decided would become part of modern Iraq under its mandated territories. In fact, the Turkish leaders were convinced that the Sheikh Said rebellion had been fomented by the British in an attempt to demonstrate the difficulties involved in ruling over a large Kurdish area and thus deter Kemalist Turkey from pursuing territorial claims over Mosul. There is little doubt that British officers supported anti-Ankara Kurdish tribes during the War of Independence (1919–1922). Moreover, the clauses of the 1920 Sèvres Treaty envisioned the creation of a Kurdish state in eastern Anatolia together with an Armenian one. Kemalist suspicion of British imperialism is thus understandable.

What is highly debatable, however, is whether the Kurdish rebellions of the 1920s and 1930s were all instigated by Britain. In analyzing Kemalist foreign policy and strategic thinking, it is critical to understand the instinctive distrust of the West as a legacy of the First World War.[22] It is important to remember the obvious fact that Turkish nationalism came of age fighting Western powers. Both during the Great War and the National Independence Struggle (1919–22), the enemies of Turkey were European countries—the UK, France, Italy, Greece—and to a lesser degree US President Woodrow Wilson and his self-determination principles siding with Greek, Armenian, and Kurdish ethnic demands. To this day, the role of the West in carving up Anatolia at the Sèvres treaty colors Kemalist suspicions of Europe and the United States. In the Kemalist imaginary, this resentment of the West stands in sharp contrast to the Russian military help received during the nationalist resistance led by Mustafa Kemal against imperialist powers. It is important to keep this benevolent image of Russian revolutionaries in mind in what later will evolve as a particularly anti-American and anti-EU brand of ultranationalism with Kemalist roots—the so-called "Eurasian" strategic alternative for Turkish foreign policy.[23]

Today, Western support for Kurdish nationalism is an ongoing bone of contention in Turkish foreign policy. This creates a very realist sense of insecurity and caution vis à vis the West most visible in the Kemalist belief that the fundamental imperative of the republic should be to focus on national and territorial integrity at home instead of embarking on regional foreign policy adventures in the name of lost grandeur and glory. The Kemalists also consider Kurdish dissent as a reaction to what is a non-negotiable achievement of the republic: the nation-state. Islamists, on the other hand, believe the Kemalist obsession with nationalism came at the expense of Islamic solidarity, which was a critical part of how the Ottoman Empire and Sultans like Abdülhamid II established networks of religious solidarity with Kurdish sheikhs and tribes. The corollary is that religious conservatives in Turkey believe there is an Islamic solution to the Kurdish question: rejection of ethnic, divisive, Turkish nationalism in favor of embracing the Muslim brotherhood of Ottoman times.[24]

As a result, while Islamists tend to blame Kemalism for the deterioration of Islamic harmony with Kurds, Kemalists have a stronger tendency to analyze the Kurdish problem as something instigated by external forces. Where the truth lies requires a balanced approach between these two views. It is important to note that no major evidence has emerged to show that British support is the main reason why Kurdish insurrections continued to the 1930s. Because the Foreign Office decided not to create a Kurdish state in its mandated territory in Iraq, supporting Kurdish nationalism became a counterproductive policy for Britain. The Sunni Kurds of Iraq provided the demographic counterbalance against the Shia Arabs for the stability of King Faisal's political regime.[25] The fact that Kurdish tribes in different parts of eastern Anatolia continued their rebellions against the Kemalist regime long after the resolution of the Mosul problem illustrates the importance of internal rather than external dynamics in analyzing these Kurdish rebellions. But these internal dynamics involved more than just the loss of Islamic solidarity. Other critical economic and political factors, such as the imposition of taxation and conscription over Kurdish lands that had no tradition of centralized state institutions, should also be taken into consideration.

At the end of the day it is important to note that the belief that British forces instigated the Kurdish uprisings in southeastern Anatolia continues to resonate in the nationalist psyche of Kemalism. And because religious conservatives are also prone to blame the West, the idea that imperialist forces are behind Kurdish nationalism and separatism became conventional wisdom in Turkey. Another crucial legacy regarding the interwar-era Kurdish rebellions was the perception that the territorial integrity and national unity of the new Turkish republic should never be taken for granted. This view was compounded by the vivid memory of Ottoman disintegration. Such concerns effectively marginalized pan-Turkic irredentism and Ottoman imperialism as utterly unrealistic and adventurist policies that were to play no role in the formation and formulation of Kemalist foreign policy. Under such circumstances, Ankara focused all of its political and military energy on the domestic project of nation building and westernization, and a cautious, sober tone came to characterize Kemalist foreign policy. There is no doubt that the Kurdish issue and its regional ramifications strongly contributed to such wariness.

Despite an attitude that can be best described as "benign neglect" toward the Middle East during the interwar era, one of the few occasions when Ankara decided to take a regional foreign policy initiative in the Middle East indirectly involved the Kurds. Although no specific mention of the Kurds was made, in the spirit of the 1937 Saadabad Pact, there was an understanding that Iran, Iraq, and Turkey would cooperate in suppressing any subversive movement associated with ethnic minority demands.[26] It is particularly telling that the Saadabad Pact was signed as Turkey was struggling to crush the Dersim rebellion, which was one of the strongest Kurdish insurrections of the 1925–1938 era. In that sense, one of the major objectives of the Saadabad Treaty was to regionalize the Kurdish question in the context of a diplomatic alliance.[27] Despite such regional cooperation among countries with important Kurdish minorities, Kurdish nationalism eventually found its full expression in Iran in the mid-1940s during the power vacuum in the immediate aftermath of Second World War.

To the dismay of Tehran, a Kurdish republic, which lasted only one year (1945–1946), was established in the province of Mahabad.[28] Although the establishment of the Mahabad republic was a Kurdish nationalist development that affected only the Kurds of Iran and Iraq, Ankara was undoubtedly relieved when the new Shah, Muhammad Reza, destroyed the Kurdish entity. In doing so, the central government in Tehran had effectively put an end to the internationalization of the Kurdish issue during the emerging years of the Cold War. Indeed, the Kurdish question was not to reappear on the international agenda for the next forty-five years.

During the first two decades of the Cold War, Turkey's general tendency of benign neglect toward Middle Eastern affairs was replaced by a stronger anticommunist and pro-Western tone. Especially after becoming a NATO member in 1952, Ankara increasingly identified its national interests with those of the West, and particularly the United States. Ironically, this absolute identification with Western perspectives and policies came under Adnan Menderes's Demokrat Parti (Democratic Party) administrations (1950–1960), whose historical mission had been to tame Turkey's radically secular westernization. In a period of political radicalism that swept the Arab world with the vocabulary of pan-Arab nationalism, Turkey zealously pursued a policy to defend Western interests without being sensitive in the least to the political aspirations of the Arab states. A series of policies, such as becoming the first Muslim state to recognize Israel, voting in favor of France at the United Nations during the Algerian war of independence, and allowing American marines to use the İncirlik air base in the Lebanese crisis of 1958, did almost irreparable damage to Turkey's relations with the Arab Middle East.

Relations with Syria were already marked by ill feelings arising from Turkish sovereignty over Alexandrette (Hatay) since 1939. As a result of the Lausanne Treaty in 1923 and the Franco-Turkish Agreement of 1921, Alexandrette had remained outside the borders of the new Turkish state. In 1936, France announced that it would grant independence to Syria and that it intended to include Alexandrette in the new Syrian state. After Turkish protest, Alexandretta became an "independent entity" in 1937 (represented by Syria in external affairs). By 1938, the international situation was so threatening that France wanted to secure Turkey's support against Germany and Italy at any price. In July 1938, elections held under Franco-Turkish military control produced a narrow Turkish majority in the Alexandrette parliament, which proclaimed the Independent Republic of Hatay. In 1939, to the great anger of Syrians, who even today depict the area as Syrian on their maps, the Hatay republic announced the union with Turkey.[29]

In addition to such tense relations with Syria, relations with Jamal Abdel Nasser's Egypt also were far from cordial. The first American attempt to construct a regional alliance in the Middle East was by bringing together Turkey and Egypt in 1951–52, but there was little enthusiasm for this option in either country because relations between Turkey and Arab countries were strained by Turkey's recognition of Israel. After 1952, as Turkey became the only NATO member in the Middle East, it began to approach the affairs of the region with a sense of moral and political superiority. In search of tightening the Western security chain around the Soviet Union, Ankara signed a treaty of cooperation with Pakistan in 1954. This was followed in 1955 by a treaty of cooperation and mutual assistance with Turkey's only friend in the Arab world, the Kingdom of Iraq under the prime ministry of Nuri al-Said.[30] Turkey actively participated in the creation of the ill-fated Baghdad Pact in 1955 by rather unselfconsciously proposing to the formal colonies of Britain to join an alliance with their colonial masters.

In 1955, Turkey told the Jordanian government that if Jordan did not join the Baghdad Pact (it never did), Turkey might find itself one day fighting on the side of Israel. This threat led to an irony: Washington and London had to warn the Turks against further alienating pro-Western Arab states. Even so, similar Turkish actions that provoked Arab ire included massing troops on the border with Syria in 1957, when the Communist Party there seemed poised to seize power, and calling for Western military intervention in Iraq to restore the monarchy after its overthrow in 1958. As Andrew Mango notes, the Baghdad Pact, which ended up including

Iran, Iraq, Pakistan, Turkey, and the UK, "was flawed from the very beginning since the United States, which had urged it, did not enter for fear
of irreversibly alienating Nasser's Egypt."[31]

Yet this identification with the West and the diplomatic distance
with the Arab Middle East slowly began to change starting with the
second half of the 1960s. This decade witnessed the emergence of the
Cyprus problem as a fundamental national security concern for Ankara.
Particularly in the eyes of Kemalist generals, Cyprus to this day remains
a primary marker of a nationalist redline over which the JDP's willingness
to compromise in 2004 created considerable consternation. It is telling that
a gradual change of heart in favor of rapprochement with the Arab world
came in the 1960s mainly because of strategic necessities on the Cyprus
front. In other words, only in return for support on the Cyprus front and
as a result of frustrations with the West was the Kemalist foreign policy
establishment—composed of the Turkish General Staff and the Turkish
Foreign Service—willing to reconsider its distance to the Muslim world.

Frustration with the West was essentially related to the first Cyprus
crisis of 1964 and the American reluctance to support Turkey. Such reluctance was clearly expressed by President Lyndon Johnson in a letter
warning that in case of a conflict with the Soviet Union resulting from
Turkish intervention on the island, NATO countries would not automat-
ically side with Ankara.[32] The letter was leaked to the press and triggered
strong anti-American feelings among large segments of Turkish society.
Most importantly, the letter traumatized the Kemalist foreign policy establishment. In effect, Turkish generals and diplomats came to realize that
their membership in NATO did not mean the unconditional application
of collective defense against the Soviet Union. As a result, the Johnson
letter convinced Ankara and especially left-wing segments within the
Kemalist ruling elite that the time had come for Turkey to become more
independent in the conduct of foreign affairs.

Turkey's short-lived flirtation with the Arab world came in this
regional context related to Cyprus. The new foreign policy aimed at grad-
ually moving toward a more pro-Palestinian position to generate support
for the Turkish position on the island. Turkey's shift was also partly due
to domestic political pressures, including the growing saliency of Islam
and religious nationalism in electoral politics. In addition to a more vocal anti-imperialist left, the religious right also made its voice heard in
this ideologically polarized domestic context. As a result, starting in the
late 1960s, Turkey went to great lengths to undo the damage inflicted on

Turkish-Arab relations in the 1950s. For instance, before the Six-Day War in 1967, Turkey sided with the Egyptian position and refused to join the group of maritime powers demanding the reopening of the Gulf of Aqaba to Israeli shipping. In its first major break with Kemalist principles in international relations, Turkey also participated in the proceedings of the Organization of the Islamic Conference (OIC) in Rabat in 1969 and became a full member of the organization in 1976. During the 1973 Israel-Arab war, Ankara denied the United States the use of American bases to help supply the Israelis and allowed Russian planes to use Turkish airspace to support the Syrians. Turkey's pro-Arab tilt continued in 1979 with the opening of the Palestinian Liberation Organization (PLO) representative's office in Ankara, which was given a quasi-diplomatic status.

Another important factor helping Turkish rapprochement with the Middle East was the 1973–74 oil crisis. Turkish governments endeavored to meet the rising oil bills from the Arab states and Iran by expanding Turkey's exports of goods and services to the region. Indeed, Turkey's exports to the region more than doubled from $2 billion in 1975 to $4.9 in 1980.[33] Trade volume with the Middle East continued to increase throughout the 1980s. The exploding volume of trade in the 1980s, during which the Middle East briefly surpassed Europe as Turkey's number-one trade partner, was essentially related to exceptionally high exports to Iraq and Iran, which were locked up in a disastrous war between 1980 and 1988. Yet, as mentioned above, the rapprochement with the Arab world proved short-lived. Despite improvements in diplomatic and trade relations, a series of other factors pushed Ankara to reconsider its Middle East policy during the second half of the 1980s.

An obvious source of discontent was the failure of the Arab countries and the PLO to support Turkey's Cyprus policy. Neither at the United Nations nor at the Organization of the Islamic Conference had the Arab world recognized the Turkish Cypriots' demand for self-determination. Indeed, many Arab states, as well as the PLO, enjoyed cordial relations with the Greek Cypriots and recognized the Greek Cypriot government as the only legitimate administration on the island. Another grievance was the Arab camp's attitude concerning Bulgaria's treatment of its Turkish minority. More than 300,000 ethnic Turks had fled to Turkey following the Zhivkov regime's forced assimilation campaign in 1986–87, leading Turkey to call for the international isolation of Bulgaria. Counting on the support of its Muslim neighbors and partners, Ankara prepared a draft resolution denouncing Sofia's behavior at the OIC summit of 1987. To the dismay of Ankara, Algeria, Syria, and the PLO refrained from supporting the resolution so as not to offend Bulgaria.[34]

In the meantime, Turkey's bilateral relations with Syria and Iraq began to deteriorate following the initiation of the ambitious Southeast Anatolia Project (GAP) in 1983. This ongoing project planned the irrigation of some 1.6 million hectares of land by using the waters of the Euphrates and the Tigris after the construction of twenty-one dams and nineteen hydroelectric stations. Not surprisingly, such prospects greatly increased Iraqi and Syrian concerns over the future volume and quality of the flow of water. Since 1983, both Damascus and Baghdad have been demanding a trilateral water-sharing treaty for the Euphrates and the Tigris. Ankara refused negotiations for a three-way water-sharing deal. Instead, it promised in the 1986 and 1987 bilateral accords with Syria to provide an average of 500 cubic meters per second on the Euphrates.[35] Unable to reach a compromise with Turkey on the water issue, Iraq and Syria signed a bilateral agreement concerning the Euphrates in April 1990 under which Syria would receive 42 percent and Iraq 58 percent of the flow arriving from Turkey.[36] The fact that Baghdad and Damascus were able to reach a consensus on the water issue despite their mutual enmity was perceived by Ankara as an all-Arab attempt to force Ankara to compromise.

The Kurdish Question and Islam in Kemalist Calculations after the 1980 Coup[37]

Starting in the second half of the 1980s, the Kurdish question reemerged as the most important factor complicating Turkey's bilateral relations with Syria and Iraq. Abdullah Öcalan, the leader of the PKK, took refuge in Syria shortly before the 1980 military takeover, a country that had control over the Bekaa Valley of Lebanon, where the PKK had training camps. Naturally, this situation exacerbated already tense relations with the Assad regime in Damascus. On the Iraqi front, it was Baghdad's own mercurial Kurdish policy in Northern Iraq that created many problems for Turkey. But once again it was the domestic dimension of the Kurdish question, with the heavy-handed repression of Kurdish activists by the military after the 1980 coup that turned the political and security dynamics in the Kurdish southeast of Turkey from bad to worse. In many ways, the military had decided to crush not only Kurdish dissent but also Kurdish ethnic identity itself.

The most important goal of the 1980 military takeover was to put an end to the ideological polarization and violence that terrorized Turkish society and had left more than 5,000 people dead and 20,000 injured between 1977 and 1980.[38] The National Security Council, which consisted of the chiefs of the Navy, Air Force, Army, and Gendarmerie, under the command of Chief of Staff Kenan Evren, took over the legislative functions of parliament, banned all political parties, and appointed a mixed civilian-military cabinet led by a retired general as prime minister.[39] Unlike the 1971 intervention, the 1980 military takeover was aimed at radically restructuring the political and legal framework of the country. This was to be done with a new constitution that would strengthen the executive power and presidential office at the expense of civil liberties. In that sense, the 1982 Constitution was drafted with an authoritarian mindset in reaction to the liberal-democratic and pluralist spirit that had characterized the 1961 Constitution.

After establishing martial law in September 1980, the army immediately resorted to a particularly brutal policy of repression in the Kurdish provinces to crush the common front of communist and nationalist activities.[40] Diyarbakır, the region's cultural and political center, became synonymous with death and torture. For instance, between September 1980 and November 1981, seventy-four detainees were unofficially acknowledged to have died in custody in the city's notorious military prison.[41] Not only activists and sympathizers, but also many villagers who had never been involved in political activities suffered greatly. Such political and military repression, coupled with cultural policies reminiscent of the 1930s, had the counterproductive effect of boosting Kurdish nationalism.[42] Therefore, a major consequence of military repression in southeastern Anatolia was the rise in the popularity of the PKK, whose leadership in Syria began to plan a counterinsurgency in eastern Anatolia.

As previously mentioned, a major goal of the military after the 1980 coup was to restructure the political system with a new constitution that would put an end to societal and ideological polarization in the country in order to restore national unity and central authority. This was a difficult task, especially after the 1960s and 1970s, which had come to be perceived as decades of debilitating ideological conflict. The top brass governed the country as a military junta for three years between 1980 and 1983—a first in terms of the time the army stayed in power since previous military interventions were shorter affairs.[43] Not surprisingly, the generals had a particularly dim view of communism. After all, Kurdish nationalists and politicized Alevi groups were closely allied with Marxist movements. Given the intellectual and organizational power of the left in academia and worker unions, the military coup leaders had a somewhat exaggerated perception of the socialist threat. Such concerns regarding the power of the Marxist-Leninist front were also validated by the state of international affairs in the late 1970s and early 1980s, a period remembered as the second Cold War with the Soviet invasion of Afghanistan.

At such a critical domestic and international juncture, Islam came to be seen as a convenient antidote against communism. This is why the Kemalist leadership of the 1980 coup did not hesitate to embrace the "Turkish-Islamic" synthesis in an attempt to use Islam to enhance national solidarity and to depoliticize the youth.[44] It was hoped that the Turkish-Islamic synthesis would generate a united national front against the ideological influence of the left and put an end to the ethnic, sectarian, and political differences that had polarized the country since the 1960s. Moreover, at a time when the army was engaged in fiercely suppressing the Kurdish provinces and leftist movements, state control over the religious establishment facilitated the co-optation of Islam in promoting a Kemalist sense of national solidarity.

Once again, the instrumentalization of religion was facilitated by the kind of secularism the Turkish republic had adopted since its inception. In other words, the control of the religious realm by the state, instead of a clear separation between state and religion, made the military's task much easier. For instance, despite their Kemalist rhetoric, the generals introduced compulsory religious lessons in primary and middle schools. Between 1980 and 1983, the number of Quranic courses rose sharply from 2,610 to 3,246.[45] The graduates of İmam-Hatip (Prayer Leader—Preacher) high schools gained the right to attend higher educational institutions. And, increasingly, higher numbers of İmam-Hatip school graduates came to be employed not only by the Directorate of Religious Affairs but also by the larger bureaucratic apparatus.[46]

General Kenan Evren, leader of the military government and president of the republic between 1982 and 1989, was particularly adept at using an Islamic rhetoric for secular purposes. His references to Islam and the Quran were used to support concepts such as literacy, positivism, and civilization. Such references highlighted his attempt to support the fundamental secular goals of the Kemalist regime. Evren easily justified the logic of introducing religious instruction into primary and secondary schools within the broader framework of Republican laicism. He argued that "Religious education cannot be given to children by every family. In fact, even if the family tried to do so, this would be improper since it may be taught wrongly, incompletely or through the family's own point of view. Secularism does not mean depriving Turkish citizens of religious instruction and exposing them to exploiters of religion."[47] The patriarchal, patronizing, and nationalist nature of Turkish secularism are clearly evident in such logic.

The first half of the 1980s marked a new stage in the interplay between state and religion in the framework of a relative "Islamization of secularism."[48] Accordingly, the Kemalist state's religious apparatus was supposed to disseminate "positivist" Islam. Article 136 of the 1982 Constitution turned the Directorate of Religious Affairs into a constitutional institution. This article set the goal of the Directorate as the "promotion and consolidation of national solidarity and unity." Article 24 of the Constitution also required the state to carry out religious and ethical education within the context of "national solidarity and unity."[49] To the charges of antisecularism concerning the teaching of religion in high schools, the military courts responded by arguing that "the Basic Law of Education encourages the teaching of love of God and the Prophet as a way of cultivating moral aspects of students that would lead to the love of their fatherland, state, and family."[50] The impetus to use Islam to consolidate the nationalist foundations of the republic went as far as rewriting secondary-level schoolbooks following the Turkish-Islamic slogan "The best Turk is a Muslim Turk—the best Muslim is a Turkish Muslim."[51]

In that sense, the "Turkish-Islamic synthesis" attempted to integrate secularism, Turkish nationalism, and Islam. This ideology was already very popular in the early 1970s among a group of conservative intellectuals involved in the Aydınlar Ocağı (The Hearth of the Enlightened).[52] Mustafa Erkal, the secretary of the organization, argued that "the love of the fatherland is the love of faith. . . . Those who reject the idea of homeland and a national flag cannot grasp the meaning of Islam as well."[53] The Heart's ideology, aimed at overriding particularistic interests by stressing the danger of anarchy and social divisions, helped shape the authoritarian-solidaristic spirit of the 1982 Constitution.[54] As a result, in the early 1980s, the military perceived the "Turkish-Islamic synthesis" as a harmless alternative to militant Kemalist secularism, which had never resonated with Anatolian masses. As Richard Tapper points out, "This synthesis was aimed at an authoritarian but not Islamist state where religion was seen as the essence of culture and social control and should thus be fostered in the education system without politicization.[55]

Depoliticization was a top priority on the military's agenda. As previously mentioned, the 1982 Constitution prohibited any connection between trade unions, professional associations, interest groups, and political parties. Because the pre-1980 political violence was often centered on university campuses, the coup created the Higher Educational Council, which had the goal of purging left-leaning professors and centralizing the curriculum and research agendas. The Higher Education Law No. 2547, enacted in late 1981, therefore banned the affiliation of the faculty and students with any political party.[56] As a result of this law, most leftist scholars either resigned or were purged and replaced with conservative ones who were willing to work in the absence of academic autonomy. In an effort to strengthen the executive body, the 1982 Constitution also significantly increased the power of the presidency. The latter remained as an unelected office in the Turkish parliamentary system, but nevertheless had the power to make appointments to the Higher Education Council; dissolve the Parliament; and appoint justices to the Constitutional Court, Court of Appeals, and Supreme Council of Judges and Prosecutors.[57]

As far as the management of the troubled Turkish economy was concerned, the military leadership supported Turkey's International Monetary Fund (IMF)-led stabilization program implemented briefly before the coup and had no major objection to economic liberalization.[58] The post-coup military leaders re-created Turkey's political economy by providing it with greater autonomy from social forces. Economic liberalism was to be promoted through a conservative-authoritarian political agenda as opposed to political liberalism. The generals therefore wanted to have a regulated and gradual transition to electoral politics. As a result, they barred more than 700 pre-coup politicians—including the leaders of the banned political parties—from politics for a period of five to ten years. The National Security Council empowered itself to screen new political parties and candidates and allowed only three of seventeen parties to participate in the general elections scheduled for 1983.[59]

The generals fully supported the pro-military Milliyetçi Demokrasi Partisi (the Nationalist Democracy Party), led by retired General Turgut Sunalp. They further tolerated a "loyal social democrat" Halkçı Parti (the Populist Party) headed by a retired high-ranking pro-coup bureaucrat. The top brass clearly distanced itself from Anavatan Partisi (the Motherland Party—the MP) of Turgut Özal. Özal was the man behind the economic liberalization program in 1979–1980 and minister of state in charge of the economy under the military regime until a series of financial scandals in

1982 forced him out of office. The unexpected success of the MP in the 1983 general elections showed how the electorate actively responded to even the smallest democratic margin permitted by the military. Despite the military's support for the two other parties, Özal's connection with informal associations and networks contributed significantly to his victory in the election.

Özal's Balancing Act between Kemalism and Neo-Ottomanism

In the 1983 elections, Özal's MP scored an overwhelming victory, polling more than 45 percent of the vote. The MP appeared to be an eclectic coalition of ideological currents and interest groups, which had joined the party because they had nowhere else to go under the military's restrictive policies. The party had electoral appeal because it embraced centrist politics with a liberal touch. The personality of Özal was crucial in balancing the conservative and liberal tendencies within party. [60] Özal had a foot in both the liberal and conservative camps: an engineer by education, he had been a successful manager in private industry in the 1970s and was very well connected to big business circles that backed his liberalization of the economy.

He knew well the Turkish and international bureaucracy because he had worked as the undersecretary of the State Planning Organization in the late 1960s and later took a position in the World Bank between 1971 and 1973. On the other hand, he had started his political career in 1977, campaigning for an unwinnable seat in Izmir for the pro-Islamic National Salvation Party. Then, after his years at the Sabancı Holding in Istanbul, Prime Minister Süleyman Demirel called him back into government service in 1979 to help handle the economy. Özal came from a conservative background in the southeastern city of Malatya and made no attempt to hide his affinity to the Nakşibendi order. Moreover, he was a member of the Heart of the Enlightened.

While campaigning in the 1983 elections, Özal did not hesitate to use the traditional networks of authority, such as the Nakşibendi order, kinship ties, and mosque associations, to build dynamic bridges with the society at large. His liberalism, antibureaucratic tendencies, and pro-Islamic attitude made him very popular in the eyes of different segments in Turkish society. In power, the inner core of Özal's administration not only included leading members of the defunct National Salvation Party and prominent disciples of Nakşibendi leaders but also liberal, pro-market, and secularist politicians.[61] These politicians coming from diverse ideological backgrounds all seemed to agree on the need to liberalize the economy. A large majority of cabinet members also supported the Turkish-Islamic synthesis and therefore encouraged religious expression and state support for religious institutions.[62]

The Islamic connections of the party proved useful beyond Turkey's borders as well. Özal was the architect of Turkey's transition from an import substitution industrialization to export-oriented economy. This necessitated an aggressive search for foreign customers who, in the 1980s, were found mainly in the Middle East because of the second boom in world oil prices. Thanks to its neutral position during the Iran-Iraq war, Turkey experienced a major increase in its trade with these two countries. Moreover, the Nakşibendi group within the party, which enjoyed good relations with the Gulf states, played an important role in promoting Turkish exports in the Middle East. The 1980s also witnessed a profound takeoff in the volume and depth of Islamic financial activity. Islamic financial institutions clearly received a boost from major inflows of Saudi capital that took advantage of the new opportunities provided by financial deregulation in Turkey.[63]

Overall, in the 1980s, the international business world and the financial community, represented by the IMF, the World Bank, and the Organization for Economic Cooperation and Development (OECD), had renewed confidence in Turkey's financial and trade liberalization program. Therefore, the flow of credits denied to pre-1980 governments resumed in the mid-1980s.[64] Özal's IMF-backed program had three main goals: to improve the balance of payments, to combat inflation, and to create an export-oriented free market economy. The means employed to achieve these objectives were a drastic devaluation of the Turkish lira within the framework of a flexible exchange rate system, a large rise in interest rates to fight inflation, and the privatization of state-owned economic enterprises. [65] The export growth strategy relatively reduced state intervention, alleviated payment difficulties, and liberalized domestic pricing.

Throughout the 1980s, small and medium-sized businesses in Anatolia greatly benefited from the economic liberalization policies of the MP governments (1983–91). They created their own financial networks, organized themselves outside the control of the state, and challenged the preeminence of state-supported large industrialists. In time, some Anatolian businesses, such as İhlas and Kombassan Holding, surpassed the level of traditional small and medium-sized companies and came to be ranked among Turkey's large holding firms. Most of these religiously oriented entrepreneurs enjoyed good relations with the conservative faction of the MP but were ideologically closer to the WP, which had emerged in 1983 as the successor of the National Salvation Party. In 1990, these Anatolian businesses formed their own organization, Müstakil Sanayici ve İşadamları Derneği (MÜSİAD), which in the 1990s became the fastest-growing and largest business organization in the country.[66] This significant rise of Islamic capital and provincial bourgeoisie during the post-1980 neoliberal era has constituted a strong financial base for the success of the WP in the 1990s.

The opportunities for profit provided by the shift to a market-oriented economy in the 1980s also encouraged religious brotherhoods and networks to engage in investment activities on a substantial scale. The Nakşibendi order and the Nurcu movement had already been playing an important role in the sociopolitical arena since the 1950s. In the 1980s, with the energizing effect of economic liberalization on civil society and state support for the Turkish-Islamic synthesis, the popularity and legitimacy of religious brotherhoods reached unprecedented levels. The 1980s, in that sense, presented important opportunities for the Sufi Brotherhoods, which have traditionally aimed to prevent the alienation of individuals and the atomization of traditional communities that occur in a fast-growing market economy and a new urban context. [67]

As a result, Muslim associations, foundations, and charities associated with religious brotherhoods greatly benefited from economic liberalization, rural migration, and urbanization. Two religious orders in particular have played central parts in the flourishing field of social Islam. One, led by Fethullah Gülen, became the richest and most important offshoot of the Nurcu movement. The other, known as the İskender Paşa community, was one of the various offshoots of the Nakşibendi order. Starting in the mid-1980s, both religious orders were able to develop powerful and active networks in business, politics, the media, and social and welfare services. In time, Fethullah Gülen's movement became the most prominent representative of the Turkish-Islamic synthesis in the 1990s. It is therefore important to note that the MP, during its tenure from 1983 to 1991, played a significant role in the mobilization of Turkey's traditionally conservative constituencies around the cause of economic liberalism. In most cases, such constituencies came to be integrated into the mainstream of Turkish politics within the framework of religious conservatism.

Although Özal had no intentions of undermining the secularist order of the state, by the end of the 1980s his laissez-faire approach to political Islam gave rise to growing concerns among secularist circles. To its dismay, the military, which had promoted the Turkish-Islamic synthesis after the 1980 coup, did not realize that, under the newly adopted policy of economic liberalization, state control over society would become much more difficult to maintain. Moreover, the late 1980s presented markedly different international and domestic conditions compared with the beginning of the decade. Most importantly, with the looming end of the Cold War and the "successful" eradication of the Turkish left, the use of religion as an antidote to communism had lost its pragmatic appeal in the eyes of Turkey's Kemalist establishment. Instead, the post–Cold War Kemalist preoccupation shifted to the need to preserve and demonstrate Turkey's Western credentials. Such an endeavor proved much more challenging with the demise of the Soviet Union. In the absence of a bipolar world and anticommunism as geostrategy, Turkey's Western identity was to come under increasing scrutiny.

Turkey's domestic Kurdish problem and Islamic leanings reemerged in this post–Cold War context. They both exacerbated Ankara's already complex domestic and foreign policy agenda. Relations with both the EU and the United States came under significant stress while problems with neighbors like Iraq, Syria, and Iran also gained new dimensions. By 1984, Ankara was facing a Kurdish nationalist insurgency group within its borders, and the leader of the PKK, Abdullah Öcalan, found safe haven and political support in Damascus. The PKK had become Damascus's Kurdish card against Turkey's leverage over water resources. Things did not look any better in northern Iraq, where two Iraqi Kurdish groups grew in strength and the PKK found a haven in the aftermath of the first Gulf War of 1991. There were also growing signs in Iran of Kurdish activism and sympathy for the PKK. Finally, to the dismay of Ankara, many European countries looked at Turkey's conflict with the Kurds as the oppression of an ethnic group whose cultural and political rights were being denied by an authoritarian state.

By the early 1990s, it was increasingly clear that there were two diverging ideological frameworks clashing over the future direction of Turkish foreign policy. While Özal seemed to favor what came to be conceptualized as an activist neo-Ottomanism in the Middle East, the military and civilian bureaucracy clearly favored traditional Kemalist norms. While the latter was clearly based on a prioritization of the Kurdish threat of separatism, the former displayed a more confident outlook in search of regional influence based on improved economic relations with neighbors and enhanced soft power. At peace with its Muslim heritage and multiple identities and void of imperialist territorial ambitions, neo-Ottomanism embraced a self-confident geostrategic vision of Turkey as an effective regional superpower in search of reestablishing its historic spheres of influences in the Arab world and the Balkans.

In that sense, Özal can be analyzed as an unconventional Turkish politician who became an early proponent of neo-Ottomanism. He believed Turkey needed to transcend the securitized, rigid Kemalist paradigm of confrontation with the Kurds at home in favor of cooperation with Kurds in the Middle East. And at home, his main goal was to co-opt rather than destroy Kurdish dissent. To do so, he became an early supporter of Kurdish cultural rights in Turkey. Özal also established working relations with Iraqi Kurdish leaders and even allowed them to travel with Turkish diplomatic passports. Late in life, he appeared to possess a vision of Turkey characterized by administrative decentralization and stronger regional autonomy. Almost three decades after his death in 1993, his vision of a federative solution to the Kurdish problem based on administrative de-centralization is still deemed too risky to discuss in the current autocratic climate of Turkish politics.[68]

His unconventional views on the Kurdish question were matched by an equally bold vision of peace and economic interdependence in the Middle East and the Black Sea region. Özal was the intellectual godfa-ther of the Black Sea Economic Cooperation Organization, established in 1989. He was also a strong advocate of the "Water for Peace" project, which envisaged the transportation of Turkish water through pipelines to Syria, Jordan, and Israel.[69] A pious and at the same time modern man, Özal established good relations with the Arab world and became the first sitting Turkish president to perform the hajj. Not unlike the JDP's ability to follow a balanced East-West policy, Özal also strongly supported and actively worked for Turkey's EU membership. In fact, Turkey applied for full membership under his government in 1987. In short, Özal's policies vis-à-vis the Middle East, Europe, and the Kurds had strong traits of a Janus-faced neo-Ottomanism.

During the first Gulf War, President Özal threw Turkey's full political and economic support behind the US military campaign. Ankara enforced UN sanctions by cutting off the flow of Iraq's oil exports through Turkish pipelines, deployed 100,000 troops along the Iraqi-Turkish border, and al-lowed the United States to fly sorties into Iraq from Turkish bases. Despite its partnership with Washington, Turkey paid a high economic price after the war. It lost an estimated $35 billion in pipeline fees and foregone trade with Iraq during the next decade. In addition, the American-encouraged, ill-fated 1991 Kurdish rebellion in northern Iraq against Baghdad led to a humanitarian crisis after Saddam Hussein's forces crushed it. Fleeing the Iraqi army, 450,000 Kurdish refugees crossed the border and took refuge in Turkey. Together with Washington's failure to compensate Turkey for its economic losses, this experience would be foremost in Turkish minds a decade later when the United States made new promises to compensate Turkey for the collateral economic costs of a proposed invasion of Iraq.

The Lost Decade of Turkish Foreign Policy and Domestic Politics

After the death of Turgut Özal in 1993, Turkey's political instability gained a chronic dimension. Nine different coalition governments ruled the county during the 1990s. The worsening dynamics on the Kurdish front during this decade undermined the Turkish economy, which suffered from high inflation, growing budget deficits, public debt, and systemic corruption. As the Kurdish insurgency reached critical dimensions, Ankara's response remained uncompromisingly nationalistic and authoritarian. Without the ideological cover of left-wing versus right-wing politics, Turkey's identity problems—Kurdish nationalism and Islam—were now out in the open. And the military had no willingness to show flexibility for any cultural or political compromise with Kurdish nationalists or Islamist politicians. While the Kurdish problem was clearly the driver of political and security concerns during the 1990s, the military soon realized it also had to deal with the rise of political Islam.

By the mid-1990s, in addition to intensification of the war against the PKK, political Islam—the second most important threat to Kemalism— also came to dominate the national agenda. Social and economic factors, such as corruption, income disparity, and frustration with center-right and center-left establishment politics, strongly contributed to the rise of Islamism. By the 1990s, Turkey's normally marginal Islamist political movement, the WP, led by Necmettin Erbakan, made significant inroads. In 1994, at the height of an acute financial crisis and the military struggle against Kurdish separatists, the WP shocked the secularist establishment by winning municipal elections nationwide and capturing Turkey's two largest metropolitan areas, Istanbul and Ankara. The new mayor of Istanbul was the young and charismatic leader of the WP youth movement: Recep Tayyip Erdoğan. A year later, in 1995, another unexpected victory, this time in parliamentary elections, put an Islamist-led coalition in charge of the entire country. The WP had received only 21 percent of the votes. Yet the notoriously fragmented nature of the center-right and center-left politics allowed the WP to form a coalition government with Doğru Yol Partisi (the True Path Party—the TPP) under the leadership of Tansu Çiller.

Faced with this success of the WP at the local and national levels, the main question that preoccupied the secularist establishment was whether the Islamist-led government would deviate from mainstream politics by adopting an overtly Islamic tone and authoritarian tendencies. It is fair to argue that during its short tenure in power, the much-feared WP shied away from political and economic policies that constituted a major break from mainstream Turkish politics. The WP followed well-established patterns of political patronage in ways similar to previous governing parties and coalitions composed of the Motherland, the True Path, and Sosyal Demokrat Halkçı Parti (the Social Democrat Populist Party) that had governed the country between 1983 and 1996. Erbakan implanted his own sympathizers and members in the ministries it held under control while he predictably adopted a narrative and policy preference in favor of religious conservatism. Yet the secularist press reacted with great alarm with sensationalist warnings about an imminent Islamic revolution.

An objective analysis of the eleven-month WP tenure in power would illustrate that no attempts were made to leave an "Islamic" imprint on important issues such as financial and economic management, internal and external security policy, the Kurdish problem, public administration, political and economic corruption, or sociopolitical liberties. To the dismay of those expecting structural political change, the WP appeared totally unprepared to govern the country. Particularly disappointing was the fact that the WP was utterly incapable of extending the government cleanup that it had pioneered at the local level to the central administration.[70] Interestingly, it was in the field of foreign relations that Prime Minister Erbakan sought a window of opportunity for following the semblance of an Islamist foreign policy. For instance, instead of an Özal-like neo-Ottoman agenda seeking EU membership, balance with the United States, and strong regional engagements, Erbakan rhetorically distanced his party and himself from the EU by calling it a "Christian Club." And his largely cosmetic efforts to forge new alliances on the basis of Islamic solidarity during trips to countries such as Iran, Libya, and Sudan irritated the military. Particularly in the case of

Libya, the official visit failed rather dramatically when Muammar Qaddafi publicly scolded Erbakan for Turkey's treatment of Kurds.[71]

Ironically, despite Erbakan's clumsy attempts at playing the Islamic card in foreign policy, it was under his prime ministry that the country witnessed a deepening of cooperation with Israel. By forging closer links with Israel, the generals turned foreign policy into a domestic political show of force, partly in retaliation to Erbakan's prior foreign policy openings to countries such as Iran, Sudan, and Libya. At the height of the stand-off between the government and the Turkish General Staff, the military went as far as consolidating Turkey's relationship with Israel without informing the Ministry of Defense.[72] Although Prime Minister Erbakan was an avowed opponent of a free trade agreement with Israel, he was forced by the military to sign this agreement during the Israeli Foreign Minister David Levy's official visit to Ankara in April 1997. Erbakan did, however, use the opportunity of his meeting with Levy to express before the media his negative views of Israeli policies and told Levy that Israel should withdraw from the occupied territories, including Jerusalem, in line with long-established UN resolutions.[73]

As far as the domestic Islamic profile of the government is concerned, Erbakan and his closest aides had an agenda based on a series of soft policy proposals. The party proposed the lifting of the ban on wearing headscarves in public buildings. More flexibility was asked for regarding working hours during the holy month of Ramadan so that the religious requirements of fasting and praying could be met. Following this micro-agenda, the WP also proposed to take away from the Turkish Civil Aviation Foundation the right of collecting and selling the hides of sacrificial sheep and give the right to religious foundations. More symbolically, the party declared its intention to build a mosque at Istanbul's Taksim Square, an area decorated with an Atatürk monument commemorating the proclamation of the Turkish republic. Finally, the party was in favor of loosening the control of the Directorate of Religious Affairs over the organization of the pilgrimage by allowing overland travel to Mecca.[74]

None of these proposals sought to radically alter the secular nature of the Republican regime. However, according to the parameters of militant laicism defined by a zero-sum approach, the WP's proposals provided sufficient ammunition for a secularist backlash. The Kemalist reaction culminated parallel to a series of individual Islamic challenges that came to be perceived as major threats to the republic's secular legacy. For instance, on November 10, 1996, during the traditional remembrance of Atatürk, the WP mayor of a central Anatolian city declared that he did not like to participate in such events.[75] A couple of months later during the month of Ramadan, Prime Minister Erbakan invited a group of religious leaders to his residence to break the fast. Finally, on February 2, 1997, the WP mayor of Sincan, a small town near Ankara, organized an event to protest Israel's occupation of East Jerusalem during which the Iranian ambassador was present and pro-Hamas and pro-Hezbollah speeches were made.[76] This last event was partly in reaction to the Turkish-Israeli "Military Cooperation and Training Agreement" signed in February 1996 under the previous Çiller government. The army had no longer the intention of tolerating such political displays of Islamic opposition to the secular principles of the republic. The next day, army tanks rumbled through the streets of Sincan. The mayor was imprisoned, and Iran had to withdraw its ambassador.

When the generals finally decided to move against the WP in early 1997, they did so with the precision and determination of a military campaign in political form. On February 28, 1997, the Turkish Armed Forces, through its presence in the National Security Council, requested from the government the implementation of an eighteen-point plan aimed at reinforcing the secular nature of the state. The army's demands, later dubbed a "soft coup" by the Turkish press, essentially called for (1) the extension of obligatory public schooling for children aged five to eight years (a measure that would bring about the closure of middle-level İmam-Hatip schools and a reduction in the number of Koranic courses), (2) close surveillance over religious orders and the investigation of their financial sources, (3) the ending of the recruitment of party members to government jobs; (4) full implementation of secular dress codes, and (5) the reexamination of relations with Iran.[77]

These requests coming from the military wing of the National Security Council (NSC) presented the beginning of the end for the WP-led coalition government. Although the government was given only two months to implement these policies, in practice the February 28 meeting of the NSC heralded the beginning of a much longer period of military pressure on political Islam, dubbed the "28 February process."[78] Despite the fact that the military, this time, was more discreet in its intervention, the message it wanted to get across was unambiguous: no deviations from Kemalist secularism would be tolerated. Ironically, the policies dictated by the NSC against organized Islam—particularly the ones regarding the closure of İmam-Hatip schools and Quranic courses—represented a total reversal of what the army had promoted in the early 1980s in its attempt to generate a Turkish-Islamic synthesis against communism. In the coming months after the February 28 NSC meeting, Erbakan tried to portray the crisis as an artificial one inflated by the anti-WP media. But this was not the way the military saw its ultimatum.

As Erbakan tried to smooth things over without really giving into the military's demands, the generals maintained their relentless political pressure on the government. The headquarters of the chief of staff set up the "Western Working Group" to monitor the economic and political activities of "fundamentalist groups" and organized a series of briefings to inform the senior bureaucrats, members of the judiciary, academics, and journalists about the vehemence of Islamist activities.[79]

In March 1997, in one such briefing the military released a list of close to one hundred corporations with which it would have no dealings in the future. These organizations were to come under investigation as financial supporters of Islamic movements. Some of these corporations were major conglomerates at the forefront of Turkish exports such as Ülker, an alimentary giant; İHLAS holding corporation; and Kombassan holding.[80] The army went on to list 19 newspapers, 20 national and local television stations, 51 radio stations, 110 magazines, and 1,200 student fraternities as engaging in "subversive Islamic activities."[81]

The military continued its campaign against the WP government during April 1997 by formulating a new "Concept of National Security Strategy." This document openly branded the Islamic movements the most important threat to the republic along with Kurdish separatists.[82] In its briefings to the different sectors of state and society, including the media, the Turkish General Staff made it clear that the military considered the "internal threat," namely Islamism, more serious than the external threat, the PKK.[83] In response to mass pro-WP demonstrations in favor of Quranic courses and İmam-Hatip schools, including a rally of some 300,000 in Istanbul on May 11, 1997, the military declared its "readiness to use force against Islamic groups."[84]

Under such mounting pressure from the military, Erbakan resigned in June 1997. The experiment of an Islamist-led government had thus come to an end after less than a year. Yet the military's anti-Islamic drive did not end even after the formation of a new minority government between Mesut Yılmaz of the MP and the veteran Bülent Ecevit, leader of Demokratik Sol Parti (the Democratic Left Party—the DLP). This minority coalition ran the country until the April 1999 elections. For the military, the ousting of the WP from government was only the first step in its campaign against political Islam. The February 28 process continued with judicial and political pressure on the WP.

In the polarized atmosphere of a Kulturkampf between Kemalists and Islamists, Ankara's secularist establishment saw with growing irritation that Turkey was being outraced by Central and Eastern European states in its attempt to become an EU member. Therefore, starting with the second half of 1996, Turkey's policy toward the EU had been focused—under the discredited leadership of Deputy Prime Minister Tansu Çiller, who had managed to stay in power thanks to her coalition with the WP—on convincing the EU that it had to include Turkey in the next round of enlargement. Çiller and other Turkish officials did not even refrain from creating an explicit linkage between Turkey's consent to an eventual eastward enlargement of NATO and entrance into the EU.[85]

Brussels, however, did not respond positively to Turkey's new assertiveness. In the eyes of EU circles, the Kurdish conflict, extrajudicial killings associated with the Turkish "deep state," the growing influence of the military in Turkish domestic politics, and the rising tension between secularists and Islamists additionally complicated Turkey's already difficult candidacy. In that sense, at a crucial time when Turkey urgently needed to improve its democratic standards to be included in the EU enlargement process, it increasingly projected the problematic image of an authoritarian country struggling with its own religious and ethnic identity. In any case, the Turkish position for full membership was somewhat handicapped because the senior leadership of the coalition government, Prime Minister Erbakan, had never made a secret of his reluctance to agree to eventual Turkish accession to the EU. As mentioned above, the outlook adopted by the WP had traditionally been that the EU was a "Christian Club" that would always discriminate against Turkey, no matter how strongly the Kemalist elite attempted to emulate it culturally.

Turkey's strategic relationship with Israel gained a more important dimension within such a domestic and international context. In February 1996—before the formation of the WP-led coalition government but shortly after the electoral victory of the Islamist Party—the Israeli and Turkish military had signed a military cooperation agreement providing for the exchange of military information, equipment, and personnel. It is also important to note that through its strategic relationship with Israel, the Kemalist establishment also hoped to gain a "back door" to Washington via the powerful pro-Israel lobby.[86] This continues to be perceived by Ankara as the best way to counter the influence of Greek and Armenian lobbies in the United States. Signing such a military partnership agreement with Israel was not an easy step even for the Turkish military, which needed some justification beyond domestic dynamics of identity politics. Arguably, the Oslo Peace Process and agreements between the PLO and Israel sheltered the Turkish military establishment from domestic and Arab criticism in forging such open military cooperation with Tel Aviv. Moreover, Ankara was in search of assistance from a country that would not attach human rights conditions to its weapon sales. Turkish military cooperation with Israel was also supposed to pressure Syria to withdraw its support for the PKK. Seen in this light, the strategic reasons for Turkey's rapprochement with Israel appeared to be sound.

Yet beyond all the strategic factors, the alliance with Israel also had an important domestic ideological and identity dimension because it above all signaled the autonomy and political determination of the Turkish military to follow a "secularist" foreign policy. This attempt becomes all the more significant when one takes into consideration the formation of the WP government and Erbakan's economic and political overtures to only Muslim countries, including Libya and Iran. In that sense, the Turkish-Israeli alliance had an important target: to embarrass the pro-Islamic government by exposing its powerlessness to halt an alliance it openly had opposed. For instance, although Prime Minister Erbakan was an avowed opponent of the free trade agreement with Israel, he was forced to sign a free trade agreement during Israeli Foreign Minister David Levy's visit to Ankara.

Indeed, Turkey's relationship with Israel brought into sharp relief the preponderant role of the military in Turkey's foreign policy, as it appeared that the civilian government did not know the exact details of the military cooperation and training agreement. Even the civil bureaucracy seemed inadequately informed. In any case, the partnership with Israel, which gained momentum parallel to the electoral rise of political Islam, can be analyzed as symptomatic of a sense of encirclement, from which Turkey's Kemalist establishment wanted to liberate itself. However, it also validates the point that the Turkish military elite sees international and domestic developments through the lens of the threats posed by political Islam and Kurdish nationalism.

When Turkey and Israel signed a military cooperation treaty in 1996, the logic for Turkey was simple: Ankara was feeling increasingly encircled in its war against the Kurdish separatists in Southeast Anatolia. There was ample evidence that Syria, Turkey's southern neighbor, was harboring the Kurdish leader Abdullah Öcalan and his organization, the PKK. Things did not look any better in northern Iraq, where the PKK and two Iraqi Kurdish groups found a haven in the aftermath of Saddam Hussain's defeat in the first Gulf War of 1991. Finally, there were also strong signs that Iran was turning a blind eye to PKK activities within its borders. This sense of Iranian, Iraqi, and Syrian encirclement in the mid-1990s was compounded by the fact that Turkey's relations with the West had also reached an impasse.

Conclusion

Turkey's lost decade of the 1990s ended with a semblance of stability, mainly because the military effectively subdued Islamists and Kurdish separatists. As we have seen, in 1997, the military forced the coalition government of Prime Minister Erbakan to resign in what came to be called the "soft coup." Shortly after taking the upper hand against political Islam, the Turkish military turned its attention to the Kurdish threat as it engaged in several cross-border operations in northern Iraq. Going one step further, in 1998, the Turkish military publicly threatened to invade Syria for supporting the PKK. Isolated after the collapse of the Soviet Union and worried by Turkish-Israeli strategic cooperation, Syria yielded to Ankara and forced Abdullah Öcalan out of Damascus. After leaving Syria for several locations, Öcalan was finally captured by Turkish intelligence in 1999 and incarcerated in a remote prison island off Istanbul. As a result, by the end of the decade, the twin threats to Kemalism, political Islam and Kurdish nationalism, both seemed to be emasculated and on the defensive.

Chronic political instability, economic stagnation, war with Kurdish insurgents, major foreign policy debacles, and a soft-military coup were primary markers of this fateful era in recent Turkish political history. As if such turbulence were not enough, the 1990s ended with two seismic events, the first one being literally the devastating earthquake of 1999. With its epicenter near Istanbul, the tremor killed close to 20,000 people and left hundreds of thousands homeless. The second calamity was the financial meltdown of 2001, which to this day is considered the worst economic crisis in the history of modern Turkey. The chronically indebted public finance system came at the brink of collapse as overnight interest rates reached 800 percent and liquidity froze with impending insolvency. The country survived this unprecedented financial crisis only thanks to a massive IMF bailout, which established fiscal discipline and austerity measures. Turkey thus entered the twenty-first century context facing daunting challenges.

Chapter 2

THE JDP'S FIRST DECADE

The lost decade of the 1990s culminating with both a real earthquake and its financial equivalent in 2001 proved to be a blessing in a disguise for a group of politicians seeking a new beginning. They were ready for a fresh start and a new political party. The politicians in question were a group of Islamist politicians convinced that their short experiment in power between 1996 and 1997 proved disastrous. Their party was kicked out from power under military pressure. Time was ripe for change and they wanted to seize the moment.

This new vision in the making was the Justice and Development Party (JDP). Founded in August 2001 by Recep Tayyip Erdoğan, Abdullah Gül, and Bülent Arınç, all former students of Necmettin Erbakan, the JDP prioritized bread-and-butter issues, good governance, and a constructive foreign policy in pursuit of European Union (EU) membership and appealed to lower middle classes, who were hardly hit by the economic deterioration of the 1990s. This political strategy worked very well, as the party won a major victory in its very first elections in November 2002 parliamentary elections and formed the government alone.

Yet the very forces that had ousted the Welfare Party (WP) were still in place. The JDP had to respect redlines and could not afford a major confrontation with this system of military guardianship and tutelage. It was therefore under the watchful eyes of the top brass and the Kemalist judiciary that the JDP crafted its domestic and foreign policy strategies in the 2000s. This chapter argues that such circumstances played a major role in tempering JDP's Islamist tendencies. The political context dictated caution and moderation.

In any case, the party leadership and especially the JDP leader himself had firsthand experience with the consequences of a clash with the secularist system.

The Beginnings: Domestic and International Context

"The minarets are our bayonets,
the domes our helmets,
the mosques our barracks
and the faithful our soldiers."

Uttered in 1997 in a public speech, it was this line of a poem that put Recep Tayyip Erdoğan in jail in 1999 and banned him from politics for five years. Erdoğan was the popular mayor of Istanbul from the WP and thus one of the political figures targeted by the military and the judiciary along with Necmettin Erbakan. In fact, when the JDP won the parliamentary elections in 2002, Erdoğan was still banned from politics. He was able to assume his duties as Prime Minister with a brief delay, only after the JDP majority in parliament passed necessary constitutional amendments.

In 2002, Erdoğan claimed to have become a different person than in 1997. He explicitly stated that he had dropped the Islamist ideology associated with Necmettin Erbakan. The bloodless coup of 1997 that ousted the WP seemed to have major, if unintended, consequences. It paved the way for serious soul-searching among Turkey's Islamists, eventually causing a generational and ideological rift within their movement. The WP's pragmatic young leaders, such as Recep Tayyip Erdoğan and Abdullah Gül, recognized the redlines of Turkish secularism and the need for genuine democratization and liberalism to change them. As stated, Erdoğan learned this lesson the hard way, having served four months in prison in 1999 for allegedly inciting religious hatred for merely reciting a poem with Islamic undertones.

The heavy-handed secularist backlash orchestrated by the military convinced moderate Islamist politicians, at least on the surface, of the benefits of liberal democracy.[1] After having participated in democratic politics for more than three decades, they had already learned to temper their views to gain electoral legitimacy. By the late 1990s, despite the soft coup and Kemalist concerns about Islamization, Turkey was not Egypt after the 2013 coup. Turkish Islamists could still operate politically and still nurtured hopes of returning to power. They were well integrated into the electoral system and had a new appreciation for the limits of what could be achieved in Turkey's secular and illiberal system. This became all the more apparent in 2001, when Erdoğan and Gül established a new political party, the JDP. They proudly announced that the JDP's ideology adhered to conservative democracy, not political Islam.

Fortunately for the JDP, all major political parties were already discredited for ineffectively tackling the political and economic problems that arose in the fateful decade of the 1990s.[2] The electoral system worked in the JDP's favor as well, putting all those existing parties out of the parliament and disproportionally rewarding 66 percent of the seats in the parliament with 34 percent of the votes in the elections. In the succeeding years, Erdoğan set out to consolidate his popularity. Fortunately the previous coalition government implemented a painful economic recovery program under Kemal Derviş. The JDP took over an economy the major fundamental problems of which were already addressed. With budgetary discipline, the JDP could put Turkish economy back on the path of continuous economic growth. Between 2002 and 2007, the Turkish economy grew from 232.7 billion to 657 billion in current US dollars. In the same period, per capita gross national income increased from $3,250 to $8,020.[3]

The benefits of this economic growth brought tangible benefits to the lives of millions. First of all, the chronic problem, inflation, which had hit hard almost all groups for a long time, considerably lessened. The average inflation rate between 1992 and 2002 was about 74 percent. By 2007, it dropped to just 8 percent. Second, the JDP government tried to protect the fixed salaries of state employees and workers against inflation pressures, systematically increasing the salaries/wages according to the inflation rates. Even in terms of the euro, for example, state employees enjoyed a big rise in their salaries even though euro/lira parity increased between December 2002 and July 2010 from about 1.4 YTL to around 1.94 YTL, an increase of at least 30 percent. The lowest employee salary in the Turkish state was about 260 euros in December 2002. During the JDP rule, the salary jumped to approximately 590 euros by July 2010, an increase of 126 percent.[4]

These two improvements, pay rise for all state employees and declining inflation rates, increased the welfare of low-middle- and middle-income families in Turkey and hence of lower-ranking bureaucracy. The betterment was visible, for example, in the renewal or upgrading of cars. With a little effort to consume less and hence save more, a typical trait of a Turkish family hard learned during decades of economic decline, many could now buy a brand-new car. Renault, the preferred car brand of low-middle- and middle-income families in Turkey, indeed enjoyed a great boom in sales in 2004. This boom came after Renault sales dropped by 61.7 percent in 2001.[5] By contrast, in 2004, Renault sales rose by a spectacular 101.1 percent.[6] Prices in the secondhand car market declined, thus giving more opportunities to Turkish families to buy younger and foreign cars. Also, prices of durable goods stabilized, helping Turkish families enjoy better welfare. A washing machine in the kitchen or a big-screen TV was a luxury before, but these are visible in many homes now in Turkey.

Many associated this improved welfare with the party in government, the JDP, and its leader, Recep Tayyip Erdoğan. As a result of economic success, the party won a landslide victory in the 2007 national elections, increasing its vote share by 11 percent since the 2002 elections, an increase hitherto unheard of in Turkish politics.[7] More critically, with this renewed popularity, the JDP elected its former leader, Abdullah Gül, to the office of the presidency soon after the elections. Thus came to an end the almost single-handed opposition of the former president, Ahmet Necdet Sezer, to the legislative and executive dominance of the JDP. From then on the JDP could pass laws much more quickly and appoint any bureaucrat without any interference from the office of the president.

Not only the domestic context but also the international context proved to be extremely conducive for the JDP. The party was formed almost exactly a month before the September 11 terrorist attacks targeting New York and Washington, DC. As the Twin Towers in Manhattan crumbled down, Samuel Huntington's clash of civilizations looked prescient. The West was now face to face with an unprecedented Jihadist threat. In the eyes of millions of Americans and Europeans, the image of Islam was at its darkest. The Muslim faith was perceived as a dangerous religion. It appeared to be incompatible with democracy, secularism, and modernity. Most tragically, it also seemed to be on a collision course with the West.

Coming to power in this international context, the JDP immediately came to be seen as a beacon of hope by Western observers paying attention to Turkish politics.[8] As a formerly Islamist movement now embracing liberalism and democracy in pursuit of EU membership, the JDP appeared to be the much-needed antidote for poisonous civilizational polarization. Needless to say, Recep Tayyip Erdoğan and Abdullah Gül were more than happy to play the part. Their pragmatism and timing seemed in perfect harmony with both global and domestic dynamics.

By 2001, therefore, both the EU and the United States were ready to improve relations with Turkey. In 1997, shortly after the soft coup, the EU had declared that Turkey was no longer part of the enlargement process. Such a rebuke naturally irritated Turkey's secularist pro-EU segments but was not totally unexpected given the state of Turkish democracy. But things rapidly changed in 1998 when a center-left German leadership under Chancellor Gerhard Schroder replaced the Christian Democrat Helmut Kohl. This new government played a critical role in reviving Turkey's moribund EU candidacy. By 1999, European leaders declared at the EU's Helsinki Summit that Turkey's eventual membership should not be ruled out as Ankara was put back on track for the enlargement process.[9] This important decision proved critical for future political developments in Turkey because it offered the newly established JDP a legitimate and widely supported reform agenda in pursuit of full membership. EU membership appeared within reach for the first time since the end of the Cold War.

By 2001, shortly after the September 11 terrorist attacks, Washington also wanted strong relations with Ankara. Turkey's Muslim and Western identity and its place in NATO suddenly gained much higher relevance in a climate where the clash of civilizations turned from a gloomy prediction into self-fulfilling prophecy. All these dynamics on the Western front favored the JDP. With Turkey's EU candidacy back on the agenda, Erdoğan correctly sensed that adopting a pro-Western reformist platform would receive the crucial support of at least three constituencies: Turkey's business community, the liberal intellectuals, and most importantly, the upwardly mobile, pragmatic middle class. The EU agenda had an additional strategic advantage: it would calm down, at least temporarily, secularist circles and their Kemalist anxieties. Europe, after all, had always been the ultimate prize in Atatürk's vision of a truly westernized Turkey.

Erdoğan correctly calculated that he needed the support of the United States and the EU against a skeptical military establishment—the very force that ousted the WP and banned its leaders. Having finished off the Islamist experiment of the WP only a few years prior, the generals and the secularist media were caught by surprise to see the JDP's democratic change. Many even blamed Western imperialism for concocting the whole enterprise, going beyond accusations of a gullible love fest with moderate Islam. In the conspiratorial eyes of the generals, the JDP's brand of "moderate Islam" seemed to be an American invention designed to erode Kemalist secularism, sovereignty, and nationalism.[10]

In an unmistakable Kemalist irony, as the JDP moved closer to the West, nationalist secularism in Turkey seemed making strides in the opposite direction. It is therefore important to remember that by November 2002, when the JDP found itself unexpectedly in power only a year after its foundation, the dominant paradigm in both Turkish domestic and foreign policy was still defined by Kemalism. The military was the primary enforcer of this paradigm, and the top brass had a very clear, dual threat perception: Kurdish nationalism and political Islam, the latter now represented by none other than Erdoğan and his party, the JDP.

Unlike their putschist counterparts in the developing world, Turkish generals never stayed in power for too long, but they seldom hesitated to intervene. Prior to the 1997 soft coup, 1960, 1971, and 1980 were the three main episodes during which elected civilian governments were overthrown by the top brass. As we have seen in our chapter on Kemalism, this pattern had established a system of tutelage whereby the generals saw themselves as the self-declared guardians of the republic. Just five years before the JDP came to power, the generals had once again delineated clear limits with the February 28 process by making sure to close the very party with which the JDP leadership identified itself.

Erdoğan's rise to hegemony was then far from inevitable. During the early years of the JDP, the high echelons of the Turkish state, the generals, the university presidents, and the heads of high judiciary had not refrained from expressing their discontent and distaste with Erdoğan and his government in every opportunity they found. The military dictum of the chief of staff against the JDP's candidate for the office of the presidency in April 2007 and the judicial attempt in March 2008 to close down the JDP were all recorded as stark instances of the opposition of high state officials to the JDP. In fact, in the latter case, there was a good chance the party could suffer the same fate as the more openly Islamist WP at the hands of the Kemalist military and judiciary.[11] The JDP, after all, survived a closure case at the Constitutional Court by only one vote that year. Erdoğan's sense of insecurity during his first decade in power was therefore understandable. Even though Erdoğan declared that he had quit the ideology of the WP and adopted conservative democracy instead, according to the Kemalist establishment Erdoğan was simply engaged in cosmetic window dressing. At his core, in the Kemalists' eyes, he remained a Machiavellian Islamist, and Islamism was an immutable ideology immune to moderation.

Erdoğan tried hard to prove the secularist establishment wrong. But his insecurity was often palpable in a narrative that embraced victimhood. Even then, instead of his banned Islamist mentor and leader of the defunct WP, Necmettin Erbakan, he seemed to politically identify more with Adnan Menderes. Menderes was the historical symbol of center-right conservatism in Turkey. As the first democratically elected prime minister of the republic, he ruled between 1950 and 1960 by winning three consecutive elections. He was eventually ousted by a coup in 1960 and sent to the gallows by a military tribunal in 1961. When Erdoğan claims he is ready for martyrdom in the name of democracy, he usually references Menderes and this darkest hour in Turkish political history.[12]

All these domestic and foreign policy dynamics were moderating factors on JDP's ideology. In such a context, there was simply no room for an overtly Islamist agenda to emerge at home or in foreign policy. In that sense, the JDP needed to adapt to conditions at hand, and it did so to perfection. Soon after the JDP won the 2002 general elections in a landslide, it passed a significant set of reforms to harmonize Turkey's judicial system, civil-military relations, and human rights practices with European norms. JDP policies were openly designed with EU accession in mind. In fact, the only time the JDP came close to picking a political fight with the Kemalist military was on a very critical issue related to Turkey's EU accession: compromise in Cyprus. In 2003, the JDP government took considerable political risks and overturned forty years of Turkish policy by pressing the leadership of Turkish Cypriots to accept a political compromise on the island. Such a deal, it was believed, would enhance Turkey's chances of joining the EU. The independent magazine *Nokta* revealed in spring 2007 that a military coup over the issue of Cyprus was barely averted in 2004 because of divisions within the Turkish general staff's top brass.[13]

The fact that the JDP took such a risk in Cyprus in terms of antagonizing the military speaks volumes about how much it valued the EU process as the legitimizing engine of domestic democratization. In other words, without the EU, the JDP would have been deprived of a much-needed combination of incentive, political legitimacy, and ideological cover for taking reformist steps toward democracy—including the most critical ones in terms of assuring civilian control over the military. In that sense, the EU was a lifeline the JDP could ill afford to lose. The way Erdoğan pushed tooth and nail for reunification in Cyprus was the clearest illustration of the EU imperative for political survival at home. No other systemic party in peace with the Kemalist system of military tutelage would have taken such risks for a simple reason: they had no existential stake in the EU process.[14] In that sense, it is important to recognize that Islamist ideology was an adventuristic risk the JDP could not afford in its domestic or foreign policy during its first two terms (2002–2007) and 2007–2011) in power when it had to contend with a powerful secularist establishment.[15]

The JDP's Neo-Ottomanism in the 2000s

Since the JDP came to power in late 2002, its foreign policy has been based on what Erdoğan's top foreign policy advisor and later foreign and prime minister, Ahmet Davutoğlu, called "strategic depth" in a widely referred-to book.[16] Davutoğlu argued that Turkish foreign policy had been unbalanced, with an overemphasis on ties with Western Europe and the United States to the neglect of Turkey's interests with other countries, particularly in the Middle East. He argues that unlike other imperial powers, for the first eighty years after its founding in 1923, the Turkish republic largely ignored relations with the states that had been formed out of the former Ottoman provinces in North Africa and the Middle East, and that Turkey needed to play a greater role there.

Davutoğlu's "neo-Ottoman" vision, it should be noted, was very different from Islamist policies advocated by WP leader Necmettin Er- bakan.[17] While Erbakan sought to create an Islamic alliance with Muslim countries like Libya, Iran, Malaysia, and Indonesia as an explicit alternative to alliance with the West, JDP leaders wanted to reach out to the East to complement their ties to the West, not replace them. Their vision, which builds on the approach of former President Özal, is one in which Turkey rediscovers its imperial legacy and seeks a new national consensus where the multiple identities of Turkey can coexist. It reminds Turks that they once had a great multinational empire that ruled the Middle East, North Africa, the Balkans, and parts of Central Europe. Such emphasis on the Ottoman legacy is not part of a plan to Islamize Turkey and Turkish foreign policy. Rather, it is an attempt to balance and broaden the horizons of Kemalism and its obsession with Turkey's Western identity and trajectory.

Three factors help define the neo-Ottoman tendencies of the JDP. The first is the willingness to come to terms with Turkey's Ottoman and

Islamic heritage at home and abroad. Neo-Ottomanism does not call for Turkish imperialism in the Middle East and the Balkans. Similarly, it does not seek to institute an Islamic legal system in modern Turkey. Instead, neo-Ottomanism favors a more moderate version of secularism at home and a more activist policy in foreign affairs. In this neo-Ottoman paradigm, Ankara exerts more "soft power"—political, economic, diplomatic, and cultural influence—in formerly Ottoman territories as well as in other regions where Turkey has strategic and national interests. This broad vision for Turkish foreign policy requires an embrace of Ottoman "great power" legacy and a redefinition of Turkey's strategic and national identity and interests.[18]

In practical terms, such a shift in the "mindset" has serious implications for policy making. For instance, because neo-Ottomanism is at peace with the imperial and multinational legacy of Turkey, it opens the door for a less "ethnic" and more multicultural conceptualization of "citizenship." As a result, neo-Ottomanism sees no major threat behind Kurdish cultural rights and the expression of Kurdish national identity as long as Kurds maintain a sense of loyalty to the Republic of Turkey.[19] Similarly, when faced with Kurdish demands for cultural and political rights, the neo-Ottoman mindset prefers to accommodate such demands in the framework of multiculturalism and Muslim identity. In other words, unlike Kemalist hardliners, who insist on assimilating the Kurds, neo-Ottomanism allows Islam to play a greater role in terms of building a sense of shared identity. Just like in Ottoman times, Islam thus becomes a crucial common denominator between Kurds and Turks.

This more flexible mindset, in turn, leads to the second characteristic of neo-Ottomanism: a sense of grandeur and self-confidence in foreign policy. Neo-Ottomanism sees Turkey as a regional superpower. Its strategic vision and culture reflect the geographic reach of the Ottoman Empire. Turkey, as a pivotal state, should thus play a very active diplomatic, political, and economic role in a wide region in which it is the "center." Such grand ambitions require a nation-state at peace with its multiple identities, including its Muslim and Ottoman past.

According to Kemalists, this ambitious vision of neo-Ottoman foreign policy is unrealistic and prone to adventurism. The idea of allowing the Kurds cultural rights and Islam more political space amounts to dangerous departures from secular, national, and other norms of the Republic. In that sense, the Kemalists consider the neo-Ottoman mindset harmful to Turkey's national interests and not that different from Islamism. Moreover,

Kemalist foreign policy rejects pan-Turkic or Islamic openings toward the Middle East and central Asia, mainly on the grounds that they are against Atatürk's precepts of a strictly "national" foreign policy. As such, Kemalist foreign policy puts a high premium on maintaining the status quo and confronting the threat of Kurdish separatism.

The third aspect of JDP's neo-Ottomanism is its pragmatic goal of embracing the West as much as the Islamic world. Like the imperial city of Istanbul, which straddles Europe and Asia, neo-Ottomanism is Janus-faced. Even on its deathbed, the Ottoman Empire was known as the sick man of "Europe" and not of Asia or Arabia. In that sense, the European legacy matters a great deal to neo-Ottomans. They are as open to the West and Western political influences as they are close to the Muslim legacy. Such pragmatism and flexibility are largely absent in the "orientalist" mindset of Kemalist hardliners, who consider Islam, multiculturalism, and liberalism as potential enemies of the Kemalist revolution.[20] Not surprisingly, the JDP's ability to embrace the West and the EU leaves many Kemalists unconvinced, as they suspect a hidden Islamic agenda. In fact, the Kemalist establishment is increasingly suspicious of Westerners—particularly the EU and the United States—whom they see as naive toward Islamists and dangerously tolerant of Kurdish nationalism.

In short, there are clear differences between Kemalism and neo-Ottomanism in these three main aspects of strategic culture. Where neo-Ottomanism favors an ambitious regional policy in the Middle East and beyond, Kemalism opts for modesty and caution. Where one favors multiculturalism and a more moderate version of secularism, the other prefers strict measures against headscarves and Kurdish ethnic identity. Where one is increasingly resentful of the EU and the United States, the other is much more pragmatic in its relations with the West, as we can see in both Özal and Erdoğan's approach to Washington and Brussels.

A major problem with Kemalism is its illiberal tendency and attachment to an anachronistic concept of "modernity and progress" based on nineteenth-century positivism. Today, it is this very success that transforms Kemalism into a conservative ideology. Kemalism, in other words, seeks to conserve what has been achieved. Especially for Turkey's politically powerful military, Kemalism represents a defensive instinct against the perceived enemies of the secular Turkish republic: Kurdish nationalism and political Islam. As mentioned in the previous chapter, concerned about the ascendance of these forces, Kemalism has become a secularist and nationalist reflex rather than a coherent ideology. Any deviation from the Turkish character of the nation-state and the secular framework of the republic presents a challenge to Kemalist identity.

Despite such differences between Kemalism and neo-Ottomanism, both share a strong sense of patriotism and attachment to the Turkish nation-state. Neo-Ottomanism represents a more pragmatic and liberal mindset than Kemalism, but it has successfully internalized the Kemalist paradigm of Turkish nationalism.[21] The concept of the nation-state and the achievements of the modern Turkish republic are not put into question or rejected by neo-Ottomans. At the end of the day, both neo-Ottomanism and Kemalism share a state-centric view of the world and Turkish national interests. In that sense, both Kemalism and neo-Ottomanism share Turkish nationalism as a common denominator. In fact, seen from the prism of rising Turkish self-confidence and nationalism, one can even argue that there is a certain convergence between neo-Ottomanism and Kemalism.

This delicate balance between Kemalism and neo-Ottomanism was also a practical necessity because of the domestic balance of power as long as the military establishment remained a quasi-hegemonic actor. In other words, the secular and nationalist tendencies of the generals and the fear of another coup similar to the one witnessed in 1997 tempered Islamist inclinations the JDP could have nurtured. Although some Kemalists considered neo-Ottomanism as an Islamist foreign policy, it is clear that neither the domestic nor the international context really favored a policy that would turn overtly Islamist during the first decade of the JDP. This is why the 2003–2011 era in Turkish foreign policy can better be appreciated in the context of a necessary balance rather than overt confrontation between the secular and Islamic.

On the other hand, the emphasis of a major clash between Islam and secularism during this pre–Arab Spring period of Turkish foreign policy is an understandable fallacy based on a familiar and conventional dichotomy. Many policy makers, analysts, and scholars tend to equate the notion of Turkish divergence from the West—or the fear of "losing Turkey"—with the idea of an Islamic revival. Moreover, this is exactly how some members within Turkey's Kemalist establishment—the military, the Republican People's Party, and the foreign service—described JDP policies vis-à-vis Iran, Syria, the Gulf, and Israel. Such an analysis gave a sense of credibility to the fallacy of an overtly "Islamist" foreign policy in Turkey.[22]

A foreign policy that can truly be labeled along the lines of described in our chapter on political Islam and the ideal of "unity of Muslims" became contextually possible only during the third term of the JDP after the party consolidated its position at home in the wake of the 2007 and 2011 elections and sidelined the military and foreign service as hegemonic Kemalist actors. In that sense, the JDP had to be able to dominate the domestic scene before the activation of its ideological tendencies in an Islamist direction infused with heavy authoritarianism. And even then, this journey toward political Islam needed the collaboration of the international context in three major ways. First, the project of EU membership had to prove elusive. Second, the Arab Spring had to provide an incentive and opportunity space for an Islamist policy in support of Muslim Brotherhood parties. And third, the United States had to see no conflict between its own objectives in the Middle East and Turkey's pursuit of an Islamist foreign policy toward the region.

While the growing importance of religion in Turkey should not be dismissed under the JDP's first decade in power, the real divergence with the West was due less to an Islamic reaction than to growing nationalism and frustration. Overall, the JDP tried hard to maintain good relations with both the EU and the United States between 2002 and 2013. The year 2013 appeared to be a turning point in the deterioration of the United States' image within JDP circles and particularly within Erdoğan's mind because of two major developments. First, the United States was silent when the Egyptian military intervened against the Muslim Brotherhood and Gezi protests in Turkey. Erdoğan quickly blamed the West and probably feared that in the unlikely case the military intervened in Turkey, Washington and Brussels would stay silent, as they had in the case of Egypt. Second, when the Obama administration began supporting the Kurds in Syria the next year, things went from bad to worse in terms of anti-Americanism in Turkey. With Turkey supporting Jihadist groups in Syria, the Islamist turn in Turkey's policies had become undeniable.[23]

Such an Islamist turn in Turkey required all these domestic and external factors—ranging from the emasculation of the Kemalist establishment to the regional upheaval that was expected to bring to power Islamists—to come together. None of this was predictable by 2003, when JDP appeared set to pursue good relations with the West. Yet even then there were signs of problems with West, it was not Turkey's religious identity or political Islam that caused the crisis: instead, it was that Turkey's own national interests clashed with American designs. What comes first to mind is the most obvious case of divergence on Iraq with a democratic Turkey that pursued its own interests in Iraq by taking the issue of whether to support the American invasion in 2003 to its parliament. The result is well-known: Ankara did not support the US military enterprise in Iraq. Tensions with neoconservative hawks in the Bush administration continued over matters related to Turkey's good relations with Syria, Iran, and Hamas and its major confrontation with Israel.[24] All of this happened during the JDP's first decade in power, during which an overtly Islamist path was not yet the case in Ankara.

During this era, one can argue that what motivated the JDP was not really an Islamist foreign policy but a sovereignty, national interest–conscious policy that did not hesitate to turn defiant, independent, self-confident, and self-centered in its strategic orientation. Beyond a clash between neo-Ottomanism and Kemalism, this stance was to some extent based on a certain harmony between the two. It was as if the JDP were following a Turkish variant of "Gaullism."[25] As in the case of Charles de Gaulle's anti-American and anti-NATO policies in the 1960s, a Gaullist Turkey in search of strategic depth under the JDP put a premium on full independence, full sovereignty, strategic leverage, and, most importantly, "Turkish glory and grandeur." The Kemalist variant of Eurasianism with a vision that seeks potential partnerships with Russia, Iran, and China is also in line with such Gaullist thinking and not directly opposed to neo-Ottomanism as long as it is not overtly Islamic and openly nationalist and anti-American.[26] In today's Turkey after the Islamist disappointment and setbacks experienced in the wake of the Arab Spring, both the neo-Ottoman and Kemalist camps embrace the same narrative vis-à-vis Europe and the United States: nationalist frustration.[27]

This frustrated and isolated Turkey appears to be in pursuit of its own strategic independence by pursuing what looks like a Gaullist policy. Erdoğan's narrative about developing Turkey's own nuclear force as a kind of Gaullist "force de frappe" and his penchant for "Realpolitik" with countries such as China and Russia are noteworthy. By 2020, now that Turkey's Islamist adventures in Egypt and Syria have largely failed and Erdoğan appears to have established a coalition with nationalists—some of them staunch ultra-secular and anti-American left-wing Kemalists—one should not underestimate the emergence of an alliance between the JDP and a much-reduced Turkish military that transcends the Islamic-secular divide. This new alliance could be based on both the Turkish military's Kemalism and the JDP's neo-Ottomanism under common denominators such as nationalism, grandeur, sovereignty, and of course anti-Americanism. In such a Gaullist Turkey, the JDP and the Kemalists will have to learn to downplay their disagreements about Islam and secularism in favor of a sort of "Muslim nationalism with an Ottoman touch" and focus instead on their common objective: strategic autonomy with the common objective of becoming a self-reliant regional superpower.[28]

It is certainly a tempting intellectual exercise to try to predict which way the ideological winds will blow for the future of Turkish foreign policy. Yet what makes much more sense for the purpose of this chapter on analyzing the JDP's Middle East policy is a focus on actual events and policies without putting Islamism, Kemalism, neo-Ottomanism, or Turkish Gaullism a priori at the forefront of the analysis. Depending on what specific context or events are driving strategies, differences between these undercurrents in Turkish foreign policy can be subtler than any sharp doctrinal dichotomy. What can be argued with more certainty, however, is that a confluence of domestic and external dynamics after 2010 opened a window of opportunity for the JDP to follow a more Islamist and hubristic policy in search of Muslim unity and regional influence. Both domestic and regional contexts enabled such an Islamist turn during the Arab Spring. It is also clear that this experiment in pan-Islamist solidarity ended in utter failure with the demise of the Muslim Brotherhood in Egypt in 2013 and the victory of the Assad regime in Syria by 2018.

One must therefore examine actual events and their contextual specificities as much as the broader strategic vision and policies to make sense of Turkey's decision in the Middle East. We do so in the next sections by looking at concrete examples since the JDP came to power. The obvious place to start is the first major event that tested the inexperienced JDP government months after its electoral victory in November 2002: the Bush administration's decision to invade Iraq.

The 2003 Iraq Debacle

Turkey had no particular ideological or security attachment to the regime of Saddam Hussain, but Baghdad traditionally provided stability on Turkey's southern border. In the eyes of the Turkish national security establishment, the Baathist regime was an effective bulwark against Kurdish separatism in Iraq.[29] Ankara had always been opposed to political or military destabilization in the region, fearing that such developments could fan ethnic separatism or sectarian conflict. Moreover, since the arrest of PKK leader Abdullah Öcalan in 1998, Turkey had enjoyed a much-cherished sense of peace and stability in its Kurdish regions. As the PKK was subdued, political and economic relations with Syria and Iran significantly improved. By the close of the century, Turkish policy makers began to speak of normalization and the emergence of a "zone of peace" as the main objective of Turkey's new Middle East policy. Davutoğlu fashioned this into a policy of "zero problems" with neighbors and regional partners.[30] Under such circumstances, the last thing the JDP, the Turkish military, and the Turkish public at large wanted was another war in Iraq.

U.S.-Turkish differences over the war came to a head in early 2003, when Ankara was pressed to respond to a US request to preposition the 4th Armored Division in Turkey for a potential invasion of Iraq from the north. In accordance with the overwhelming majority of Turkish public opinion, the JDP government was against the war, but it also wanted to maintain good relations with the Bush administration that hailed Turkey as a democratic model for the region. The Kemalist military establishment was as usual quite cautious about any major involvement in the Middle East. The generals were at the forefront of negotiations with Washington but remained reluctant to commit the Turkish army for a joint ground operation, especially in the absence of a United Nations or even NATO consensus for the invasion decision.[31] Yet, as the Pentagon seemed determined to move forward unilaterally with a coalition of the willing, Turkish generals became particularly disturbed by the American-Kurdish military cooperation and the joint buildup in Iraqi Kurdistan. They feared that the Kurds would emerge as the main beneficiaries in a post-Saddam Iraq, because the dynamics on the ground might lead incrementally to the emergence of an independent Kurdish state.

On top of these problems, there was also clear distrust between the Turkish military and the JDP. The military considered the JDP an Islamist party and was not convinced by its EU reform agenda. The JDP had already irritated the military and the Kemalist national security establishment by promoting a plan for reunification and compromise on Cyprus. Given this state of affairs in Turkey's civil-military relations, the generals seemed happy to see Washington's relations with the "Islamist" JDP deteriorate. The JDP top leadership also seemed divided over the issue of supporting the United States. Foreign Minister Abdullah Gül believed Turkey could avert the war by mobilizing Iraq's neighbors behind a regional peace initiative.

The government postponed several times the parliamentary vote on allowing the US military to use Turkish soil for the invasion of Iraq. On the other hand, there was consensus about the need for a large compensation package, and the JDP bargained hard with the United States over what Ankara would receive in return for its cooperation. The negotiations were difficult and often acrimonious—the Americans believed Ankara should be willing to help its strategic partner, while the Turkish government resented the "reality" that it could be "bought off" to support a war considered ill-advised.

Weeks before the war, the JDP brought together six key regional powers—Turkey, Egypt, Iran, Jordan, Saudi Arabia, and Syria (Kuwait did not participate) in a series of regional conferences. This Turkish initiative led to the "Istanbul Declaration," which was explicitly aimed at heading off a US military attack. Although some analysts in the United States and Turkey saw the motivation behind the initiatives as "Islamist," the initiative was based not so much on Muslim solidarity as on a Turkish self-perception as a regional leader.[32] The JDP policy was dictated by a strong sense of self-confidence and national interest—both part of the neo-Ottoman and Kemalist framework described above.

Yet in the end, Turkey's ambitious initiative failed to produce concrete results. Negotiations between Ankara and Washington eventually resulted in a US offer to provide Turkey with $15 billion in grants and loans along with an agreement that some 20,000 Turkish troops could enter northern Iraq to protect Turkish interests there.[33] Despite this deal, the Turkish parliament shocked the United States, and perhaps itself, on March 1, 2003, when it narrowly voted against allowing the United States to open a northern front against Baghdad from Turkey. Washington's frustration with Turkey's decision was enormous. Three years after the vote, Defense Secretary Donald Rumsfeld was still partly blaming Turkey for the Iraqi insurgency: "Had we been successful in getting the 4th Infantry Division to come in through Turkey in the north when our forces were coming up from the south out of Kuwait," Rumsfeld said, "I believe that a considerably smaller number of the Ba'athists and the regime elements would have escaped. More would have been captured or killed, and as a result, the insurgency would have been at a lesser intensity than it is today."[34]

Relations between Turkey and the United States over Iraq got even worse after the war started, when, on July 4, 2003, US forces in northern Iraq detained eleven Turkish special forces members suspected of planning to participate in the assassination of a local Kurdish politician. The Turks were released after forty-eight hours, but not before they were hooded and treated as prisoners by the Americans, causing great humiliation and resentment in Turkey. The Turkish general staff spoke of "the worst crisis of confidence" between Ankara and Washington in more than fifty years, and Foreign Minister Gül warned that "this harm cannot be forgotten."[35] Although the two sides eventually issued a joint statement of regret about the incident, for many Turks "July 4" came to symbolize America's hostility to Turkey in the same way that for the Bush administration "March 1" came to symbolize Turkey's lack of support for the United States. The strategic partnership that was supposed to bind the two countries together was crumbling in the sands of Iraq.

JDP's Zero Problems in Action

The post-invasion chaos in Iraq drove Turkey more deeply into the Middle East. After the invasion, Ankara's worst fears were realized. Iraq became a breeding ground for international terrorism and descended into sectarian and ethnic violence. Tehran's influence was greatly increased in Iraq and in the region more broadly. The Iraqi Kurds' drive for autonomy—and perhaps eventually formal independence—gained momentum. Once believed to have dissolved, the PKK took up arms again. Beginning in January 2005, the PKK launched repeated attacks on Turkish territory, killing several hundred Turkish security forces. Although the PKK maintained some guerilla and urban presence in Turkey, most Turkish observers believed its main attacks were being organized from sanctuaries in the Kandil Mountains in northern Iraq.[36]

Turkey's Kemalist instincts and neo-Ottoman tendencies shared the main objective as far as the Kurdish question was concerned: to stop the emergence of an independent Kurdish state in the region. Yet the way the two camps wanted to achieve this goal often differed. The nationalist-Kemalist position traditionally refused even open dialogue with the Iraqi Kurdish authorities, mainly because of the PKK presence in Kandil. For instance, when he was president of Turkey (2000–2007), Ahmet Necdet Sezer, a staunch Kemalist, objected to any dialogue with Iraqi President Jalal Talabani, mainly because the latter was Kurdish. The JDP position proved much more flexible and pragmatic. In 2007, Foreign Minister Gül had to cancel the scheduled visit to Turkey of Kurdish Regional Government Prime Minister Nerchivan Barzani when the chief of the Turkish general staff publicly announced his opposition to such contacts. Only when Abdullah Gül became president in August 2007 did Turkey invite Jalal Talabani to make an official visit. This clear display of clashing tendencies proved that while the JDP was willing to co-opt the Kurds and play "big brother" to them, the Kemalist position remained stubbornly against any major diplomatic engagement.[37] At the end of the day, the potential of several billions of dollars in Turkish investment and trade in tipped the balance in favor of engagement in with Iraqi Kurds as Ankara emerged as the Kurdistan Regional Government (KRG)'s main trading partner.

Another issue that created tension was the sectarian question in Iraq. The Sunnis of Iraq found themselves marginalized in post-Saddam Iraq, as the Shiite majority gained politically and demographically the upper hand. The JDP's very active diplomacy with Iraq's Sunni minority, particularly in terms of encouraging them to participate in elections and join the government, did not find much support among Kemalists, who were generally averse to sectarian approaches to Iraq. The Kemalists feared that any sectarian Turkish approach toward Iraq would backfire and pave the way for Iraqi attempts to play the Kurdish card against Ankara. It is in this context that the JDP's "zero problems" served a critical purpose with the Kemalist establishment: the message that there would be no Islamist adventurism. Instead, the JDP's main message was constructive engagement in the framework of multilateral diplomacy.

Sending troops to Afghanistan in the framework of NATO and International Security Assistance Forces (ISAF), contributing to UN forces in Lebanon, active diplomatic mediation between Israel and Syria over the disputed Golan Heights, trying to avert a nuclear standoff between Iran and the United States by engaging in nuclear diplomacy, and assuming a leadership position in the Organization of Islamic Cooperation between 2005 and 2013 were some of multidimensional policies followed by the JDP during its first decade of zero problems with Middle Eastern neighbors. Overall, despite some reservations on Cyprus, most of these policies based on constructive engagement received praise from Kemalists.[38]

Echoing Atatürk's slogan "Peace at Home, Peace in the World," the JDP signaled peaceful engagement in the pursuit of constructive mutually beneficial diplomatic, economic, and cultural relations as the ultimate strategic objective. Of all the foreign policy initiatives of the JDP vis à vis the Middle East, it was not surprisingly relations with Syria and Iran—two difficult neighbors in the eyes of both Kemalists and the West—where domestic and international scrutiny was at its highest for the potential of Islamization.

Engagement with Syria and Iran

Turkey's relations with Syria improved dramatically during the first decade of the new century before declining rapidly again in 2011.[39] Hafiz Assad's decision to expel Abdullah Öcalan opened the way for a gradual improvement in economic and diplomatic relations after the Adana Agreement in 1998.[40] This rapprochement was underscored by Syrian President Bashar al-Assad's visit to Ankara in January 2005—the first trip by a Syrian president to Turkey since Syria gained independence in 1946. As with Iran, the main driver of the Turkish-Syrian rapprochement was their common interest in dealing with Kurdish separatists. Both Ankara and Damascus worried that the Iraq War had unleashed a serious threat of Kurdish nationalism that both must work together to contain.

Like Iran, Syria sought to use the rapprochement with Turkey to break free of isolation, especially that imposed on it by the West after the assassination of Lebanese Prime Minister Rafik al-Hariri in February 2005. It did so in part by developing its economic relationship with Turkey. Between 2005 and 2007, Syrian authorities approved more than thirty Turkish investment projects in the country with a total value of more than $150 million.[41] Bilateral trade was approximately $1.5 billion in 2007, more than triple the figure when the JDP came to power in November 2002. Also, the number of Turkish tourists to Syria increased nineteenfold between 2000 and 2005. Ankara and Damascus agreed in 2006 to establish a free-trade zone; and with Damascus encouraging Turkish investment in Syria, the two countries established a joint company for oil exploration. In March 2010, Turkey and Syria lifted visa requirements for their nationals and signed a "High Level Strategic Cooperation Council Agreement," which aimed to boost economic integration and regional stability. Later in the year the visa restrictions were extended to Jordan and Lebanon, thus creating a Turkish-Syrian-Jordanian-Lebanese zone of free movement of goods and persons.[42]

Ankara also started brokering indirect Syrian-Israeli contacts in 2007, and in May 2008 these talks were made public and intensified. However, the mediation was suspended in the wake of Israel's war on Gaza in

December-January 2008–2009. Turkey's role in these talks greatly raised its diplomatic profile, especially at a time when the Bush administration had all but abandoned the peace process. Turkish-Israeli relations took a nosedive in late January after a very public dispute between Erdoğan and Shimon Peres over the Gaza war at the Davos World Economic Forum and deteriorated further in the wake of the Gaza flotilla incident in late May 2010.[43] As Turkey's relations with Israel deteriorated, Turkey grew even closer to Syria, with warm visits by the two leaders. As we will see, all of this rapprochement came crashing down in the midst of the Syrian uprising in 2011.

In short, the decade before Syria collapsed into chaos saw Ankara invest heavily in further attempts to shore up influence with the new Assad government. During this time, Erdoğan and Assad became the first leaders on either side of the border to visit the other country. Erdoğan saw Syria's foreign policy as stuck in another time and used its influence to try to bring in Syria from the cold by supporting the country in the aftermath of the Syrian withdrawal from Lebanon in 2005. In line with this, in 2007 and 2008 Turkey played a key role in fostering negotiations between Israel and Syria over the Golan Heights issue. Relations reached their zenith in late 2010 when, along with Lebanon and Jordan, the two countries formed the Levant Quartet, an organization with the goal of an EU-like political union in the region.[44] Thus, through diplomatic, economic, and political measures focused more on a thaw than combativeness, Erdoğan believed he had achieved new heights in influence and control over his Southern neighbor.

Relations with Iran

Iran was another neighbor where dynamics of engagement characterized Turkey's relations during the first decade of the JDP in power.[45] Turkey and Iran come from rival imperial and religious traditions. The Ottomans were historically the defenders of Sunni Islam against the Shi'i Persians. Particularly after their conquest of Mecca and Medina in the fifteenth century, Ottoman Sultans who assumed the title of caliph came to see the Shi'i Safavids as heretic contenders on their eastern borders. Ottomans and Safavids fought major wars during the sixteenth century. On the other hand, as Turkish officials are quick to remind their Western partners concerned about Iran's ascendency, the last major war fought between Turks and Persians was almost 400 years ago. In addition to a long and peaceful relationship since then, Atatürk's Turkey became a secular and Western model for Iran's Pahlavi dynasty during the first half of the twentieth century. In fact, Iran's White Revolution in the 1960s was greatly inspired by Turkey's Kemalist cultural revolution. By contrast to Ankara's negative image in the Arab world (as a former colonial master that turned its back on Islam), the image of secular Turkey in Pahlavi Iran was largely positive during most of the 1960s and 1970s. As two important allies of the United States, Turkey and Iran put their imperial competition and religious rivalry aside during most of the Cold War. However, this harmony with Tehran ended abruptly in 1979 after the Islamic revolution in the country. When Ayatollah Ruhollah Khomeini emphasized "exporting" the Islamic revolution, Turkey with its secular and pro-Western political regime, came to see itself as a natural target of such efforts. As a result, by the 1980s, the historic rivalry between Turkey and Iran reemerged—this time in the context of a secular Turkey versus an Islamic Iran. Yet despite such difficult and antagonistic dynamics, Ankara maintained a traditional Kemalist policy of nonengagement and noninvolvement in the Middle East. Thanks largely to this policy, Ankara managed to remain neutral during the Iran-Iraq war of the 1980s. Throughout that long and bloody conflict, Ankara's neutrality served the Turkish economy well. Turkish exports to both countries increased sevenfold.

By the mid-1990s, as Iran's Islamic revolution lost steam, political relations between Ankara and Tehran also slowly began to improve. This rapprochement was also helped by political Islam gaining some social and cultural ground in Turkey with the arrival of the WP to power. In fact, it was under the Islamist-led coalition government of Erbakan that Ankara signed a $23 billion deal for the delivery of natural gas from Iran to Turkey. After coming to power in 1996, Erbakan quickly launched new openings to the Islamic world. Because the Turkish military was vigilant about any departure from secularism at home, Erbakan's overtures to the Islamic world were partly designed to compensate for the absence of a domestic Islamic agenda. Yet it did not take very long for Erbakan's high-profile state visits to Iran and Libya to upset both Washington and Turkey's secular military establishment. Given its official policy of isolating Iran, a major energy deal between Tehran and Ankara was not welcomed by Washington. In time, the Turkish military and secularist public opinion also began to worry about Erbakan's outreach to the Islamic world. Erbakan's short tenure in power—he was forced from office by the soft coup of 1997—included visits to Egypt, Malaysia, Pakistan, Indonesia, and Nigeria.

Erbakan's interest in improving Turkey's economic and political ties with the Islamic world reached an unprecedented level in 1997, when his government took a leadership role in the establishment of the "Developing Eight" (D-8) organization, a Muslim countries' version of the G8. The establishment of the D-8 was announced officially in Istanbul at an economic summit with the heads of state of Bangladesh, Egypt, Indonesia, Iran, Malaysia, Nigeria, and Pakistan.[46] Progress in Turkish-Iranian relations during the late 1990s was not confined to economic relations or the Islamic solidarity of Erbakan. As trade relations between Ankara and Tehran improved, the two countries also increasingly began to focus on the Kurdish issue. Iran, home to 5 million Kurds, has historically been concerned about Kurdish separatism.

Although Tehran has traditionally been more tolerant than Turkey of Kurdish cultural rights, the Islamic regime still shares Ankara's concerns about an increasingly independent Kurdish region in Iraq. As a result, Turkey and Iran began cooperating on the security front in the framework of the Turkey-Iran High Security Commission established in 1988. However, this body became more active after the fall of the Saddam regime and after the formation of Party for Freedom of Kurdistan or PJAK, a sister terrorist organization of the PKK active in Iran. Although the PKK and PJAK are organizationally distinct, both have their main training camps in the Kandil mountains of northern Iraq, where they logistically cooperate and profess allegiance to PKK founder Abdullah Öcalan. In October 2011, both Turkey and Iran were involved separately in attacks on PKK and PJAK military bases in Iraq's Kandil mountains.[47]

Since the emergence of the PJAK in 2004, the Turkey-Iran High Security Commission has met several times, and the agenda has been dominated by discussions about intelligence cooperation against the PKK and PJAK. In 2004, Ankara and Tehran signed a security cooperation agreement that branded the PKK a terrorist organization. For Tehran, Turkey's Kurdish obsession proved a useful issue to press Turkey to stay out of an economic embargo or a coalition of the willing with the West in case of a U.S.-Iranian military confrontation. During visits to Ankara, Iranian officials often stress the troubles created for both nations by the PKK.

Strong Turkish-Iranian relations also led to a remarkable role for Turkey in Iran's nuclear dispute with the West and the international community. In May 2010, as the United States moved to secure international sanctions against Iran, Turkey along with Brazil negotiated a nuclear deal with Iran in which Iran would exchange 1,200 kilograms of its low-enriched Uranium for 20 kilograms of 20 percent enriched uranium for the Tehran research reactor. The deal met with an angry US response, although Ankara argued that the deal was in line with what US and Western negotiators had been trying to get Tehran to agree to. The United States and other permanent members of the UN Security Council secured a vote for sanctions against Iran a few days later, while both Turkey and Brazil voted against the sanctions.

Even Turkey's secularist establishment appeared willing to engage in more direct relations with Iran. For instance, it is quite remarkable that in June 2002, shortly after President George W. Bush declared Iran part of the "axis of evil," the Turkish President Ahmet Necdet Sezer, who had excellent relations with the Turkish military, visited Iran. Iran's welcome extended to letting Sezer become the first Turkish president to visit the Turkish-Azeri regions of the country and to give a lecture in Tehran (on Kemalism and Atatürk). Of course, Iran was then under President Muhammad Khatami, who declared to Sezer that Tehran strongly supported Turkey's EU membership as a symbol against the supposed "Clash of Civilizations."[48] One of the greatest elements that has ensured that this positive engagement would continue is the dependence of both parties on energy flows.

Beginning in 1996, Iran and Turkey signed a gas agreement, promising that a pipeline would be laid down to carry natural gas from Iran's northern gas fields near Tabriz directly to Ankara.[49] The 2,577-km pipeline, commissioned in 2001, has the capacity to carry 14 billion cubic meters of natural gas from Iran to Turkey. In addition, the agreement obligated Turkey to buy at least 8.6 billion cubic meters of gas from Iran annually for 25 year.[50] Today Turkey imports 70 percent of its energy from outside the country and will continue to be dependent on foreign gas in large part at least until its large energy infrastructure projects conclude in the future.[51] Since the opening of the Tabriz-Ankara pipeline, Turkey has signed numerous Memoranda of Understanding on energy with Iran, further drawing the two countries together and enhancing the degree of mutual dependence and cooperation that the two countries share.

Iran's nuclear ambitions, however, are a source of serious concern for Turkey. Although Turkey does not see Iran as a threat, it is conscious that a nuclear-armed Iran could have a destabilizing impact on the Persian Gulf region and force Turkey to take countermeasures for its own security.

Because of the destabilizing nature of the Iranian nuclear program and rather than working to develop its own program to counter the threat of a possible nuclear Iran, Turkish leaders sought a diplomatic settlement, which would peacefully end or at least considerably scale down the Iranian nuclear program. This further enhanced the visibility of joint Turco-Iranian interests and most importantly allowed Erdoğan and Davutoğlu to prove to the world that they had emerged from second-rate power status to a new position of preeminent regional influence and respectable global weight. Moreover, it would allow Turkey's leaders to use their temporary position on the UN Security Council to change perceptions of Turkey around the world. To this end, Turkey inserted itself into nuclear negotiations, attempting to moderate between Iran and the West on a peaceful resolution.[52]

By 2010, Iran had gained the support of Turkey and Brazil on a preliminary deal that would trade highly enriched nuclear fuel for lower-enriched fuel, giving Western powers a reassuring sign that Iran was willing to negotiate. Turkey's proactive move to insert itself in the Iran nuclear issue showed Turkish leaders' interest in protecting and enhancing the cooperative elements of their relationship with Iran and clearly showcased their desire to become a regional power broker. As time drew on, however, Turkey was marginalized in the negotiation process and was entirely sidelined when the United States opened direct talks with Iran in March 2013. The Joint Comprehensive Plan of Action, which would be signed between the P5+1 in 2015, formally showed little of Turkey's efforts to secure a deal for Iran, but certainly served the interests of Turco-Iranian coordination.

At the end, during its first decade in power Iran has been a testing ground for the JDP's relations with the United States. Despite its willingness to defy American financial sanctions and venture in its own nuclear diplomacy efforts, the JDP also discovered the limits of its strategic autonomy with Iran in 2011 when the Obama administration heavily pressured the JDP to host a NATO radar and ballistic missile defense system to closely monitor Tehran. Despite its discontent with being so actively included in efforts to contain Iran, the JDP caved and had to accept the deployment of the NATO radars. While Ankara had to swallow its pride, the deployment of this NATO radar system proved to be a major victory for the Obama administration. It firmly anchored Turkey's position in Western efforts to contain Iran's nuclear ambitions. Compartmentalizing relations with Tehran—cooperation against Kurdish nationalism but sectarian rivalry in Iraq—continued to be difficult for Ankara. By 2012, Syria would emerge as a much more troubling irritant in bilateral relations.

With the exception of bilateral relations with Israel, which began to deteriorate after 2010, it is clear that the JDP strongly engaged in highly positive engagements in the Middle East. Critically important was the fact that despite such strong relations with the Muslim neighborhood, the West was not neglected. Turkey began accession negotiations with the EU in 2006, and the United States remained a strategic military partner despite the Iraq debacle. This balancing act helped Erdoğan to secure his position as responsible statesman vis à vis the secularist establishment, where suspicions of a hidden Islamic agenda were never really far from the surface. In that sense, one of Erdoğan's primary goals was to remain in power by assuring that no major destabilization would take place in relations with the Kemalist establishment. This is why the era of zero problems that characterized the JDP's first decade was also a decade during which the JDP tried to have zero problems with the military.

Yet by 2007 this endeavor at peaceful coexistence between Erdoğan and the generals appeared to have reached its limits, as a serious confrontation seemed increasingly inevitable regarding the selection of a new president to replace the staunchly secularist Ahmet Necdet Sezer, whose term was up. The fact that the JDP felt confident to challenge the top brass regarding the presidency showed Erdoğan's growing level of confidence. It was also indicative of how the party also appeared ready to shift from caution to Islamist adventurism a few years later in the context of the Arab Spring. It is tempting to focus solely on the political and strategic in analyzing this important transition. However, the victory of the JDP on the domestic and foreign policy fronts against the old Kemalist guard would have been impossible without the strong performance of the Turkish economy and rising living standards for average citizens. In other words, Erdoğan had the economy and, together with such strong economic performance, the support of Turkish public opinion behind him.

Economy-Driven Foreign Policy: "the Rise of the Trading State"[53]

There was also a strong economic rationality behind Turkey's foreign policy during the JDP's first decade. It was during the Turgut Özal era that Turkey began adopting market-oriented neoliberal reforms in the mid 1980s, which marked the end of import substitution industrialization (ISI) and the beginning of export-oriented industrialization. Under Özal, thanks to structural reforms liberalizing the financial and trade sectors, Turkish exports began to increase together with the manufacturing performance of the country.

Since the mid-1980s, despite the lost decade of the 1990s, Turkey had made considerable progress in changing its domestic economic structure: the share of agricultural products in Turkey's exports decreased from 86 percent in the period of 1923–1930 to a mere 7.1 percent by 2000. More significantly, in due course, a new entrepreneur class came into being, centered in major Anatolian towns such as Gaziantep, Denizli, Kayseri, Malatya, and Konya, and threw their support behind the JDP. However, mostly Anatolian in origin, this class lacked international expertise and was further haunted by the language barrier to seek new markets abroad. Hence, they needed strong political support on their side to open up new markets to grow further. Furthermore, without active political support, they could hardly compete with much stronger international companies.

Erdoğan's high international profile and activist economic policies with the EU, the Middle East, and Africa and would play into their hands. What Erdoğan himself called "merchant politics" referred exactly to this project of opening up new markets all around the world for Turkey's Anatolian-based bourgeoise. A new Turkey with a new business community composed of so-called Anatolian tigers characterized this vibrant pro-JDP entrepreneurialism. In time, it became customary for the JDP leadership to travel with hundreds of businessmen around the world to establish commercial links and obtain contracts for them. Erdoğan and his team helped Turkey's exports increase from $36 billion in 2002 to $132 billion in 2008. As a sign of remarkable overall economic performance during the same years, Turkey's GDP more than doubled, and income per capita reached $10,000 in purchasing power parity.

When analyzing Turkey's relationship with countries such as Israel, Iran, and the Arab world, one has to consider this economic necessity: economic liberalization has created a thriving, export-oriented economy in Turkey; from agriculture to manufacturing, from construction to the service sector, tens of thousands of small, middle-, and large-scale family enterprises entered new markets to further their growth. Erdoğan tirelessly worked to help Turkish companies gain market share in all these new areas of investment and growth. In any case, receiving governmental support for exports either at the political level or with substantial subsidies was a well-established practice from the Özal years during the transition from ISI to export-led growth. Only a handful of Turkish companies did not need any political interference on their side to compete in new markets with much stronger international companies. And even the giants of Turkish construction companies needed political support to get big contracts, even in the Arab world.

Iran and the Arab world, in the most immediate geographical vicinity of Turkey, have acquired particular significance as Erdoğan's favorite foreign market search. Under Erdoğan governments, while Turkey's exports to EU countries almost tripled from $20 billion to $52 billion, between 2002 and 2010, Turkish exports to the Middle East and North Africa increased more than six times from $4.7 billion in 2002 to $30 billion in 2010. Improving relations with the Arab world and Iran did not cost the loss of Israel as an export destination either: exports to Israel increased by 2.4 times from $861 million in 2002 to $2 billion in 2010. The share of the MENA region in Turkey's total trade volume was particularly impressive during the JDP's first decade.

Turkey's exports to the region increased in relative terms from 13 percent in 2002 to 26 percent in 2002, while those to EU countries decreased from 56 percent in 2002 to 46 percent in 2010. It is also important to note that trade also created room for cultural and tourism-oriented rapprochement with the Middle East. Between 2002 and 2010, Turkey had become one of the top tourist destinations for Middle Eastern travelers: the number of Iranian and Arab tourists to Turkey increased from about one million in 2003 to about 2.8 million in 2010, adding a further boost to the Turkish economy.

Combined, all these factors—strong economic performance, rising regional influence, and political stability at home—meant that when the time of reckoning with the secularist establishment came in 2007, the JDP was in a much stronger position than when it first came to power in 2002. And the same dynamics apply to foreign policy adventurism in 2011. In other words, it is impossible to understand how the JDP managed to shift from caution to Islamist adventurism during the Arab Spring without analyzing all these dynamics. This is the issue we are turning to in the next chapter, which focuses on JDP's transformation after its first decade in power.

Chapter 3

THE ARAB SPRING

The JDP's pursuit of an Islamist foreign policy during its first two terms in power (from 2002 to 2007 and from 2007 to 2011) would have been a premature departure from traditional Kemalist norms. Neither the domestic nor the regional context would have supported it. Such adventurism would have been ill-advised at a time when the JDP had to contend with a powerful secularist establishment. An ideological posture was in that sense an unaffordable luxury that had to wait for more opportune times when conditions would be ripe. Prime Minister Recep Tayyip Erdoğan had learned this lesson well in his political journey from prison to the commanding heights of hegemonic power in Turkey. When the JDP managed to consolidate power in a quasi-uncontested way at home by 2011, the party was finally able to afford the luxury of its Islamist ideals, aspirations, and dreams. In other words, idealism and ideological thinking became "pragmatically and realistically" affordable only when the secularist military was no longer an impediment.

In what Erdoğan probably saw as a sign of divine providence, just when the domestic context seemed ripe for Islamism, external dynamics in the Middle East began to favor political Islam as well with the toppling of autocratic regimes. Islamists were to become the main beneficiaries of autocratic collapse in Tunisia and Egypt. More importantly, this ascension to power was not through violence, revolution, or autocratic repression. In Tunis and Cairo, the Muslim Brotherhood–oriented political formations assumed power with elections. Instead of overtly supporting political Islam, the electoral ascent of the Muslim Brotherhood allowed the JDP to make the critical claim that what the region needed was democracy.[1] Because it looked like democracy, elections, and political Islam went hand in hand, there was no need to single out an Islamist agenda. Democratization, after all, was a much more noble and legitimate process to support compared with Islamization.

Erdoğan famously paid lip service to secularism in a visit to Egypt after the collapse of the Mubarak regime.[2] His strong belief that Islamists would win elections was most likely part of his motivation in inviting the Islamists to respect the democratic and secular rules of the game. There was no need to challenge the secular and democratic system. On the contrary, there was a need to allay secularist fears both in Egypt and in the West that Islamists would destroy the system that had helped them come to power. In that sense, Erdoğan was also projecting Turkey's own model whereby the ballot box legitimized his party and his agenda. Plausible deniability against accusations of Islamism was thus conveniently established.

Erdoğan and Davutoğlu clearly believed that Islamists in Egypt and Tunisia, once in power, would see the JDP's Turkey as their natural part-ner and a model to emulate.[3] Yet behind such idealism and support for democratic change there were also realpolitik and mercantilist interests at play. After all, Turkey did not have major economic, trade, or financial equities in either Tunisia or in Egypt. This was not the case in Libya, where the authoritarian Qaddafi regime was a major partner because of lucrative and vast construction projects. In that sense, there was always some realism behind Erdoğan's Islamist idealism. A sober cost-benefit analysis showed that the JDP did not have much to lose by supporting the new regimes in Egypt and in Tunisia.

Similar dynamics applied to Syria, where the JDP had financial and political interests. Ankara initially hesitated and maintained the hope of reforming the regime. In a sense, the luxury of ideology was missing be-cause of realistic concerns. Caution was in order. Yet once reforms proved elusive in Syria and the cycle of internal opposition and repression gained momentum, the context changed, and the JDP's ideology gained the upper hand in strategic evaluations and action. By 2012, the JDP threw such caution to the wind and decided to sail full force toward Islamist waters. The fact that the Turkish reaction to Tunisia, Egypt and Syria differed is a strong reminder that context matters as much as ideological inclinations. The delicate balance between pragmatism and idealism may not create a clear winner unless the context favors one or the other. This is why how the actor sees the context is of critical importance for the activation of ideology or for pragmatic restraint. This is also why this chapter analyzes the JDP's calibrated dance between idealism and pragmatism in tandem with the domestic and international context.

The Domestic Struggle: The Emasculation of the Military

Today, what confuses many analysts of the JDP is that before the autocratic turn in the country, Turkey witnessed considerable liberalization and de-mocratization under the same political leadership.[4] It is indeed very hard to deny the political success of the JDP during its first decade in power. For a while, it looked like Erdoğan would truly transform Turkey into a more liberal democratic country. Soon after coming to power in 2002, the JDP passed an impressive series of reforms to harmonize Turkey's judicial system, civil-military relations, and human rights practices with European norms.[5] The European Union (EU) began accession negotiations with Erdoğan's Turkey in 2005, rewarding the JDP's democratic reforms and Ankara's constructive approach to Cyprus. The JDP's efforts were not confined to democratization. Following the guidelines from an IMF stabilization program adopted after the 2001 financial meltdown, the JDP reaped the economic benefits of belt tightening and structural reforms. It pursued fiscal discipline, lowered a very high inflation rate to single digits, and prioritized good governance and social services in the areas of health care, housing, and urban infrastructure.[6]

Between 2002 and 2008, the Turkish economy grew by an average of 7.5 percent. Lower inflation and interest rates fueled domestic consumption. Thanks to good relations with the EU and a disciplined privatization program, the Turkish economy began to attract unprecedented amounts of foreign direct investment. The average per capita income nearly tripled, from $2,800 in 2001 to approximately $10,000 in 2011, exceeding those of some new EU members.[7] With its ever-expanding grassroots network and thanks to an improved economic climate, the JDP understood that the key to gaining even more political support was to target Turkey's large lower-middle class. Therefore, in addition to distributing food, subsidizing coal, and improving basic infrastructure in poor urban districts, the JDP governments prioritized upward economic mobility with housing credits for first-time home buyers and increased grants for students, favorable loans to the business community, and new public investment projects helping small and medium companies—the Anatolian tigers.[8] As a result of higher productivity and production, Turkish manufacturing and agriculture also took off. Turkish exports to the Middle East, Africa, Central Asia, and of course Europe—which remained the largest market for Turkish goods—increased almost fourfold between 2003 and 2008.[9]

Erdoğan's JDP proved equally adept in relations with the West. Thanks to a series of rapid democratic reforms and the promotion of minority rights, the JDP came to embody, at least in the eyes of progressive European political parties, a rare compatibility between Islamic tradition, secularism, and good governance.[10] Washington also admired and supported Erdoğan's brand of "moderate Islam." Turkey's mediation efforts between Israel and Syria received high praise. Despite its disappointment with Ankara's lack of support for the invasion of Iraq, the Bush administration still considered Turkey a model for the "freedom agenda" it supported in the Middle East. And as late as in 2012, President Barack Obama named Erdoğan as a friend with whom he established a regular line of communication about developments in the region.[11] Finally, by 2009, after having won two consecutive elections (2002 and 2007), Erdoğan took positive steps toward tackling Turkey's most daunting democratic challenge: the Kurdish question. Secret negotiations with the PKK and the organization's jailed leader Abdullah Öcalan began despite objections from nationalist circles and the military. These were bold initiatives that no other Turkish political party had dared to take in the long history of this ethnic conflict.[12]

However, as the JDP adopted a more liberal order, Kemalist segments of Turkish society grew increasingly suspicious that it had a hidden agenda. They feared that the JDP was exploiting the EU membership process to diminish the military's political role and, eventually, the Kemalist legacy.[13] They balked, for instance, at JDP measures to increase the ratio of civilians to military officers on the National Security Council, elect a civilian to head the National Security Council, remove military representatives from the boards of the Higher Education Council and the Radio and Television High Council, and grant broadcasting and cultural rights to Kurds.

As mentioned earlier, on foreign policy, Prime Minister Erdoğan's willingness to compromise on the question of Cyprus had already polarized relations with the generals. The JDP backed a United Nations plan to reunify the island; the military adamantly opposed the plan. The deadlock was an important obstacle to EU membership—and the pro-Islamist party actually appeared more willing to compromise than either the secularists or the military. Although the JDP did not seek confrontation, Turkey's internal divisions deepened between 2006 and 2008 over symbolic religious issues.

The JDP had long wanted to lift the ban on Islamic dress—or wearing of headscarves—in universities and end discrimination against graduates of İmam-Hatip schools (such as special criteria for their university entry exams). The JDP had strong popular support for both steps. Party leaders preferred to promote reform by building a national consensus rather than by challenging the secularist establishment head-on. But secularists remained wary. They pointed to Erdoğan's brief attempt to criminalize adultery in 2004, his appointment of religious conservatives to bureaucratic positions, and JDP attempts to discourage the sale of alcohol.[14]

There was another issue of much more serious nature that polarized the secularist debate over Islamization: the role of Fethullah Gülen in politics. The JDP's de facto coalition with a movement led by the influential cleric whose followers had gained critical positions within the intelligence, security (police), judiciary, and bureaucracy played a major role in fueling the secularist threat perception. Although they came from ideologically different Islamic backgrounds, both Erdoğan and Fethullah Gülen shared a common enemy: the ultrasecularist generals. They therefore established a marriage of convenience.[15] Erdoğan and Gülen had legitimate reasons to fear the powerful Turkish military. They both had served short prison sentences—Gülen in the 1970s and Erdoğan in the 1990s—in the wake of military interventions. And both men were suspect in the eyes of the top brass for nurturing hidden Islamist agendas behind their moderate façades.

The Kemalists were dismayed by the fact that both Erdoğan and Gülen seemed to fool naive Westerners in search of democratic models in the Islamic world. A nationalist and secularist sense of anger began to build up among Kemalist circles against the United States and EU. Some within the military even voiced the need to forge a new alternative strategic orientation for Turkey by building alliances with Russia and China. This "Eurasian" vision of Turkey's future was also in clear reaction to Washington's support for Kurds in post–Saddam Hussein Iraq. The fact that Fethullah Gülen already lived in self-imposed exile in the United States by the time the JDP came to power did not help to fight the conspiracy theory that he was controlled by the "West."

Gülen had become infamous after the soft coup of 1997 because of a leaked sermon in which he encouraged his followers to quietly pursue careers in government "until the time is ripe."[16] By the time he left for Pennsylvania in 1999, he was the most powerful and influential cleric in Turkey. His religious movement was known for having invested in education, interfaith dialogue, the media, and private economic enterprise since the late 1970s. Gülen had established hundreds of schools in Turkey and encouraged his graduates to serve in the government bureaucracy as well as in all the educational, social, media, and economic sectors where his movement was active. His self-imposed exile was a clear indication that he feared prosecution by the military's anti-Islamic campaign. In the eyes of the staunchly secularist army, Erdoğan and Gülen were made from the same Islamic cloth.[17] They tried to appear moderate but shared the same long-term objective: to topple the secular regime founded by Atatürk. And in 1999, the year Gülen left Turkey, Erdoğan began his four-month sentence in prison.

Erdoğan and Gülen openly supported each other between 2002 and 2012. They had a mutually beneficial coalition. The Gülen movement traditionally maintained good relations with centrist parties and kept a safe distance from Islamist politicians. This is why Fethullah Gülen stayed away from the WP's Necmettin Erbakan. When the JDP entered the Turkish political scene as a center-right party that repudiated its Islamist past, the Gülen movement became its natural ally. Erdoğan needed help, particularly educated and pious cadres in running the state. When he came to power in 2002 after his unexpectedly strong victory, he needed civil servants he could work with in the government and was unprepared to run the whole state apparatus. There was mutual distrust between the secular bureaucracy and the JDP. Erdoğan also needed protection from ultrasecularists within the military. After toppling the pro-Islamic Welfare Party, the generals remained highly skeptical of the JDP's agenda.

The Gülen movement proved ready to help. Fethullah Gülen had been investing in education, and his graduates had acquired mid-level positions within the bureaucracy since the early 1980s.[18] The relationship Fethullah Gülen forged with the JDP was strategic and highly useful for his movement. Gülen needed a powerful governing political party to support his movement's educational, media, business investments in Turkey, and beyond. In return, he was happy to provide the human capital the JDP needed to run the bureaucracy with Gülen school graduates and loyalists. In any case, these civil servants were already working in a wide array of governmental institutions ranging from the Ministry of Education to the police department.[19] Now they were to gain upward mobility and much more influence. Moreover, the JDP's brand of "moderate Islam" was in perfect harmony with Gülen's positivist Islamism and the kind of ethnoreligious "soft power" the Gülen brand represented. By the 2000s,

Gülen schools were mushrooming all over the world and had a strong reputation for excellence thanks to dedicated, missionary-like teachers.

In time, the biggest loser from this "coalition of the pious" proved to be the common enemy of Erdoğan and Gülen: the Turkish military. The generals knew that they had to act against this alliance and took a risky step in that direction in April 2007 when the Turkish General Staff issued a thinly veiled threat to the JDP not to nominate JDP cofounder Abdullah Gül to the presidency.[20] The generals appeared ready to once again take matters into their own hands. The presidency, a symbolic and ceremonial position in Turkey's parliamentary system, was traditionally associated with the secular establishment. Feeling strong in great part thanks to the popularity of his economic and social policies, Erdoğan did not bow to the intimidating tactics of the military.

Instead he pushed back, called early elections, and won the July 2007 general elections in a landslide. Soon after this victory, a jubilant Erdoğan and JDP-dominated Turkish parliament once again designated Abdullah Gül for the presidency. Shortly after Abdullah Gül's ascendance to the presidency, the military establishment once again challenged Erdoğan, this time by using Kemalist allies in the judiciary branch. The JDP was charged by a staunchly Kemalist prosecutor for promoting an Islamist agenda. The matter came before the Constitutional Court, a bastion of Kemalism, as a case for closure of the JDP on the grounds of anticonstitutional activities. The JDP narrowly survived this potential "judicial coup" in 2008 by only a couple of votes.[21]

On the one hand, Erdoğan had emerged victorious from these two major confrontations—one with the military, the other with the judiciary—with the Kemalist establishment. On the other hand, a day of reckoning between his newly emboldened JDP and the weakened Kemalist political system had become unavoidable. Shortly after the judicial coup failed, the Erdoğan-Gülen alliance launched a widespread investigation aiming to prosecute activist generals and other alleged coup plotters within the state bureaucracy. Between 2009 and 2011, the Ergenekon investigation emasculated Turkey's once very powerful military in great part thanks to the leading role of Gülenist prosecutors and informants within the security and judicial establishment.[22] Although some of the evidence against military officers appeared to be fabricated, Erdoğan and Gülen now had the upper hand against the Kemalist establishment. As the Ergenekon investigation moved forward in full force during 2009 and 2010, the

JDP consolidated its gains against the military with a growing sense of confidence. Despite the political turbulence, Turkey weathered the global financial crisis of 2008 with remarkable success. The economy continued double-digit growth rates in 2009 after a brief recession. By 2012, Turkey's unemployment rate and budget deficit were at record lows.

In June 2011, the JDP won its third consecutive electoral victory with nearly 50 percent of the vote. A month later, on July 29, 2011, the military's chief of staff resigned after a disagreement with Erdoğan about staff promotions. The same day, the heads of the army, navy, and air force requested early retirement. By early 2012, half of all Turkish admirals and one in ten active-duty generals were in jail for plotting against the government.[23] It was a paradigm shift for a country that had experienced three military coups and constant military meddling for almost a century. The JDP also consolidated its supremacy over the military—a first since the creation of the modern state.

The country's global stature also reached new heights. As uprisings shook the Middle East, reformers in Egypt, Jordan, Libya, Morocco, Syria, and Tunisia often cited Turkey and the JDP as models. The JDP government feigned modesty about its standing in the Islamic world. "We are not presenting ourselves as a model," Erdoğan told an audience of Turkish journalists in 2011. "Maybe we are a source of inspiration or a successful example in some areas."[24] Yet Turkey's experience with Islamist politics—no longer simply an experiment—was widely cited both inside and outside the Muslim world.[25]

With the military sidelined, the road seemed wide open for a new liberal and democratic constitution that would consolidate the political reforms in a post-Kemalist Turkey. There was growing expectation that the JDP would also solve the Kurdish problem by engaging the jailed leadership of the PKK and the pro-Kurdish Halkların Demokratik Partisi (Peoples' Democratic Party—PDP) in a constructive dialogue. With the Arab Spring in full swing, Erdoğan appeared to be at the vanguard of this democratic wave in the Middle East. Very few could have predicted that in a couple of years this sense of hubris in Turkey would turn into gloom and doom.

The Arab Spring and the JDP's Islamist Hubris

Like everyone else, Ankara was caught unaware by the sudden eruption of pro-democracy protests around the Arab world.[26] As we saw in the second chapter, Turkey had tried hard to pursue a "zero problems" policy with its Middle Eastern neighbors and had managed to forge considerably strong diplomatic and economic relations with most of the region. Now the outbreak of conflict between governments and their populations made this policy no longer tenable: Ankara had to take sides.[27] It was caught between several considerations: a legacy of having built good relations with rulers in the region, large contractual and business interests with many regimes, and a public political platform built on a democratizing image and good governance. Erdoğan had a high profile in the region as a legitimate, democratically elected, strong, and principled leader with growing acclaim and credibility in the eyes of Sunni Muslims, in part because of his confrontation with Israel over the Gaza siege.

This crisis between Israel and Turkey as well as the issue of Iran in Turkish-American relations had already created a temporary perception of an Islamist turn in JDP policies by 2010. In that sense, the Arab Spring came at a time of some turbulence in Turkey's relations with the United States and Israel. The uneasiness emanated from growing Western concerns about an Islamist turn in Ankara's foreign policy. Tensions began mounting in 2010 with the Gaza flotilla crisis, which ended with Israeli forces killing nine Turkish citizens. Weeks later, Turkey's "no" vote to a new round of UN sanctions against Iran triggered a heated "who lost Turkey?" debate in Washington. As relations with Israel and Washington continued to sink, Turkey appeared to have found new allies in Syria, Russia, and Iran. The resulting perception of an Islamist "axis shift" in Turkey led observers like columnist Thomas Friedman to suggest that Ankara was now joining the "Hamas-Hezbollah-Iran resistance front against Israel."[28]

In the midst of this growing negativity toward Erdoğan, the Arab Spring erupted when on December 17, 2010, a street vendor named Muhammad Bouazizi self-immolated in protest of the local police's maltreatment and the local officials' negligence. Bouazizi was rushed to the hospital and lost his life two weeks later on January 4, 2011. Yet he had already lit the light of the revolution. Hundreds of thousands of Tunisians had gone to the streets across Tunisia and demanded the fall of the regime. Unable to calm down or suppress the protests, Tunisia's president, Zein Al-Abidine bin Ali, resigned on January 14, 2011, and went to Saudi Arabia, where he had lived as an exile until his death there in 2019.

Turkey acted cautiously during that fateful month.[29] Turkey's Ministry of Foreign Affairs did not issue any press release on Tunisia until January 14, 2011, the day Bin Ali stepped down. On the other hand, in the same period the Ministry issued press releases on a range of developments as different as the signing of a treaty between Israel and (South) Cyprus; a parliamentary vote of confidence on the new Iraqi government, terrorist attacks in Pakistan; and in Alexandria, Egypt, Israel's destruction of Shepherd Hotel in East Jerusalem from December 17, 2010, to January 14, 2011. The Ministry's first press release on Tunisia issued on the day Bin Ali resigned was a short and still cautious statement: Turkey expressed its "deep regrets" that the demonstrations cost many lives and injuries and its wishes that order and peace be rebuilt soon. The Ministry issued another press release two weeks later on January 28, 2011, and finally declared Turkey's full support for the Tunisian people's demands for a more democratic and free society.

When the protests erupted in Egypt, Turkey dropped the cautiousness it had adopted on Tunisia and instead enthusiastically declared its support for the protesters. That declaration, coming within one week after millions gathered in Tahrir Square on January 25, 2011, was issued by Turkey's strongman, then prime minister Recep Tayyip Erdoğan. Speaking to his party group in parliament, Erdoğan explicitly called on Husni Mubarek, Egypt's long-ruling president, to step down.

> I want to give a very sincere advice, a very genuine warning to Egypt's President Mr. Hosni Mubarak; . . . listen, let us listen, to the people's callings and their most humane demands. Respond without any hesitation to the desire of change coming from the people. . . . You take the first step for Egypt's peace, security and stability. Take steps that will satisfy the people. Freedoms cannot be delayed and ignored in today's world.[30]

Having just made a powerful, and even passionate, statement of support for the protesters in Egypt, Turkey did not withhold its support for the protesters when they went to the streets in massive numbers in Libya, Yemen, Bahrain, and Syria. Even in the case of Bahrain, Turkey declared its support for the protesters, thus risking its vital interests in such Gulf States as Saudi Arabia, the UAE, and Qatar, which extended generous financial, diplomatic, and even military assistance to the ruling dynasty in Bahrain. Even after these Gulf states militarily intervened and sent their troops to Bahrain, Turkey called on all sides to "refrain from violence" and urged the regime "to listen to the legitimate expectation and demands on the path of reform and democracy."[31]

As the case of Bahrain painfully illustrated, the new cases, where protests and revolutions broke out, turned out to be more complicated than the leaders of Turkey could possibly fathom. Turkey was not the sole player in the region. Other regional and global players had their own stakes and therefore began to intervene. Furthermore, in these new cases of the Arab Spring, the leaders were not willing to easily succumb to the protestors, unlike what had happened in Tunisia or Egypt, and could resort to violence if necessary. Furthermore, both the regimes and the protestors had no qualms in seeking foreign assistance to change the balance of power in their own favor.

Turkey came to this realization most vividly in the case of Libya. Turkey was basically asked to make a simple choice: whether or not to join a NATO-led direct military intervention on the side of the rebels. Even though NATO's military intervention received the blessing of the other Arab states, Turkey vehemently opposed it. In fact, Erdoğan himself expressed this opposition on several occasions. In one instance, for example, Erdoğan said, "should NATO intervene in Libya? Can there be more nonsense? What does NATO have to do with Libya? . . . As Turkey we are against this. Anything like this cannot be mentioned, anything like this cannot be contemplated." Erdoğan saw an ulterior motive driving the NATO intervention and said it explicitly: "We see Tunisia belonging to Tunisians. Egypt belongs to Egyptians, Bahrain to Bahrainians, Libya to Libyans, Morocco to Moroccans, Algeria to Algerians. The people of those countries have to themselves determine their own future. No one else. No one should calculate the number of oil wells in those countries. This is the problem."[32]

Yet Turkey's vehement opposition impressed neither the rulers nor the masses in the Arab world. This became apparent when the Arab League, followed by the African Union, called for the imposition of a no-fly zone over Libya so that the regime could not use its air forces against the protesters-turned-rebels. The UN Security Council then passed a resolution and paved the way for a NATO-led intervention. Turkey could have vetoed it in the NATO, as its membership gave it that right, but did not, apparently not to be sidelined by the regional and international powers in shaping the future of Libya. Turkey even sent four frigates, a submarine, and a support vessel to join the NATO operation.[33]

Turkey faced the most difficult dilemma in Syria, where it had to make two difficult choices. First, it was facing a regime that had been so open to developing extremely cordial relations. By the time the protests erupted,

Turkey and Syria had mutually cancelled visa requirements, expanded trade relations (Turkey's exports to Syria jumping from $266 million in 2002 to $1.8 billion in 2010), held joint military exercises in April 2009,[34] and even agreed that the Turkish army would train the Syrian army.[35] Second, Turkey had to make a choice in the ongoing rivalry between Iran and Saudi Arabia. This rivalry dated back to the 1979 Iranian revolution and had ebbed and flowed since then, but reemerged with a new vigor in the second half of the 2000s.[36] In reigniting this rivalry, Saudi Arabia was basically reacting to what it perceived as Iran's expanding sphere of influence in the Middle East, especially in the aftermath of the US invasion of Afghanistan in 2001 and of Iraq in 2003.[37] In the midst of this ongoing rivalry, Turkey had steered its own foreign policy and successfully remained bipartisan, taking no side and developing cordial relations with both Iran and Saudi Arabia.[38] The crisis in Syria put Turkey in a dilemma, as any choice would put Turkey on the side of either Iran, which was strongly pro-regime in Syria, or Saudi Arabia, which was strongly against.

Turkey's immediate solution was to delay making any definitive choice. Even after the regime began to crack down on the protesters, Turkey continued to implore Syria to implement necessary reforms to appease the protesters. Only after the much-publicized visit of Turkey's minister of foreign affairs, Ahmet Davutoğlu, to Syria in August 2011, Turkey lost its hope to effect a change through diplomacy and dialogue with the regime. Expressing his desperation with the regime, on August 15, 2011, Davutoğlu would say, "from now on there is nothing left to talk about with Syria."[39]

While Turkey had kept channels of communication with the Syrian regime open during this period, it also allowed both armed and non-armed opposition to Damascus to freely organize in Turkey, again illustrating the dilemma Turkey was facing. After nine long months, in November 2011, Erdoğan finally called on Bashar Assad to step down for the first time.[40] Four months later, Turkey took another step and closed its embassy in Damascus. In May 2012, it expelled Syria's diplomats. By the summer of 2012, especially after Syria's shooting down of a Turkish fighter and killing two of its pilots, Turkey began to voice support for an international military intervention in Syria. To its dismay, however, neither the United States nor the EU was interested in that option. Turkey, with Saudi Arabia and Qatar, had to rely on its own resources to change the balance of power on the ground.

As this brief discussion illustrates, Turkey had not adopted the exact same position on the protests that had erupted across the Arab World during the Arab Spring. It early on called on the leader of Egypt to step down but waited for months to do the same for the leader of Syria. It opposed military intervention in Libya, but later changed its position. When it came to Syria, Turkey itself began to call for a military intervention. On Yemen and Bahrain, Turkey left the direction of developments in the hands of the Gulf States while elsewhere it saw its historical responsibility to become involved. It is still possible to claim, however, that Turkey had adhered all along to one basic principle: to call on the regimes that faced protesters, rebels, and revolutionaries to implement the political reforms that would satisfy them.[41]

Turkey's positive stance toward and welcoming of the Arab Spring had brought enormous complications for Turkey in the near future. We visit two prominent cases.

Egypt: The End of the Arab Spring

Seven months after Mubarak resigned, Turkey's then Prime Minister Erdoğan visited Egypt in September 2011 and received a hero's welcome. Most Egyptians regarded the JDP's track record in finding a balance between moderate Islam, democracy, and economic growth a successful experience worth learning from. The Egyptian Muslim Brotherhood, who stood to benefit from the Egyptian revolution, also looked closely and positively at the JDP's experience. Egyptians appreciated Turkey's principled stand with the pro-democracy revolution; and many Islamists looked to the JDP as an example of a successful, moderate, and pragmatic Muslim political party. They decidedly preferred it to the Iranian model of government, or the Saudi, Taliban, al-Qaeda, and other strict or radical variations.

During his visit to Cairo in September 2011, Erdoğan publicly defended the Turkish model with an unexpected emphasis on secularism. Erdoğan's remarks were as follows:

> Turkey's constitutional secularism means the state is equidistant to all religions. Secularism is definitely not atheism. I, Recep Tayyip Erdoğan, am a Muslim, I am not secular. But I am the prime minister of a secular state. In a secular state, people have

the liberty of being religious or not. I advise Egypt to have a secular constitution. Because secularism is not an enemy of religion. So not be afraid of secularism. I hope Egyptians' view of secularism will change following my remarks.[42]

This defense of secularism was well received in the West among those who wanted to avoid an Islamization of Egyptian politics. Yet in the eyes of his critics, Erdoğan was just warning the Muslim Brotherhood to proceed with caution and avoid haste and confrontation when it came to pursuing its political projects.[43]

Erdoğan also brought with him a large business delegation to Cairo, as Turkey was eager to expand its economic relations with the largest Arab country. Although Ankara was to suffer considerable economic losses as a result of sudden change and instability in the Middle East, it generally looked positively at the Arab Spring as a long-overdue correction toward more accountable and hence sustainable and effective governance. Turkey's ties to prerevolutionary Egypt had also improved under the tenure of the JDP. Egypt and Turkey exchanged numerous state visits, and both shared common strategic positions. Both were allies of the United States, and both had established diplomatic relations with Israel. Both had had strained relations with Iran since the Iranian revolution, although Turkey's relations with Iran had markedly improved, and both countries wanted to tamp down radical Islam.

When, in the 1990s, Welfare Party leader and Prime Minister Erbakan launched the D-8 as a global bloc of key Muslim states, Egypt was the only Arab member. Turkey also had an agreement with Egypt to deliver Egyptian natural gas to Turkey (via Jordan and Syria), although the pipeline has not been completed yet. The two countries signed a free trade agreement in 2005 and a memorandum of understanding to improve and further military relations and cooperation between them in 2008. Despite this, Mubarak's Egypt had been reluctant to encourage Turkish involvement in Arab affairs in ways that might shift the geopolitical balance or overshadow Egypt's influence in Arab affairs. After all, Cairo's "strategic rent" vis-à-vis the West partially depended on its role as a shepherd of Arab affairs. With Mubarak gone, Erdoğan naturally nurtured hopes of greatly improving trade relations with Egypt. Yet it was obviously on the ideological and political fronts that Ankara had much larger strategic designs for the future.

It did not take long for Davutoğlu and Erdoğan to realize that embracing the Arab Spring was a clear vehicle to achieve a sense of Muslim unity under Turkish leadership. The Islamist reflex of neo-Ottomanism slowly gained the upper hand in this context and turned into a sort of Muslim hubris infused with nostalgia for the centuries of Islamic unity under one caliphate. As discussed in more detail in the next chapter, Ahmet Davutoğlu's view of the Arab Spring often reflected a flamboyant narrative with the argument that since the collapse of the Ottoman Empire, the Middle East had gone through tragic experiences with Western colonialism and the Cold War. The good news, however, was that this "one-hundred-year parenthesis" of humiliation and tragedy was now coming to an end with the normalization of the natural flow of history.[44] "The template drawn by Sykes-Picot," as he called it, was finally coming down and bringing to power political parties that truly represented the peoples of the Middle East and the Islamists of the region. In a speech he delivered at Dicle University in Diyarbakir, Turkey, in March 2013, Davutoğlu declared in a similar spirit of Muslim unity: "We will render the borders meaningless in these winds of change [blowing] in the Middle East, [working] together with the administrations that came to and will come to power."[45]

In Turkey's growing Islamist vision of Muslim unity, Egypt was to have the seat of honor. In an interview with the *New York Times*, Davutoğlu laid out his view on the importance of the Turkish-Egyptian relationship and explained that

> Egypt would become the focus of Turkish efforts, as an older American-backed order, buttressed by Israel, Saudi Arabia and, to a lesser extent, prerevolutionary Egypt, begins to crumble. Turkey seeks to create a new axis of power at a time when American influence in the Middle East seems to be diminishing . . . an axis of democracy of the two biggest nations in our region, from the north to the south, from the Black Sea down to the Nile Valley in Sudan.[46]

The emphasis on democracy in the Turkish-Egyptian axis mentioned by Davutoğlu is important to underline. The fact that Turkey supported democracy, not political Islam, remains an important talking point and has some merit because the Muslim Brotherhood was clearly the main beneficiary of a post-autocratic Egypt. Despite its autocratic tendencies, it is also hard to argue that Egyptian Islamists did not come to power with free elections. The post-Mubarak Egypt was still a highly illiberal country, but it was certainly making strides toward becoming an electoral democracy. This is why there is veracity in the Turkish narrative of supporting democracy in the context of supporting the Muslim Brotherhood.

Turkey, as Davutoğlu mentioned in this *New York Times* interview, also believed it was filling a vacuum in the Middle East left by the United States. Yet, as Ankara was soon to realize, there were other powerful regional actors that were willing to fill the vacuum in different ways than Turkey envisioned. In that sense, one of the major failures of Turkey was its inability to realistically analyze the regional context and the ways in which Saudi Arabia and Iran had agendas that clashed with Turkey's support for the Muslim Brotherhood. While Riyadh opposed this Turkish Islamist project in Cairo, Tehran was firmly against it in the context of Syria and Turkey's support for Sunni Islamists groups. Both Iran and Saudi Arabia proved to be winners compared with Turkey because they managed to eventually achieve their strategic objectives in Syria and Egypt, respectively. Turkey's exaggerated sense that it could fill the vacuum left by Washington with an Ankara-Cairo axis of democracy—in Davutoğlu's words—proved wishful thinking based on Islamist idealism.

At the end of the day, Turkey not only felt isolated because of Iran's victory in Syria and Saudi Arabia's in Egypt, but it also felt sidelined by the United States when the Pentagon began arming PKK-affiliated Kurds in Syria against jihadists, and the Obama White House stayed practically silent about Egypt when General Abdel Fattah Al-Sisi seized power in Cairo with a military coup toppling the Muslim Brotherhood. In short, Turkey proved equally as inept at reading the Western context as it had the regional one. The Islamist lens through which the JDP looked at the region with idealism faced the harsh realities of realpolitik.

To be sure, Turkey tried to create its own sphere of influence with economic and military power. In December 2011, Turkey and Egypt held joint naval exercises in the Mediterranean.[47] Once the Muslim Brotherhood–affiliated Muhammad Morsi was sworn in as Egyptian president in the summer of 2012, Erdoğan pledged a $2 billion aid package to revitalize the Egyptian economy at a time when Egypt was having difficulties obtaining credit from international financial institutions. There was even some hope that Ankara and Cairo could act together in Syria. The two countries conferred frequently on Hamas and Israel, often with the hope of finding diplomatic solutions. The Islamist hubris of the JDP reached a climax in September 2012 during its party convention. Muhammad Morsi was a guest of honor along with Hamas leader Khalid Mashaal at the JDP convention. Both referred to Prime Minister Erdoğan and President Gül as "brothers" in an expression of solidarity and praised Turkey's leadership in managing regional problems ranging from Syria and the Palestinians to the need to defeat Western support for tyranny.

During Morsi's tenure in power, Erdoğan and the JDP could have advised him to adopt a very liberal and democratic approach toward the opposition in the spirit of being magnanimous in victory. Yet Morsi proved to be an inexperienced politician with autocratic tendencies. His government rushed to consolidate power with a controversial constitution that polarized Egyptian society. Instead of warning Morsi to respect minorities and the secular opposition, Erdoğan came to Cairo in November 2012 with the goal of signing as many economic, financial, and trade agreements as possible. Morsi and Erdoğan ended up signing twenty-seven agreements ranging from transportation to health care.

When Morsi's mismanagement of the economy and authoritarian tactics led to a governance crisis with the deterioration of law and order in the country, public protests against the Muslim Brotherhood started filling the streets. In the last few days before the military takeover, Ankara had a window of opportunity to provide some constructive advice to the Egyptian government. Instead, Erdoğan encouraged Morsi to stand firm at a time when Washington was pushing for a compromise such as a transfer of power to a newly appointed prime minister to avoid a full-blown crisis.[48]

Erdoğan continued to misread the Egyptian domestic context after the military coup as his government backed civilian resistance in the form of sit-ins in defiance of military rule and curfews. Ankara still nurtured hopes that Morsi could be returned to power. Such civilian resistance tragically resulted in massive casualties when the Egyptian military fired on Muslim Brotherhood supporters and activists camping in Rabia Square. The way the Muslim Brotherhood was violently ousted increased Erdoğan's righteous indignation. And the fact that Saudi Arabia, the United Arab Emirates, and Israel supported the ousting of Muhammad Morsi only worsened Turkey's sense of Islamist victimhood and frustration. Erdoğan to this day often employs the "R4BIA" signs, with his four fingers a symbol of Islamic solidarity and criticism of General Abdel Fattah al-Sisi following the July 3, 2013, coup in Egypt.[49] The fact that the West stayed silent and US Secretary of State John Kerry went as far as claiming that the Egyptian was restoring democracy made things worse by adding salt to the injury.[50] In sum, all the idealistic hopes invested in the Arab Spring with the dream of Islamic unity came to a rude awakening in Egypt, the country that mattered the most for the future of political Islam.

Events in Egypt with the bloody military coup against the Muslim Brotherhood had an almost traumatic impact on Erdoğan's reading of Turkish domestic events as well. When mass mobilization during the Gezi Park protests during the summer of 2013 spread all around Turkey, Erdoğan blamed the West and showed signs of insecurity about his hold on power. According to some analysts, he also feared he could be ousted by a military-led coup, even though he had emasculated Turkey's Armed Forces.[51]

Given the primacy of domestic dynamics for Erdoğan, at the tactical level, it is important to note that his support for the Muslim Brotherhood helps Erdoğan with his Islamist, nationalist, populist, anti-West, victim-hood-oriented agenda. What happened in Egypt in the summer of 2013 was the best way to expose American and European double standards to his domestic audiences and remind them the West would have no problem with a military coup in Turkey as well. The fact that the United States failed to quickly condemn the failed coup in Turkey in July 2016 proved his point. Today, when the Western press describes Erdoğan as a dictator, the Turkish president accuses them of Islamophobia, complicity with coup plotters, and dishonesty.

The Syrian Quagmire[52]

If Egypt was certainly the high point of Erdoğan's Islamism during the Arab Spring, Syria should come as a close second. As discussed before, in the face of this unfolding crisis in Syria, Turkey had painfully avoided taking a decisive stance in the early months in large part because it had enviably cordial relations with Syria before the Arab Spring. It therefore had kept channels of communication with the regime and encouraged it to undertake political reforms. By the end of the summer, Turkey's hopes that the regime would introduce reforms were totally dashed. In November 2011, nine months after the protests started, Turkey made its first call to the Syrian president to step down and introduced a number of sanctions against the regime. Four months later, in March 2012, Turkey closed its embassy in Syria and in May 2012 expelled Syria's diplomats.

Severing diplomatic ties with the Asad regime was rather the easier part of the decision. The more critical decision to be made of course was what kind and level of support to extend to the armed rebel groups. As early as the summer of 2011 Turkey actually allowed the formation of the Free Syrian Army (FSA) in its territory. The FSA continued to coordinate the rebel activities inside Syria from Turkey in the ensuing months. But it is unclear when Turkey began to provide actual weapons and money to the rebels. By the beginning of 2012, however, Turkey along with Saudi Arabia and Qatar seemed to have independently or jointly concluded that the regime of Bashar Asad must go, or, if necessary, be brought down. By March 2012 they had begun to extend financial and military support to the rebel groups in Syria, the FSA serving as their focal point to reach out to the rebel groups.[53]

Yet this outside financial and military support proved to be detrimental for the viability of the FSA as more and more rebel groups formed and vied for the rather easy, but limited resources these states provided. Coordination among ever increasing number of armed groups became a more and more challenging task. As the FSA could not transform itself into a monolithic organization or a true army with a hierarchical chain of command, it became rather a label for otherwise independent rebel groups adopted or dropped at will.[54]

By the end of 2012, the FSA had declined as a major fighting force in Syria, and in its stead Salafi-Jihadist groups filled the ensuing vacuum. These groups had enjoyed certain advantages that the FSA had not. First, they were ideologically more committed than the FSA, claiming to be fighting an infidel regime in the path of God and therefore better able to motivate its fighters. Second, Salafi-Jihadists were simply better at providing social services and local governance; hence they could deepen their roots in the society by improving the daily lives of ordinary people. Finally, Salafi-Jihadist groups had benefited from their access to the international pool of kin groups elsewhere. They therefore could not only recruit fighters from, but also raise funds in other countries.

A number of journalistic reports suggest that Turkey and Qatar had at the very least benignly neglected the funding and recruitment activities inside their territories undertaken for Salafi-Jihadist groups in Syria.[55] To be added as well is that Turkey had become a major transit road for international jihadists and turned a blind eye to their logistical efforts, such as medical treatment inside its territories.[56] There are two possible reasons for Turkey's support or benign neglect of Jihadist groups. First, the radical Islamists within groups like the Jabhat al-Nusra Front had proven to be the most efficient fighters against the Assad regime. Second, the same groups and the Islamic State in Iraq and al-Sham or ISIS considered the PKK-affiliated Partiya Yekitiya Demokrat (Democratic Union Party—PYD) their rival. With American support to the PYD, Turkey's main threat perception in Syria shifted from Assad to the Kurdish aspirations for autonomy. It is within this context that Turkey began to support jihadists in Syria. All these dynamics had the potential to turn Turkey's role into something similar to that of Pakistan during the Afghan jihad in the 1980s.

In the meantime, the military support of Iran and Russia helped the survival of the Assad regime. The radicalism of ISIS and the Jabhat al-Nusra Front fatally damaged the international reputation of the Syrian opposition. Yet Turkey's reluctance to consider jihadist groups as its main threat and its willingness to turn a blind eye to ISIS fighters crossing the border from Turkey did perhaps even more damage to Turkey's own reputation. What began as Turkish support for the Muslim Brotherhood in Syria evolved to Turkish support for radical Islamist groups and came to symbolize the Islamization of Erdoğan's foreign policy in the Middle East.

In early 2015, Turkey, along with Saudi Arabia and Qatar, once again boosted its efforts to topple the Asad regime. In late April 2015, two major Salafi-Jihadi groups, Jabhat al-Nusra and Ahrar al-Sham, and a number of FSA-affiliated groups formed Jaish al-Fatah. Having allegedly received significant military aid from Saudi Arabia and Turkey, Jaish al-Fatah scored a number of critical victories against the regime in both the south and the north, for example, capturing strategic towns such as Idlib and Jisr al-Shughour.[57] Four months later, Russia militarily intervened in the Syria conflict and changed the balance of power in favor of the regime. As the United States had busied itself more with ISIS than with the Asad regime and refrained from countering Russia's intervention in Syria, the rebel cause in Syria seemed to have hit a wall. Turkey's shooting down of a Russian jet in November 2015 met with a harsh Russian reaction, which in turn limited Turkey's capability to intervene in Syria.[58]

In the meantime, Russia's military intervention in Syria and the United States's prioritization of defeating ISIS provided the PKK-affiliated PYD a valuable opportunity to expand its sphere of influence in Northern Syria as it fought against ISIS and thus turned itself into a useful ground force for the United States in the latter's fight against ISIS. The rise of the PYD alarmed Turkey. In retrospect, however, the rise of the PYD in

Syria also provided Turkey a legitimate reason to militarily intervene in the Syrian conflict.

First Turkey reconciled with Russia in June 2016.[59] Two months later, it militarily intervened in the Syrian conflict and effectively prevented the PYD's westward territorial expansion. More than a year later in January 2018, Turkey made another military incursion into Syria and expelled the PYD from its westernmost enclave in Northern Syria, Afrin. While directly targeting the PYD, Turkey also included the Syrian rebel forces in its military incursions and in the administration of these newly captured territories. By investing in the military and administrative capacity of the Syrian rebel forces and engaging in some welfare-improving activities in territories it captured, Turkey seemed to be actively helping the Syrian rebels build their own states in northern Syria.[60]

It is undeniable that Turkey now sees its involvement in Syria as vital for border security, the suppression of Kurdish terrorism, and the resettlement of the nearly 4 million Syrian refugees in Turkey. Turkey began its largest incursion into Syria, Operation Peace Spring, in October 2019 after the withdrawal of US troops began.[61] According to Erdoğan, the operation is primarily intended to expel the PYD from the border region as well as to create a resettlement zone in northern Syria where some of the 4 million Syrian refugees in Turkey would return—the operation is considered controversial for numerous reasons. Since the formal end of Turkish-Syrian relations in late 2011, Erdoğan has continued to ratchet up the pressure on his protégé-turned-foe. From supporting and hosting opposition groups to occupying swathes of Northern Syria, Erdoğan has played almost every card in an attempt to once again gain influence over and control Damascus.[62] All in all, however, Turkey paid a heavy price for its involvement in Syria: from terrorism to refugees, a host of problems has already been troublesome for Turkey.

Last, but not least, it is important to note that Erdoğan's policies in the Middle East have badly tarnished Turkey's image in the West as a country that supports political Islam. As the Middle East became the new center of gravity in the bilateral Turkish-American agenda in the 1990s, things went from bad to worse. Not only the Kurdish question, but also the Israeli-Palestinian conflict and the role of the Muslim Brotherhood in Egypt—all poisoned the relationship between the NATO allies, Turkey, and the United States. To be sure, Turkey has had its problems with radical Islamist groups like ISIS and therefore had common strategic interests with the West. But at the end of the day, the real threat that emanates from the Middle East for Ankara is ethnic Kurdish terrorism rather than terrorism with jihadist roots.

This is also why the Syrian uprising turned into a nightmare for Turkish-American relations. The American decision to arm Syrian Kurds to counter the jihadist terrorist threat ISIS posed came as a shock to the Turkish national security establishment. In Ankara's eyes, Washington was arming a terrorist organization—its Kurdish nemesis—in the name of fighting another terrorist entity. Washington, on the other hand, had its own axe to grind. To the American military, Turkey was in bed with radical Islamist groups linked to al-Qaeda and was turning a blind eye to ISIS supporters entering Syria over its porous border with the country. Having different threat perceptions was tolerable to a certain degree. But in Syria, Ankara and Washington were each supplying military aid to the other's existential threat. All this proved too much to stomach for what was left of a partnership that had always depended on a common threat rather than shared democratic values. In short, Turkey's Islamist turn in Syria came at a heavy price not only in terms of deterioration of political dynamics at home and regional isolation in the Middle East. Erdoğan's Turkey is paying a heavy price in relations with Washington as well.

Domestic Unraveling with Authoritarianism

As Turkey's Islamist adventure in foreign policy resulted in failure in both Egypt and Syria, Turkey's democratic journey at home also came to an end. Already by 2013, there were clear signs that the country was turning increasingly autocratic, nationalistic, and conspiratorial under the same leader who received so much praise during his first decade in power.[63]

In retrospect, events that unfolded in 2013 proved to be a major turning point in the JDP's democratic journey. The brutal suppression of young environmentalist protesters at Istanbul's Gezi Park and subsequent cycles of violence against protesters across the country unveiled the fragile nature of civil liberties in Erdoğan's new Turkey.[64] The crackdown on protests and the suppression of freedom of speech and assembly clearly revealed the absence of rule of law in the country. The same year, the clash between Erdoğan and the Gülen movement turned the political climate from bad to worse. The absence of an independent judiciary became obvious when Erdoğan sacked the Gülenist prosecutors who launched a major corruption investigation against him. There was clear and undeniable corruption within the JDP ranks. It was a well-known fact within JDP circles that Erdoğan himself distributed government contracts and big infrastructure projects to cronies. Yet Erdoğan managed to portray the corruption investigation against him as a coup attempt orchestrated by Fethullah Gülen.

Once their shared enemy—the military—was politically sidelined, the Erdoğan-Gülen alliance rapidly turned into a debilitating competition for power.[65] Erdoğan went after the education network of the Gülen movement, and Gülenist prosecutors came after Erdoğan's corrupt network of patronage in a system of crony capitalism. Erdoğan responded to the corruption investigation by launching an all-out war against the Gülen movement.[66] His policies included sacking the prosecutors involved in the corruption investigation, reassigning hundreds of police chiefs, and rewriting laws in ways that would allow government control over the judiciary and corruption probes. After the resignation of four implicated ministers, Erdoğan reshuffled half of his cabinet. In addition to the total number of ninety-six prosecutors and judges who were replaced, the government decided to push through draconian new laws giving it more control over the judiciary and tightening monitoring of telephones and the internet. The new legislation also enhanced government control over the High Council of Judges and Prosecutors, which is responsible for judicial functions and the appointments of judges, and thus severely undermined the separation between the executive and judiciary branches. Nothing much was left in the name of rule of law in Turkey as Erdoğan began to call all the shots.[67]

As his alliance with Gülen came to an acrimonious end, Erdoğan forged a new partnership, this time with the ultranationalists he had sidelined only a few years earlier. The military was of course more than happy to see the alliance that brought the tutelage system down crumble. The generals were equally happy to see the end of the Kurdish peace process under the weight of authoritarianism at home and the Syrian civil war where the United States was supportive of Kurds aligned with the PKK.[68] By 2015 the dynamics of war were once again dominating the Kurdish question in Turkey. In many ways, Ankara had returned to the old days of illiberalism, authoritarianism, and reactionary nationalism that characterized the lost decade of the 1990s.

It is once again obviously clear that the country lacked a strong civil society, an independent judiciary, and a free media. In other words, institutions that are bedrocks of liberalism were absent. What is left of

Turkish democracy was therefore reduced to elections and majority rule. As a result, today's Turkey has turned from a once hopeful model of democratic governance into a textbook example of illiberalism where elections legitimize the tyranny of the majority. Despite mounting political polarization and unrest since the 2013 Gezi Park protests, the JDP managed to win almost all the local, parliamentary, and presidential elections between 2014 and today. Especially after the transition to a presidential system in 2017, Erdoğan monopolized power and consolidated his hegemony.[69]

Starting with his open fight with Gülen in 2013, as a corruption probe swirled around his government and his family, Erdoğan also returned to the familiar tactic of blaming his problems on a vast international conspiracy as part of an orchestrated effort to weaken Turkey. Partly because Gülen lived in the United States and has been critical of Turkey's confrontations with Israel, Erdoğan hinted that corruption allegations were the result of attempts by Israel and the United States to frame his government. By 2013, Turkey's relations with Israel were still severely strained because of Turkey's support of Hamas. Erdoğan even threatened to expel the US ambassador on the grounds that he held meetings with opposition figures. Yet there was one additional factor that had caused considerable insecurity and alarm in relations with Washington: the US failure to see the Egyptian military coup in Egypt as a coup. This only worsened the Islamist instincts of Erdoğan based on a partly justified perception of Western double standards.

Conclusion

Turkey's Islamist approach to Syria and Egypt was made possible thanks to Erdoğan's consolidation of power at home against the Kemalist establishment. Had the military still been able to call the shots in Turkey in the 2010s, Turkey would have followed a much more cautious foreign policy vis à vis Egypt's Muslim Brotherhood and the Islamist groups in Syria.

All the strategic factors behind the JDP's support for the Muslim Brotherhood are infused with both idealism and ideology. This should not come as a surprise given that Erdoğan's own political background is in Islamist politics. When the domestic and international context allowed it, these ideological instincts quickly resurfaced. On the other hand, Erdoğan has plausible deniability against accusations of being an Islamist because he can portray his ideological agenda, at least partly, as support for democracy in the region. He genuinely and firmly believed that democratic elections in the Middle East could only produce victories for the Muslim Brotherhood. And such victories, he assumed, would produce a strategic victory for Turkey because Muslim Brotherhood–oriented parties considered Turkey as a model state and Erdoğan as the regional leader. As a result, according to Erdoğan's calculations, the rise of electoral democracy could only increase Turkey's political, economic, and diplomatic soft power in the Arab world.

Chapter 4

ISLAMISM AT WORK

When Turkey's strongman Recep Tayyip Erdoğan called Husni Mubarak to listen to "the people's callings and their most humane demands" on February 1, 2011, just one week after the massive protests broke out in Egypt, he committed Turkey to embrace the unfolding Arab Spring. And Turkey did indeed embrace the Arab Spring unusually enthusiastically. Turkey had consistently and repeatedly expressed its full, unconditional support for the demands of the protesters, be it in Egypt, Libya, or Syria. In his very first statement on the Arab revolutions, Recep Tayyip Erdoğan unequivocally declared that he wanted "democracy, prosperity, justice, freedom for . . . our fellow nations."[1] This embracing turned out to have disastrous consequences for Turkey that of course could not have been foreseen. Three years later, Turkey found itself totally isolated in the region and deeply embroiled in the civil war raging in next-door Syria and Libya across the Mediterranean.

No obvious or compelling economic or political reason seems to have driven Turkey's embracing of the Arab Spring. We argue instead that Turkey's attitude toward the Arab Spring was ideologically driven or Islamist. More specifically, we claim that Islamism provided an interpretative framework or prism through which foreign policy makers in Ankara interpreted the regional and the world developments. Hailing from an Islamist background, the leadership of Turkey's ruling JDP saw in the Arab Spring a historic opportunity that could sweep away the culturally alienated ruling elite in the Arab world and bring the "true voice" of the people to power. In the minds of the JDP leaders, the masses in the Arab world were, as a majority, naturally inclined toward Islamists, and any democratic opening would bring to power opposition groups such as the Muslim Brotherhood that reflected the piety of the Arab street. As understood by Turkish Islamists, the Arab Spring then was unleashing a transformation that could potentially help Turkey's Islamists realize their long-held dream of "İttihad-ı Islam [The Union of Islam]" across the Muslim world.

To illustrate these claims, we look more deeply into Islamism in this chapter. First we look at how Ahmet Davutoğlu, the chief architect of Turkey's foreign policy before and during the Arab Spring, interpreted the Arab Spring. Then we ground Davutoğlu's interpretation within Islamism.

Interpreting the Arab Spring

We argue that Turkey's unusually enthusiastic embracing of the Arab Spring was ideologically driven. More specifically, we argue, the Islamist ideology of the leaders, then totally in control of foreign policy in Ankara, led them to analyze the developments in the Arab world through a particular interpretive framework or prism. This interpretative framework can readily be constructed through Ahmet Davutoğlu's own speeches and statements. To be remembered, Ahmet Davutoğlu had greatly influenced Turkey's foreign policy both before and during the Arab Spring in his capacity as the chief foreign policy advisor to Turkey's prime minister from 2002 to 2009, then minister of foreign affairs from 2009 to 2014 and prime minister from 2014 to 2015. Furthermore, Davutoğlu represented not just himself, but a school of thought, Islamism. It is discussed later in this chapter that Davutoğlu's reading of the Arab Spring is an application of the Islamist interpretive frame of modern history of the Middle East.

As Turkey's minister of foreign affairs, his tenure coinciding with the eruption and unfolding of the Arab Spring, Davutoğlu delivered several speeches on different occasions on what was happening in the region. These speeches provided critical clues on how he viewed the Middle East history.

Before analyzing those speeches, however, it is helpful to look first at an illustrative anecdote. In late July 2014, Kemal Kılıçdaroğlu, the main opposition leader, criticized Turkey's foreign policy and uttered the following sentence: "do not drag Turkey into the Middle East swamp." The "swamp" analogy received an unusually harsh response from Ahmet Davutoğlu. "We," he said, "have come to know Damascus, what they called swamp, as the honored Damascus (Şam-ı Şerif). We have come to know Mecca, Medina in the Middle East, what they called swamp, as our Ka'ba. We have come to know Baghdad in the Middle East, what they called swamp as brother (kardeş). We have come to know Kirkuk in the Middle East, what they called swamp as saint (aziz)."

"The Middle East is not swamp," Davutoğlu continued, "but the center of that saintly revelation that uplifted consciences and humanity." The Middle East was "the center of Hira." It was "the mountain of Sina," "the Olive Mountain," "Jerusalem," and "Cairo." All these places have special religious significances in the history of religions. Hira is the name of the cave where the Prophet of Islam was claimed to have received the first revelation. The Mountain of Sina was the mountain where the Prophet of Judaism was claimed to have received the Ten Commandments. From the olive mountain, Christianity's Son of God was claimed to have made his last march to Jerusalem. Davutoğlu then challenged, "the main opposition leader and some others called it 'swamp.' We will not allow the Middle East, where the Cave of Hira that enlightens humanity is, to be called swamp."[2]

He was not a mere demagogue. Davutoğlu had certainly held the Middle East in high esteem. The Middle East was like no other place on earth. It was saintly, almost divine, where God made himself known to humanity. He had expressed this view of the exceptional and saintly Middle East earlier in a speech he delivered on September 7, 2012, to an audience mainly composed of leaders of various religions.[3] Early in his speech, Davutoğlu recounted his first-ever visits to the Olive Mountain, the Mountain of Sina, and the Cave of Hira. Davutoğlu's point was that the Middle East had been the birthplace and center of an ancient (kadim) civilization; a civilization of compassion, justice, and mercy. This civilization was not just another human civilization; it was Godly, through the history of which God had revealed and manifested itself through revelations to successive great Prophets.[4]

This civilization, Davutoğlu noted, had nurtured cities of interfaith tolerance, such as Medina, Damascus, Jerusalem, Cairo, Marakesh, and Istanbul, where "Muslim, Christian, Sunni, Shia, Catholic, Orthodox, Jewish had lived together. When the word peace (Selam) was uttered, no matter whichever language it was uttered in, peace unto you (Aleyküm Selam) was uttered back and to that person, who said peace, was said you are in safety and trust. The names of our cities became the place of safety (darüleman), the place of peace (darüsselam). Our ancient and long-standing tradition had always voiced safety and peace." This ancient civilization also nurtured and respected pluralism, Davutoğlu claimed:

people were neither homogenized nor excluded as the others, nor made hostage to a certain group feeling (asabiye). Their color, gender, or race did not matter. Humanity was one and could not be divided.

Davutoğlu's view of the Middle East is obviously civilizational, the base of which is revelation. The peoples of the Middle East are identified not by their nationalities, ethnicities, or sects, but by their religions. There are thus Muslims, Christians, and Jews in the Middle East, not Turks, Iranians, Kurds, or Arabs. And because all these religions are revelations from God, their adherents are one people.

Davutoğlu was not blind to the reality of today's Middle East, however. Today's Middle East was "a geography of wars, ethnic and sectarian conflicts, major massacres." It did not have "deeply rooted political culture" and was the scene of "violence and hatred." Implicitly as well as explicitly, Davutoğlu was suggesting, that ancient civilization or tradition, which had kept the Middle East peaceful, harmonious, and pluralistic, had been lost some time in the past and had to be recovered to revive the old Middle East. But why did it happen? Or, according to Davutoğlu, what went wrong?

Davutoğlu blamed the transition to modernity. National identity formation integrated people in Europe, Davutoğlu suggested, but destroyed the unity of the peoples of the Middle East. "We began to become alien to our neighbors. We became aliens through ethnic identity. We became aliens through religious identity. We became aliens through sectarian identity." The Middle East was, as a result, steadily shattered into more and more parochial and exclusionary identities.

According to Davutoğlu's reading of Middle East history, the Ottoman Empire was the last embodiment of that ancient civilization, and with its demise, Davutoğlu suggested, had gone the ancient civilization, which had not reincarnated since. Its collapse paved the way for further alienation among the peoples of the Middle East. Davutoğlu referred to the post-Ottoman alienation among the peoples of the Middle East in at least three of his speeches. The first was delivered at the Sixth Al-Jazeera Forum held in Doha, Qatar, on March 13, 2011; the second on the occasion of the centennial anniversary of the Turkish Houses, held in Istanbul on March 26, 2011; and the third was at Dicle University in Diyarbakir on March 15, 2013.

Let us look at Davutoğlu's Al Jazeera speech.[5] Davutoğlu claimed in this speech that since the collapse of the Ottoman Empire, the Middle East had gone through two tragic experiences, each of which simply deepened, if not created, the alienation among the peoples of the Middle East. The first experience was colonialism. "Colonialism in the 1930s, 40s and 50s," Davutoğlu declared, "divided the region into colonial entities and separated the natural links between tribes and communities." As Syria and Iraq were divided by the French and the British, respectively, into colonial states, "the historical link was cut off. The economic links were cut." The other tragic experience that the Middle East had gone through was the Cold War, which simply continued to divide the peoples of the Middle East by making "them enemies as members of different blocs . . . Those countries who lived together for centuries became enemies to each other, like Turkey and Syria. We were in NATO. Syria was pro-Soviet. Our border became not the border of two nation states, but the border of two blocs."[6]

The whole period, during which the peoples of the Middle East had increasingly become alien to one another, was an unnatural aberration, an abnormality in the history of the region. With the end of the Cold War, this abnormality should have ended. But it did not. This is critical to note. According to Davutoğlu, this did not happen because, he claimed, the region had not been democratized. In his Al Jazeera Speech, Davutoğlu said, "some people," "or some countries said that Arab societies do not deserve democracies." Davutoğlu claimed that these people or these countries let authoritarianism continue in the Arab world "in order to keep the status quo," and "in order, at that time in the 1990s, to prevent radicalisation or Islamic radicalism or others." Among them were countries and leaders "who were proud of their own democracy" but still claimed democratization could entail "certain risks and certain potential risks of insecurity in our region."[7]

Under the JDP leadership, Davutoğlu believed, Turkey was leading the normalization of Middle East history, correcting the said aberration or abnormality. Turkey was doing this in two ways. First, Davutoğlu suggested in a television interview, Turkey became an inspiration for the peoples of the Middle East by strengthening its democracy. "In Turkey democracy did not lead to chaos or feed radicalism. Moreover, it has not been a source of weakness against countries like Israel, but rather the strengthening of democracy in Turkey greatly helped voicing Palestine's rights in higher volumes. Thus the legitimacy of the Arab regimes that have been based on these reasons was shattered."[8]

Second, Davutoğlu suggested, Turkey led the normalization of Middle East history through its foreign policy. In his Dicle speech, Davutoğlu said that Turkey's foreign policy had been seeking to establish a new regional order, an order closely connected to Asia, the Indian Ocean, and Africa. "This is the pillar of our economic restoration. For this reason we cancel visa requirements; with high level meetings of strategic cooperation, we in fact open the way for a major restoration, regional restoration."[9]

Coming after Turkey's efforts to "normalize" Middle East history, the Arab Spring was in fact the normalization of Middle East history. Davutoğlu stated in the Al Jazeera Forum, "the events around us today are normal developments. Of course, they develop spontaneously, but we have to see them as natural reflections of the natural flow of history. We are going through a natural flow of history."[10]

The Arab Spring, in another Davutoğlu's metaphor, was closing a "100-years old paranthesis." It was 100 years old because the Ottoman Empire "had disintegrated into shreds" beginning 100 years before the Arab Spring in 1911, and as a result "its constitutive elements were torn apart, and psychologically and historically separated from one another." Starting in 2011, what needed to be done was "to integrate again the severed, dissolved and torn apart elements of the nation."[11]

The objective was to construct the region anew. "In this new region," Davutoğlu envisaged, "there should be less violence, no violence. There should be fewer barriers between countries, between societies, between sects. There should be more economic interdependency, more political dialogue, more dialogue between intellectuals. There should be a common zone of security and respect for each other."[12] To this end, Davutoğlu declared in his Dicle Speech, "We will render the borders meaningless in this wind of changes [blowing] in the Middle East, [working] together with the administrations that came to and will come to power." Davutoğlu boldly stated, "we will break that template drawn for us by Sykes-Picot," and added, "no one can prevent this [from being realized]."[13]

Davutoğlu was not that straightforward in explaining why in his view the Arab Spring was normalizing Middle East history. Still, we can conjecture. In his Turkish Houses speech, Davutoğlu declared Turkey's desire to lead the normalization in the Middle East. Every state would respect the existing borders, but would not "serve as walls any more," to be transformed "into flexible and penetrable borders." Davutoğlu also said in the same speech, "It is our desire that the peoples of the Middle East are not separated from each other under new authoritarian structures."[14] Davutoğlu thus linked the prevalence of authoritarianism in the Middle East to the disconnectedness of the peoples of the Middle East.

Davutoğlu was more explicit in stating this link in a speech he delivered at a panel organized by Ankara-based think tank SETA in March 2012. In this speech, Davutoğlu described the agents who brought about the Arab Spring as the ordinary peoples of the region, who were "tired of being humilitiated sometimes by Israel . . . sometimes by their own rulers." The ordinary peoples of the region simply desired to determine their own fates. This was a quest for dignity on their parts, similar to, Davutoğlu suggested, the people's quest for dignity in Turkey. The latter voted for the JDP in 2002 to assert their dignity so as to be "respected both as individuals in the political system and as a country in the international system."

With the Arab Spring, the other peoples of the Middle East were demanding the same: dignity abroad, rule of law, respect for human rights, transparency, and democracy at home. They were demanding a political system "based on the will of the people." Once such political systems were founded across the Middle East, Davutoğlu prophesized, the region would be more integrated, as the political systems would reflect the peoples' preferences. Davutoğlu argued that this would happen because the peoples of the region were culturally akin to one another. For example, "a democratic Syria will integrate with Turkey much more than before. A democratic Egypt will be much more integrated with a democratic Libya, because this is the peoples' will. These peoples do not want iron walls to be built between one another, do not want Berlin walls to be built. They want to unite and return to history together."[15]

As far as we can see, Davutoğlu had never said it explicitly, at least in the public. But, reading between the lines, he seemed to hold that the existing political regimes and systems were not truly authentic to the region. Or, much like the borders dividing the peoples of the Middle East, the regimes were also artificial, to be swept away in the giant waves of history.

The Arab Spring was just doing that, normalizing Middle East history by bringing to power political parties that truly represented the peoples of the Middle East. From Davutoğlu's perspective, the Arab World was simply replicating what Turkey had done after the JDP's rise to power in 2002. It was Turkey that had started the Arab spring in the Middle East. The Arab Spring was also "the spring of the region" and "of Turkey." Because Turkey experienced that spring before, it was leading the normalization in the Middle East.[16]

To better grasp this latter claim, it is essential to see Davutoğlu's negative view of the Ottoman/Republican modernization. In their modernization efforts, Davutoğlu believed, the Ottoman statesmen and the founders of the republic worked to detach Turkey from Islamic civilization and make it a member of Western civilization. Yet this project failed. Turkey could neither become truly Western nor remain Islamic.[17]

In Davutoğlu's view, the whole process of modernization estranged the elites in Turkey from the masses: while the former became westernized, the masses remained Muslim. To put it another way, the state and the nation had been estranged from one another in Turkey. In Davutoğlu's view, the JDP's coming to power in 2002 was the correction of a historical estrangement between the state and the nation. This was because under the JDP the state and the nation became one again. The same moderniza-tion process also determined Turkey's place in the international system. During the Ottoman period, it was the political center of the Islamic civilization. But, with modernization, Turkey became estranged from that civilization and moved to the periphery of another civilization, Western civilization.[18] In Davutoğlu's view, therefore, Turkey and the other Mid-dle East countries had undergone the same transformation, as a result of which the elites and the masses became estranged from one another: while the former became westernized, the latter remained culturally and traditionally religious.

This estrangement between the elites and the masses had also im-pacted interstate relations in the Middle East. Artificial borders divided not only the states, but also the peoples, imagined to be culturally and traditionally unified. Such estranged elites, Davutoğlu also seemed to believe, could only rule in an authoritarian fashion. By undermining authoritarianism in the region, the Arab Spring, Davutoğlu believed, was paving the way for the reintegration of the region. This would happen because the estranged elites would surely lose elections and give way to the authentic representatives of the peoples of the Middle East. And this was a welcome development, a development to which Turkey had worked to contribute before the Arab Spring. Not surprisingly, Turkey adopted a positive stance toward and welcomed the Arab Spring.

Davutoğlu's interpretation of the Arab Spring is not solely his own interpretation or personal construction, but rather should be grounded into the broader Islamist interpretive framework. At the end of the day, it was that broader framework, skillfully applied by Davutoğlu to a contemporary development, that influenced foreign policy makers in Ankara to interpret the Arab Spring in a particular way and embrace it enthusiastically.

The Origin and the Context

I wandered around the world of unbelief (küfr),
I saw cities, luxurious mansions,
I traveled through the world of Islam,
I saw only ruins.

—Ziya Paşa (1825–1880)

Turkish Islamism has its intellectual roots in the nineteenth century. It was in this century that Ottoman statesmen and men of letters painfully realized the stark and still growing power disparity between the West and Muslim countries. This power disparity could be conveniently ignored if it did not create a hostile international environment for the Islamic world starting in the late eighteenth century. The European powers, especially Britain, France, and Russia, were becoming increasingly aggressive, bit by bit colonizing the Islamic world. Meanwhile, the Ottoman Empire, the last great Muslim Empire, was failing to stop the whole descent.

Even though the Empire had been ambitiously reforming its military, administration, education, and justice systems since the beginning of the same century, it was still losing territories in the Balkans, Caucasus, and North Africa. Not only the superpowers of the period, but also the Empire's Christian subjects, such as Greeks, Bulgarians, and Serbians, had been rebelling one after another and cutting their own territorial pieces out of the Empire. By the end of the nineteenth century, the other remaining religious and ethnic groups, such as Albanians, Armenians, Arabs, and Kurds, also began to long for their own independent state.

The whole historical process concerned religion, Islam, in multiple ways. In the first place, and most obviously, Islam could be held responsible for the overall backwardness of the Muslim world. Prior to the nineteenth century, various European thinkers, and especially Christian men of religion, had generally spoken negatively about Islam.[19] In the nineteenth century, they continued to do so, but now did so in a superior position of military and economic power over the Muslims. And, therefore, the charge against Islam became no longer theological. In a lecture delivered at Sorbonne University in 1883, for example, Ernst Renan, a prominent French Orientalist, held Islam responsible for the backwardness of the Muslims: "Anyone with even the slightest education in matters of our time," declared Renan, "sees clearly the current inferiority of Muslim countries, the decadence of states governed by Islam, the intellectual sterility of races that derive their culture and education from that religion alone. All who have been to the Orient or to Africa are struck by what is the inevitably narrow-mindedness of a true believer, of that kind of iron ring around his head, making it absolutely closed to science, incapable of learning anything or of opening itself up to any new idea." For Renan, "Islam" was "an indistinguishable union of spiritual and temporal," "the reign of dogma," and "the heaviest chain that humankind has ever borne." And as such it was the prime reason for the backwardness of the Muslims.[20]

The rise of Europe and the concomitant decline of the Ottoman Empire posed a related and even more serious problem for Islam, and that problem concerned the overall place of Islam in the state administration. The problem arose acutely because in order to stop the decline, the Ottoman political elites implemented state-modernizing reforms in the imitation of Europe, which brought about fundamental changes in all fields where religion had been fundamental, especially the fields of justice and education. First and foremost, the Ottoman elites founded new courts and borrowed from Europe laws to apply in these courts. The Ottoman elites also founded new state schools and borrowed from Europe materials to teach in those schools. New courts and schools initially ran in parallel with, but eventually dominated, religious courts and schools.[21]

Furthermore, various European ideas and ideologies, such as materialism, positivism, rationalism, and the like, began to penetrate the Ottoman Empire, gaining adherents among the future bureaucrats and intellectuals of the country through various means, such as missionary or newly founded state schools and mushrooming print media. In the late nineteenth century, the amalgam of ideas and ideologies that circulated in the Ottoman intellectual and academic space was, Şükrü Hanioğlu observes, by and large antireligion and by twist of fate came to influence an influential group of bureaucrats: the Young Turks. It was this group of bureaucrats who "were destined to rule the Islamic caliphate [the Ottoman Empire] for almost a decade, and then to go on to craft a secular nation-state out of its remains."[22] All in all, as a result, the wholesale ideational invasion in effect undermined religion's traditional status as the fountain of truth, knowledge, and wisdom.

Islamism's Core Belief

This ideational milieu, shaped and reshaped within the background of an ascending Europe and descending Ottoman Empire, gave the intellectual impetus to the formation of what became Islamism's core beliefs as a number of religious scholars and intellectuals in the Ottoman Empire and across the Muslim world proposed various theological theses to defend Islam against what seemed to be a total assault. These theses essentially attributed to Islam certain key features, some of which can readily be derived from the main sources of Islam, but interpreted and reinterpreted in the particular context of the age.

All in all, to keep it short, Islam was claimed to be God's last and unadulterated religion and hence "the most perfect and best of all religions."[23] As such, Islam was, for example, "the most humane religion" and "the most complete and highest form of human civilization in its spirit and in its signification."[24] Islam preached the highest ideals and the best virtues for humans, such as "genuine principles of liberty and solidarity,"[25] "hard work,"[26] and "unity, solidarity and mutual assistance among believers"[27]; and it forbade the worst vices, such as, "disunity,"[28] "enmity, animosity, dissension, conflict and laziness among Muslims."[29] Commanding "consultation in social and political matters" and establishing principles of "liberty, equality and justice," Islam "formed the basis of an ideal government, hitherto never seen in human history."[30] Islam was also claimed to be "a rational religion," "the true friend and protector of the arts and sciences." As such, Islam was perfectly "compatible with science and could not "contradict any scientific facts."[31] The cause of "the decline and backwardness of the Muslims" was, therefore, not Islam, but Muslims' "failure to properly implement the tenets of" Islam or of "the real and genuine Islam.[32] If properly observed, Islam guaranteed not only "the unearthly, heavenly happiness of mankind," but also "the material/temporal and mundane happiness of the people."[33] What needed to be done, therefore, was that Islam should be properly interpreted and lived up to and thus could be a great moral and ideational source to generate progress and development in Muslim countries.

A number of individuals expressed these and similar ideas about Islam. It might be illustrative to take a look into the writings of one of them, Said Nursi (1878–1960), a member of the first generation of Islamists in Turkey, who also lived through the Republican period—hence a critical link between the Ottoman and the Republican periods.

Said Nursi was born in 1878 in Nurs, a village in the mountainous region south of Lake Van, and passed away in 1960 in the southeastern city of Urfa.[34] He thus lived his formative years in the turbulent last decades of the Ottoman Empire.[35] Even though Nursi received a religious education, thus posed either as a religious student or as a religious scholar, he also became familiar with major political and intellectual debates of his period. His early writings show that he was well aware of a broad spectrum of arguments raised against Islam. In the very beginning of his Devaü'l Yeis (the Medicine of Despair), for example, Said Nursi warned against an intellectual current working against Islam, leading people to either become irreligious or disrespect religions or become Christian or suspect the truthfulness of Islam. One argument this current could bring was, Said Nursi warned, "Oo, Muslims. Look wherever a Muslim is, he is comparatively poorer, ignorant and uncivilized. Wherever a Christian is, he is comparatively civilized, enlightened, rich."[36] This argument essentially implied that Islam could be held responsible for the great disparity in material wealth between the Islamic world and Europe.[37]

It is obvious in his writings that Said Nursi denied any responsibility of Islam in the material backwardness of the Islamic world. Said Nursi claimed to the contrary that Islam had all the potential needed for material progress. For example, only Islam could unite hundreds of millions of Muslims as one soul. Compatible with the findings of modern sciences, Islam directed Muslims towards the most exalted aims, furnished them with a desire to progress, and destroyed such maladies as envy, malice, and rivalry.[38] To prove his point, Nursi also made a bold statement: "History shows that the people of Islam became more civilized and progressed to the extent they acted in accordance with the truths of Islam, and history also shows that they fell into savagery, decline, disaster and defeat to the extent of their weakness in the truths of Islam."[39] Said Nursi claimed that other religions were different. "Their adherents progressed and became more civilized to the extent their adherence to their religions weakened and they regressed and fell into revolutions to the extent they strengthened their devotions to their religions."[40]

Said Nursi also believed that Islam provided effective solutions for a variety of political and economic problems humanity faced. In Europe, for example, two phrases reflected the causes of all revolutions, upheavals, factionalism, debauchery, and similar vices in Europe. The first one was "As long as I am full, I do not care if others die from hunger," and the other was, "You work and I consume." Islam, Nursi claimed, commanded the rich to help the poor by distributing alms and charities and rejecting usury. With these two commands, Islam roots out two sources of various economic and political problems from Muslim societies.[41]

Nursi further believed that Islam would even appeal to Europeans and gain adherents among them. More specifically, he argued that in the past Islam could not penetrate into Europe because of some intellectual and institutional barriers such as Europeans' ignorance, savagery, and fundamentalism in their religions, the power of the clergy over Europeans, and Europeans' blind obedience to them. As Europeans became more civilized and questioning because of the spread of modern sciences and enlightenment, they would look for a religion whose truths would be ascertained by rationality and evidence. Nursi believed that humanity could not live without religion, for only religions could give meaning to human life. Only Islam, however, which called for humans to employ their reason and reflect on its truths, could satisfy humanity's need for a religion. Therefore, Nursi declared, only Islam would dominate in the future.[42]

In defense of Islam against what they considered to be a total assault, a number of religious scholars and intellectuals proposed a variety of theses about Islam; not all these theses have remained popular. But all contributed to the formation of the core belief of Islam: that Islam, as God's last and most perfect revelation, could provide not only humanity's natural need for religions, but also solutions for all sorts of humanity's problems; or as Said Nursi memorably put it, "the prescription for a diseased age, an ailing nation, and a disabled organ is to follow the Quran." Nursi also added, "the prescription for once great, but now unfortunate continent, once glorious, but now ill-fated state, once precious, but now weakened people is the union of Islam."[43]

The union of Islam or the unity of Muslims was not Said Nursi's call only, but many others', and in fact it became and has since remained Islamism's most often cited ideal that Muslims should aspire to achieve, an ideal that directly concerned international politics. The powerful appeal of this call, however, lay in its rootedness in the Quran and early history of Islam. To understand its appeal then and now, we have to look at its roots.

The Union of Islam or İttihad-ı Islam: The Roots

"The Arabs will not recognize the rule of anyone but this tribe of Quraysh. They are the most central [=noble] of the Arabs in lineage and abode." This was how Abu Bakr, the Prophet's close companion, was claimed to have told the Medinans who met at the Saqifat Bani Saida to elect a leader of their own after the Prophet of Islam passed away. With this declaration, Abu Bakr staged his own succession to the leadership, or to the caliphate, of Muslims in that meeting.

As Wilfred Madelung observed, Abu Bakr's justification was essentially pragmatic. The leadership must be from Quraysh simply because the Arabs would obey only a Qurayshi, no one else.[44] Hence Abu Bakr's emphasis was not on some inherent, divinely acquired right of the Prophet's tribe to rule, but rather on the necessity of electing a leader who could protect the unity of the community of believers or, as popularly called, the ummah.

Abu Bakr's obsession with protecting the unity of the ummah is understandable: first of all, in the prior two decades or so, the Prophet and his Companions (Abu Bakr being one of the most loyal ones) had undergone such trials and tribulations that they had developed a very powerful sense of brotherhood. An oft quoted verse in Islam's Holy Book, the Quran, reflects this sense of brotherhood: "the believers are indeed brothers (49:10)." In a similar vein, another verse portrays Muslims as "comrades/protectors of one another (9:71)," and yet another verse describes them as "merciful among themselves," but "resolute/firm against the disbelievers (48:29)."

The Quran commands Muslims to preserve this unity: a famous verse, for example, states, "And hold firmly to the rope of Allah all together and do not become divided." That brotherhood was God's favor upon them: the Quran continues, "And remember the favor of Allah upon you—when you were enemies and He brought your hearts together and you became, by His favor, brothers. And you were on the edge of a pit of the fire and He saved you from it (3:103)." The Holy Book also commands Muslims to avoid actions that might harm their unity: for example, one verse commands Muslims not to "dispute and [thus] lose courage and [then] your strength would depart." Muslims have to "be patient" instead (8:46). If some Muslims dispute one another, the Quran commands other Muslims to intervene and make a settlement between them. "The believers are but brothers, so make settlement between your brothers (49:10)." The Quran goes even further and commands, "Do not insult one another and do not call each other by nicknames (49:11)"; "avoid much [negative] assumption . . . and do not backbite each other." For backbiting, the Quran declares, "would one of you like to eat the flesh of his dead brother? You would detest it (49:12)."

Early Muslims desperately needed this unity, for at almost every stage during his mission, the Prophet and his companions had made powerful enemies of different kinds, such as the polytheists/associationists of Mecca, the hypocrites of Medina, the rival prophets, the pagans, the Jews, and even the Christians of the Arabian Peninsula. The hostility early Muslims faced throughout was quite expected because the Prophet's religious message was radical for the predominantly pagan populations of the peninsula as he preached the absolute oneness of God. One short surah says it all: "Say: He is Allah, the One. He is Samed [on whom all creatures are dependent, but He is dependent on none]. He neither begat, nor was begotten. Nor has he any equal (112:1–4)."

The Prophet's religious message was also exclusive, claiming monopoly over the ultimate truth about God and condemning all other views to falsehood: regarding Islam, the Quran unequivocally declares, "the Truth has come and the falsehood vanished (17:81)." The Quran also judges adherents of all other views extremely harshly: the Quran's most famous and opening Sarah, al-Fatihah, even claims that all others incurred God's wrath: "It is You we worship and You we ask for help. Guide us to the straight path. The path of those upon whom You have bestowed favor, not of those who incurred Your wrath or of those who are astray (1:5–7)."

Even though the Quran is not specific in the opening surah regarding to whom God directs his wrath, elsewhere it is: in speaking of the polytheists and hypocrites, the Quran states, "Allah is wrathful with them and He has cursed them and prepared for them Hell, and what an evil destination it is (48:6)." The Quran also informs that God is wrathful with Jews because ""they disbelieved in the signs of Allah and killed the 26 prophets unrightly." And therefore, "they were afflicted by humiliation and poverty and incurred the wrath of Allah (2:61)."[45]

The Prophet and his Companions thus perceived themselves as the adherents of God's only and true religion in the sea of peoples all adhering to false religions. The Quran also reflects this self-perception of transcendence: "You are the best community ever brought forth to humankind, you command what is right, forbid what is evil, and believe in God (2:143)." Commanding what is right, forbidding what is evil, the Quran in essence entrusts Muslims with the task of inviting the rest of humankind to God's only and true religion. Even though the Quran preaches Muslims to employ persuasion in this task, it also allows Muslims to resort to brute force if necessary: "Fight them until there is no fitnah and the religion is only for Allah (2:193)." Or "Fight those who do not have faith in Allah nor in the last Day, nor forbid what Allah and His Apostle have forbidden nor practice the true religion, from among those who were given the Book, until they pay the tribute out of hand, degraded (9:29)."

All in all, then, the Quran adopts various rhetorical strategies to strengthen the internal unity and cohesion of Muslims or of the ummah, emphasizing the ummah's divine origin, entrusting it with a transcendental mission, claiming its exclusivity over the truth about God, and directly commanding its members to strengthen their internal unity and cohesion.

That unity faced a formidable challenge when the Prophet passed away.[46] It is critical to note that the challenge did not concern the question of whether Muslims should have a leader or not, but rather concerned the question of who should be the leader(s) after the Prophet. Even though most of Medinans and Meccans pledged their allegiance (bayah) to Abu Bakr after he staged his succession to the leadership, many Muslims across the Arabian Peninsula did not, most likely considering that their allegiance was formerly paid to the Prophet, not to some imagined community of believers. Abu Bakr disagreed: when the Prophet passed away, Abu Bakr seemed to have concluded, the ummah did not become obsolete, but rather had to be kept together, if necessary, by force. And he did. He declared a total war not only against rival prophets and their adherents but also against those Muslims who did not recognize his leadership. In what came to be known as the Ridda Wars or the Wars of Apostasy in Arab-Islamic history, Abu Bakr defeated both groups, reunited the ummah under his leadership, and unleashed a great conquest movement.

Yet Abu Bakr's success proved to be short-term. Almost two decades after his death, centrifugal forces had already set in and shattered into pieces the ummah's unity. Even the close companions of the Prophet fought two bloody wars, known as the War of Camel and the War of Siffin, during the caliphate of Ali and shed each other's blood: in the notorious War of Camel, the Prophet's wife Aisha was on one side and the Prophet's cousin and son-in-law Ali on the other.

The whole episode left an indelible mark on the later development of the Sunni political theology, which evolved to prioritize the unity of the ummah as the ultimate political ideal and condemn all actions that might threaten that ideal. Hence the Wars of Camel and of Siffin and the development of different sects such as Kharijism and Shiism came to be called fitnahs (or futun). The choice of wording is interesting, for the Quran declares "fitnah" worse than killing (2:217). Yet the various meanings the Quran attaches to the word "fitnah" do not necessarily connote the same sense that the word came to acquire. More significantly, the Sunni political theology developed a strong distaste for rebellion against rulers even if they are unjust and tyrannical.[47] Hence the infamous maxim "tyranny is better than anarchy." The Quran's ultimate political objective of building a tightly knit community of believers, strengthening the unity of that community, and deterring Muslims from undermining that unity thus became the foundation of the Sunni political theology's ultimate political ideal of building a political order and deterring Muslims from undermining that order.

İttihad-ı İslam: The Nineteenth-Century Revival

The unity of the ummah as a political ideal was revived again in full strength in the nineteenth century in the form of a multitude of calls for the development of closer cooperation and stronger relations among Muslims of all ethnicities and sects across the world. Coined as İttihad-ı İslam in Ottoman Turkish or Wahdat al-Islam in Arabic (yet, in both cases, literally meaning unity or union of Islam), this call found an echo among statesmen and bureaucrats of the Ottoman Empire, the state that many Muslims had turned to for financial, military, and diplomatic aid throughout that long century.[48] In the late nineteenth century, the Ottoman Empire even pursued pan-Islamism, the phrase coined by Europeans to refer to what the Ottomans called "İttihad-ı İslam" as a foreign policy during the reign of Sultan Abdülhamid II.

In the hostile international context of the nineteenth century, the idea appeared appealing: by cooperating with one another, Muslims could have stood up against Europe and protected their interests. In the same century also emerged political movements of the same kind, such as pan-Germanism, pan-Slavism, pan-Hellenism, pan-Turanism, pan-Arabism, pan-Turkism, Zionism, and others.[49] In fact, Kemal Karpat, a prominent Ottoman historian, argued that "the idea of establishing a Muslim union first emerged as a reaction to Russia's pan-Slavist propaganda among the Slavic Orthodox Christian population of the Ottoman Empire and Austria." The unity of Muslims was "to counter Russia's pan-slavism with a Muslim version of their own devising, possibly modelled on 'pan-Germanic' ideas."[50] The Ottoman state's own policy of Ottomanism or ittihad-ı anasır (literally the unity of elements) was itself inspirational. It should not, therefore, require much imaginative stretching to apply the same idea to Muslims.

The strong emphasis on the Quran and the Prophetic Traditions, as discussed before, made the idea all the more natural especially at a time of successive waves of Muslim migration into Anatolia from the Caucasus and the Balkans to escape persecution at the hands of Russians or the Balkan Christians.

The idea of the unity of Muslims became popular in the hands of the Young Ottomans. Seemingly the first ever publication to use the term İttihad-ı Islam, an anonymous article published in the Young Ottomanist journal *Hürriyet* in 1869 stated, "all Islamic governments today are in a state of total collapse and the greatest solution for our salvation is unity."[51] Similar articles calling for and explaining the potential benefits for the Ottoman Empire of the unity of Muslims appeared in other young Ottomanist journals.[52] As to the question of how to realize the unity of Muslims, an article published in another young Ottomanist journal, *Basiret*, in 1872 suggested that unity of the Muslims would naturally come about with the implementation of the Shariah and no force could stop its realization.[53]

In many of the Young Ottomanist publications, the unity of Muslims appeared to be a political solution to a pressing problem, not necessarily a religious obligation. A pamphlet published in 1873 by Esad Efendi,[54] who also published in Young Ottomanist journals, however, argued that it was also a religious obligation. That obligation came from first and foremost from two Quranic declarations: the first was, "Obey Allah and obey the Messenger, and those in authority among you (4:59)," and the other was "the believers are indeed brothers (49:10)." The article thus tied together religious brotherhood, unity of Muslims, and obedience to the ruler as a package and unsurprisingly declared the Ottoman Sultan as the only legitimate authority to be obeyed by Muslims.[55]

As the Ottoman Empire lost territories in the succeeding decades, İttihad-ı Islam continued to appeal to statesmen and men of letters from diverse backgrounds.[56] More strongly than others did the early generations of Turkish Islamism embrace it, presenting it not only as a measure to strengthen the Ottoman Empire to better confront European imperialism, but also as an antidote to rising ethnic nationalisms of different Muslim ethnicities, such as Albanians, Arabs, Kurds, and Turks.

One of them, Mehmet Akif, the future writer of the lyrics of the Turkish national anthem, for example, suggested that unity of Muslims was a religious obligation. Quoting the famous Quranic command "And hold firmly to the rope of Allah all together," Akif declared, "let us leave aside

Muslims in foreign countries. There are many ethnicities in the Ottoman country: Albanian, Kurd, Circassian, Bosnian, Arab, Turk, Laz . . ." Akif then rhetorically asked, "what is the tie among them?" and answered, "the tie of religion." Christians could be ethnic nationalists, Akif believed, and live with it. "But, we cannot. If religion departs, there is no life for us." Disunity inspired by ethnic nationalism, Akif declared, was "the prime cause of the current catastrophe."[57]

Another member of the early generation of Turkish Islamism, Ahmed Naim, declared "the Muslim brotherhood" as "one of the pillars of Islam" on the authority of the famous Quranic declaration that "the believers are indeed brothers (49:10)." Various values and duties, Naim claimed, were in fact imposed by Islam to serve this brotherhood. For the same purpose, Islam, Naim believed, prohibited ethnic nationalism and racism. "Ethnic nationalism is," Naim declared, "a harmful and alien ideology to Muslim culture and it poses a dangerous threat to the unity of Islam. Ethnic nationalism is like a deadly contagious disease that could cause the demise of Islam. Ethnic nationalism is an evil ideology whose roots extend to the period of Jahiliyyah, the age of darkness and ignorance that existed before the advent of Islam in Arabia."[58]

It is critical to add that the early generation of Turkish Islamism categorically rejected racial and/or ethnic nationalism, but not nationalism per se. Hence they generally used two different terms, "kavmiyetçilik" for the former and "milliyetçilik" for the latter. As for nationalism as milliyetçilik, the early generation of Turkish Islamism even embraced it, albeit with nuanced differences. Some, for example, argued that there was no nationality in Islam, but religion: therefore all Muslims were one nation. "Islam," Ahmed Hilmi declared, "is one nation." As Muslims were none but brothers, "they all make up one nation," Ahmed Hilmi added, and this nation was "called the Muslim nation," or the "nation of Islam.'" Whatever one's race is, he or she was "one of this nation." "Those who consider them as separate and different from each other," Ahmed Hilmi warned, were "sowers of discord."[59]

Some, on the other hand, argued that Muslims could have different nationalities, yet still had to strive to build stronger relations with other Muslim nationalities. According to Said Halim, for example, "it is not possible to argue that the fundamentals of Islam reject or weaken nationalism." Islam rejected, however, Said Halim argued, "the perversion, superstition, bigotry and selfishness of racism." Yet, Said Halim added, "whether a person is Turk, Arab or Iranian or Indian . . . s/he should value solidarity among Muslim nations as much as s/he values her/his own national solidarity. Then, s/he can be a good Turk, a good Arab, a good Iranian, or a good Indian . . . S/he should know that national and intra-Islam assistance complement each other."[60]

Despite their nuanced differences on the question of nationalism, however, the early generation of Turkish Islamism promoted the idea of unity of Muslims as a political solution to the pressing problems of the Ottoman Empire, justifying it not only on geopolitical grounds, but also on theological grounds. With that, union of Islam, or İttihad-ı Islam, entered Turkish Islamism as a core belief, a belief that directly concerned international relations.

The early generation formulated not only the two core beliefs of Turkish Islamism, but also the nucleus of what later became an elaborate interpretative framework. This framework assumed the existence of an internal enemy that always worked against Muslims and in certain ways assumed conspiratorial features.

Conspiratorial Interpretative Framework

In Mecca, the Prophet of Islam was in a position of political weakness, and his foes, the polytheists, constituted the formidable political and economic elites of the town. In Medina, however, the Prophet was himself in a position of political power yet still faced formidable foes: the hypocrites and the Jews. The so-called hypocrites were those Medinan Arabs, who like their fellow Medinans converted to Islam, but unlike them were not sincere in their beliefs. As the Quran describes them, the hypocrites say, " 'We have faith in Allah and the Last Day,' but they have no faith. They seek to deceive Allah and those who have faith (2:8–9)." The Quran furthermore declares that the hypocrites will receive the harshest punishment in the hereafter: "Inform the hypocrites that there is painful punishment for them . . . Allah will gather the hypocrites and the faithless in hell all together (4:138, 140)." In fact the hypocrites will get the worst: "Indeed the hypocrites will be in the lowest reach of the Fire (4:145)."

The Jews were the Prophet's other and even more formidable foes in Medina. Divided into a number of tribes and economically powerful, the Jews posed a different kind of challenge for the Prophet than those the polytheists of Mecca or the hypocrites of Medina posed: the Jews could theologically challenge the Prophet. This is because the Prophet claimed that he was the last Prophet God sent to humanity and hence many before him preached God's same message: hence the Quran commands Muslims to "Say, 'We have faith in Allah, and in what has been sent down to us, and what was sent down to Abraham, Ishmael, Isaac, Jacob and the Tribes, and that which Moses and Jesus were given, and the prophets, from their Lord. We make no distinction between any of them, and to Him do we submit (3:84).' " Judaism and Christianity were therefore based on God's earlier revelations, yet later distorted and corrupted by the Jews and the Christians: the Quran was simply reiterating and reconfirming God's eternal message. The Prophet was even claimed to have descended from Abraham through Ishmael's grandson Adnan.

The Jews' conversion would therefore not only put human and economic resources in the hands of the Prophet, but also boost his claim to Prophethood. Yet to his disappointment, except for a handful of them, the Jews in Medina refused to leave their own religion and enter the new one. Still the Prophet worked to make a deal with them in his early years in Medina and thus must have hoped at least to pacify them in his struggle with the Meccan Polytheists. However, his efforts proved to be in vain. Quite the opposite, the Jews joined the opposition to the Prophet, being even suspected to have helped the polytheists of Mecca and the hypocrites of Medina in the latters' fight against the Prophet.[61] For one or another reason, the Prophet had forcefully driven the three most powerful Jewish tribes out of Medina. Not surprisingly, the Quran is extremely harsh about the Jews, much more so than it is about the Christians. One famous verse, for example, declares, "Surely You will find the most hostile of all people towards those who believe to be the Jews and the polytheists and surely you will find the nearest of them in affection to those who believe to be those who say 'We are Christians' (5:82)."

Both living in and around Medina, the hypocrites and the Jews constituted the internal enemies for Muslims. Yet there was a critical difference between the two. The hypocrites were hidden. Only God knew who they really were. The Prophet also knew them, informed by God but not allowed to expose them. The Jews were on the other hand visible, and their identities were perfectly known by Muslims. Furthermore, the Quran blurs the distinction between the hypocrites and the Jews by attributing similar traits to both groups. For example, the Quran also accuses the Jews of trying to deceive God and Muslims by pretending to be believers:

"When they [the Jews] meet the faithful, they say, 'We believe,' and when they are alone with one another, they say, 'Do you recount to them what Allah has revealed to you, so that they may argue with you therewith before your Lord? Do you not apply reason?' Do they not know that Allah knows whatever they hide and whatever they disclose?" (2:76).

As David Nirenberg puts it, "Within the Qur'an the concept of hypocricy is closely tied to Judaism. The hypocrite is like the Jew, sometimes seduced by the Jew . . . or related to the Jew." Yet for the Quran, the two groups are still distinct. This distinction serves as a useful rhetorical device; as Nirenberg aptly describes, "it explains how 'Jewish' attributes (lying, envy, enmity, greed, cowardice, materialism, preference for this world over the next) can infect the 'non-Jewish' followers of God." With this conjugation, the Quran provides "a theory of seduction" that explains the persistence of falsehood in the world "despite the warnings of the prophets and the revelation."[62]

More critically, perhaps, the Quran creates an eternal enemy within, the hypocrite Jew, and warns Muslims to be always vigilant about this enemy's desire and activities to deter Muslims from God's path and hence undermine their unity, a unity that depends on Muslims' full adherence to the Quran's teachings and instructions. The Quran's portrayal of such an enemy must have contributed to the development of two interrelated tendencies: one is the "attribution of a Jewish origin or ancestry in order to discredit an individual, a group, a custom or an idea" and the other the attribution of "subversive and extremist doctrines to Jewish origins or instigation."[63] In the most famous case, for example, the great schism between the Sunnis and the Shia has generally been attributed to the work of a single Yemenite Jew, Abdullah bin Saba.

The Quran's portrayal of the Jews as such must have contributed to Muslims' overall negative view of the Jews in the succeeding centuries. Yet in the context of the Ottoman Empire, the Jews had not assumed the role of evil internal enemy even during the troubled nineteenth century. This was for the obvious reason that unlike Christian minorities, the Jews had neither rebelled against the Empire nor been under the protection of any major European power. Economically as well, they had been much less well-to-do than Christians and Muslims.[64] In other words, there was no reason for many Muslims to accuse them of, or suspect their involvement in, acts against the Empire. This was to change in the Empire's last decade.

Interpretative Frame of
Early Generations of Turkish Islamism

Early generations of Turkish Islamism sought the causes of the Muslim world's decline in the Muslims' own weaknesses. To give an example, Ahmed Hilmi declared,

"O brothers in the Faith! Now I will speak to you a word more bitter than poison, bitterer than hell-fruit; I will speak to you a word of great truth. I will tell you the reason why we are despicable, wretched, poor, enslaved. It is because we have not harkened to nor understood the commands of our God and of our Prophet; because we have been shameless and ignorant; because we have tyrannised over ourselves, over our brothers, overall servants of God."[65]

Yet Ahmed Hilmi also believed that Muslims had enemies who would work to keep this state of affairs. "The enemies of Islam," Ahmed Hilmi argued, "know that if we Moslems give up our evil ways and unite we shall become masters of our honour. That is why they do not wish us to open our eyes and unite." To prevent that from happening, or "in order to leave us poor and ignorant as of old," Ahmed Hilmi claimed, "they have bought with money such traitors to their religion and their nation as there are amongst us."[66] To achieve their objective, "these accursed ones," Ahmed Hilmi warned, would sow discord among Muslims and thus keep them weak.[67]

Ahmed Hilmi thus laid out the basic architecture of Turkish Islamism's interpretive framework. To that framework, Derviş Vahdeti, a rather obscure figure among early generations of Turkish Islamism, made his own peculiar contribution, a contribution that proved to be quite fruitful in the future enrichment of the framework. Derviş Vahdeti made that contribution as the owner and chief editor of a short-lived newspaper, *Volkan*, by raising the "Jewish question" or, more specifically, by suggesting the idea that the Jews were one of the most, if not the only, formidable internal enemies. How so?

The Ottoman Sultan Abdülhamid II (r. 1876–1909) continued apace the modernization/state-building reforms of his predecessors. But, unlike them, he pursued a much more ambitious pan-Islamist foreign policy and employed Islam more extensively to legitimate his rule.[68] Abdülhamid II's increasingly autocratic rule came to an end in 1908 when a number of officers mutinied and demanded that Abdülhamid II reinstate the constitution he had abrogated thirty years earlier. Unable to suppress the mutinies and subsequent popular demonstrations, Abdülhamid II conceded and restored the constitution. Behind the mutinies against the Sultan was a clandestine organization, known as İttihat ve Terakki Cemiyeti (the Committee of Union and Progress—the CUP), which had its members in the military and civilian bureaucracy.

Almost five months after the restoration of the constitution, in December 1908, Derviş Vahdeti began to publish *Volkan* and soon afterward came to accuse the CUP of corruption, authoritarianism, maladministration, and so forth.[69] Vahdeti also complained bitterly about the spread of irreligiosity and moral laxity among Muslims.[70] Vahdeti believed that the Freemasons formed the most formidable irreligious (dinsiz) group in the empire. Claiming to serve all of humanity, not any particular religion, the Freemasons, according to Vahdeti, were a transnational revolutionary organization that aimed and worked to spread freedom of religion. For this advocacy, Vahdeti claimed, the Freemasons were even ostracized from Christianity. Vahdeti also claimed that the Freemasons were a secret organization, having developed special signs and codes to recognize one another and instituted their own holidays. [71]

More controversially, Vahdeti claimed that Freemasonry spread and gained strength in the then-Ottoman town Salonika. It was also in Salonika, Vahdeti exclaims, that the CUP was established and gained adherents. Vahdeti also pointed out that the CUP and the Freemason lodge in Salonika had similar internal organizations.[72] Taking this one step further, Vahdeti pointed out that the followers of Sabatai Sevi, who claimed in the seventeenth century that he was the awaited messiah of the Jews, were also from the same city. Known as the dönme or the converts, they were not genuine Muslims, according to Vahdeti, but secret Jews.[73]

Vahdeti certainly believed that secret/crypto Jews and Freemasons penetrated the CUP. But to what extent and at what hierarchy they did in Vahdeti's imagination is difficult to determine. When he was hanged for his role in the instigation of and participation in the 1909 countercoup attempt against the CUP, he was just thirty-nine. He thus could not leave much writing behind. Yet his writings in *Volkan* over a period of fewer than five months left an indelible legacy for the future evolution of Turkish Islamism's interpretive framework. That legacy essentially suggested that there were internal enemies, crypto-Jews appearing to be Muslims, but in essence conspiring against Islam and Muslims.[74]

The Evolution: The Republican Period

In the evolution of Turkish Islamism, the foundation of the republic in 1923 and the subsequent reforms truly constituted a watershed. Former Young Turks, the founders of the republic, implemented a series of reforms, such as the abolition of the caliphate, the office of Sheikh al-Islam, and the Şer'iyye ve Evkaf Vekaleti (Ministry of Shariah and Religious Foundations); the closure of religious seminaries, religious courts, and Sufi orders; the adoption of the hat and promotion of European-style clothing; secularization of family law, the then-last vestige of the Islamic law in Turkey; the change of the alphabet from the Arabic script to the Latin; the recitation of the Islamic call to prayer (ezan) in Turkish; the grounding of the national identity not in religion, but in ethnic Turkishness; and the removal of the religion clause and institution in its place of the secular character of the state in the constitution.[75] Along the same lines, the republic also changed its foreign policy, dropping whatever pan-Islamist elements had remained: Mustafa Kemal, the founder of the republic, gave the hint of this change quite early: in December 1921, he stated,

> Every one of our compatriots and coreligionists may nourish a high ideal in his mind; he is free to do so . . . But the government of the Grand National Assembly of Turkey has a firm, positive, material policy, and that, gentlemen, is directed to the preservation of life and independence . . . within defined national frontiers. The Grand National Assembly and government of Turkey, in the name of the nation they represent, are very modest, very far from fantasies, and completely realistic . . .[76]

The reforms undertaken by the founders of the republic were not meant to eradicate Islam but to depoliticize religion and put it under the exclusive service of the state. For example, in place of the office of Sheikh al-Islam and of the Ministry of Shariah and Religious Foundations, the republic instituted the Directorate of Religious Affairs to administer all religious ritualistic services through mosques and offices of religious counsels (müftülük).[77]

Mustafa Kemal Atatürk, the founding father of the republic and its first president, was quite explicit in defining the task of this Republican religious institution: "Our Republican government," declared Atatürk, "has an office of the Directorate of Religious Affairs. Under this office work many state employees such as many religious counsels, preachers and prayer leaders. These individuals' level of knowledge and wisdom is known." Yet, Atatürk complained, "I also see many people who are not employed here [the Directorate] . . . I came across among them very ignorant, even illiterate ones. Especially in some places these ignorants act as leaders of the people as if they are their representatives . . . I want to ask people like these: From whom did they take this right and responsibility?"[78]

With the said reforms, the republic essentially established a monopoly over religion, and that monopoly came along with the authority to define what religion was and was not. The republic also assumed in this vein such religious services as research and publication on religion between 1924 and 1950. The Directorate of Religious Affairs, for example, financed translations of the Quran and the Prophetic Traditions (Hadith) into Turkish and multivolume commentaries on the Quran and the Prophetic traditions in Turkey. More significantly, the Directorate distributed thousands of copies of these state-approved translations and commentaries across mosques in Turkey.

The republic jealously protected its monopoly over religion. Several biographies from the 1920s to 1950s consistently show that the Turkish state inflicted severe hardships on individual religious figures who did not collaborate with the regime and tried to break the state monopoly over religious teaching and research. Religious figures such as Said Nursi, Mehmet Esad Erdebili, İskilipli Mehmet Atıf, Ali Galip Keskin, Abdülhakim Arvasi, Mehmet Vehbi, and Süleyman Hilmi Tunahan faced severe punishments from the regime ranging from exile to death because of their continuation of activities that were distasteful to the republic.

The repression on independent religious activity considerably lessened starting in the late 1940s as Turkey made a transition to multiparty politics. Yet the republic still maintained control over the religious field in the succeeding decades. The republic had continued to be the largest religious service provider in Turkey, leaving limited space for any independent religious activity. Still, independent religious activity continued in Turkey and gained further strength in the succeeding decades. The challenge then was how to keep intact the secular nature of the state in the face of this religious activism.

Meeting that challenge fell on the shoulders of the court system and the military. By the time Turkey made a transition to multiparty politics, the Turkish penal code had articles that penalized certain religious activities.

Most notoriously, Article 163, which was introduced in 1949 just before the transition, made it a punishable crime to found, lead, and/or help an association that worked to alter Turkey's social, economic, political, or legal system in accordance with religious fundamentals and beliefs. The same article also made it a punishable crime to make propaganda of any such association and furthermore augmented the sentences for the same crimes if committed by state employees. Applying this and similar articles, the court system in Turkey continued to monitor independent religious activity in the post-1950 period. The court system in fact frequently invoked relevant articles to punish independent religious activism.

Apart from the court system, the military was even more critical in safeguarding the secular nature of the Turkish state. It is critical to note that the leading founding figures of the republic were military men. These men enjoyed not only great legitimacy, but also impeccable prestige among officer corps thanks to their leadership and nationalistic credentials proven during and even before the War of Independence. More critically, the founders of the republic had been educated in the same schools and gone through the same traumatic experiences with many of the high-ranking military officers. Thus the founders and the military had shared similar, if not exactly the same, ideological orientations that concerned the state and religion. Not surprisingly, the military grew quite restive during the long one-party period.

More critically, the republic entrusted the military with the task of its ultimate guardianship. The 1935 Army Internal Service Law clearly stated, "the duty of the armed forces is to protect and defend the Turkish homeland and the Turkish Republic." This clause, repeated in the 1961 Turkish Armed Services Internal Service Law, came to justify the military's repeated interventions into politics during the multiparty period.[79] The military directly intervened in politics four times, in 1960, 1971, 1980, and 1997. Neither in 1960, nor in 1971, nor in 1980 was the military's primary target independent religious activity. This was simply because until the 1980s, Marxism-Communism, which appealed especially to the youth and intellectual-academic circles, posed a much more serious challenge to the republic than independent religious activity. In the same period, independent religious actors marshaled their resources against Marxist-Communist groups and thus voluntarily served the republic.

More importantly, independent religious activity began to flourish and expanded its societal base in the 1980s. The flourishing of independent religious activity, which became most manifest in the Welfare Party's winning of major municipalities in the 1994 local elections and emergence as the leading party in the 1995 national elections, paved the way for the military's fourth direct intervention in politics, known in Turkey as the 28 February soft coup. On that day in 1997, the government, headed by Necmettin Erbakan, the leader of the Islamist Welfare Party, was forced by the military to sign a document that essentially advised the government to implement a series of measures to curb independent religious activity, which was declared to be threatening the foundations of the republic. Even though he signed that document, Erbakan proved unable to satisfy the military and a few months later resigned from government. In early 1998, the Constitutional Court of Turkey closed down the Welfare Party and banned its leaders, including Necmettin Erbakan, from politics for five years.

All in all, the republic created and quite successfully sustained a relatively hostile and extremely restrictive environment for all sorts of independent religious activism in Turkey. Islamism survived and evolved in the same environment.

The Republican Islamism

Islamism was born in the late Ottoman period not as an organized movement, but rather as individual efforts to defend Islam against what seemed to be a relentless total attack on this last monotheistic religion. The hostile environment the republic created and sustained in Turkey had deeply shaped and reshaped Islamism in Turkey.

First and foremost, the republic came to preach a particular understanding of Islam across its mosques.[80] This understanding was best formulated in a treatise titled *Islam Dini* (Religion of Islam) penned by Ahmed Hamdi Akseki, who had worked in the Directorate first as a member of its Consultative Council (1924–1939), then as its vice-president (1939–1947), and finally as its president (1947–1951).[81] Laying out Islam's basic beliefs (itikad), rituals (ibadet), and moral principles (ahlak), *Islam Dini* was recommended by the then president of the Directorate, Rıfat Börekçi, for publication and distribution to all preachers and prayer leaders.[82]

According to *Islam Dini*, religions are essentially moral teachings, established by the Creator, Allah, to lead humans toward happiness, teach them the purpose of creation, and inform them of the good deeds. "Without religion," *Islam Dini* argues, "no morality and virtue can be observed in individuals. There will be no trace of order and harmony in a society formed by such individuals. Nothing can substitute religion."[83] As a corollary, irreligiousness is harmful for societies, for it will bring about the end of morality, the dissolution of moral ties that unite individuals, and hence the collapse of human societies.

"There is no doubt," *Islam Dini* argues, that "human societies will degenerate and plunge into a merciless anarchy with no end. From the perspective of individual, familial and societal happiness religion is the most necessary societal institution."[84] *Islam Dini* further claims that human societies have always had religions not only because religion is necessary, but also because it is in human nature. As time passed, religions have been updated by the Creator and eventually have reached perfection in Islam. Islam is indisputably the final religion, its rulings being valid across all time and places until the end of the time.

According to *Islam Dini*, Islam is a natural religion (tabii bir din), for its rulings are based on human reason and the obvious truths, and hence in no conflict with human nature and the natural laws. Islam's beliefs are in no conflict with natural sciences and modern ideas and therefore require no adjustments in their rulings. Islam's moral principles are so salient and sublime that they can challenge even the most sound and perfect philosophy. Islam highly values human reason, science, and wisdom. It sets forth the principles of freedom and equality before law in the soundest possible way. Islam's biggest enemies are ignorance, superstition, repression, and injustice. Islam always commands its adherents to be just and pursue knowledge, wisdom, and art. With all these features, "we argue," *Islam Dini* states, "the only natural and universal religion is Islam."[85]

The republic's Islam, as formulated in *Islam Dini*, was in essence not so different from that of the Ottoman Islamism. Both argued that religions were necessary in modern life and Islam as the most perfect of all was especially apt for it. By defining religion in this way, the republic, paradoxically perhaps, helped consolidate Islamism's core belief about Islam.

Characterizing religion as such created a safe space for independent religious activism. As long as claims about religion remained within that space, religious activism was on the same side with the Turkish state. Preaching a more comprehensive Islam, however, an Islam that encompassed not only a set of beliefs, rituals, and morals, but also definitive commands and rulings that concerned legislation, public administration, or interstate relations, would be troublesome, as it would amount to questioning the fundamental character of the republic.

Islamism's struggle in Turkey in fact has been to consolidate that safe space as firmly as possible. To this end, Islamism has not only reiterated the same view, but also sought the causes of a variety of personal, social, economic, and political problems in the spread of immorality, which was ultimately linked to the loss of religion. Islamism became oppositional in Turkey when it also sought to breach and expand the boundaries that were drawn by the Directorate as much as possible and to this end portrayed Islam as more than a set of beliefs, rituals, and morals.

Even Said Nursi, who was otherwise a staunch critic and opponent of the founders of the republic, seemed to share the same view of Islam. In fact, long before the foundation of the republic, Nursi declared, "the Shariah is ninety-nine percent about morality, rituals, the hereafter and virtues. It is only one-percent about politics." Said Nursi expressed this statement in a court defense in 1909, which was published as *Divan-i Harb-i Örfi*. Yet he also included it in his biography, *Tarihçe-i Hayat*; hence he seemed to have continued to embrace the same view during the Republican period as well.

Unlike the Directorate, however, Said Nursi believed that there was a more immediate and pressing problem: individual faiths were under the assaults of such dangerous philosophies as atheism, naturalism, materialism, deism, secularism, positivism, and so forth. Nursi therefore devoted his scholarship to strengthening individual faiths in God and Islam. It might be telling to look into the content of Said Nursi's magnum opus, *Sözler*. *Sözler* mainly deals with the fundamentals of belief, which Said Nursi set out to strengthen. For example, the first nine sections enumerate the benefits of having a faith and abiding by Islamic rituals, such as praying and distributing charity; the tenth section argues for the necessity of the existence of an afterlife; the eleventh section discusses the Divine reasoning behind the creation of the universe and of humanity; the twelfth and the thirteenth sections compare and contrast the Qur'an and philosophy; the nineteenth section deals with the Prophethood of the Prophet of Islam; the twenty-fifth section shows the miraculousness of the Qur'an; the twenty-sixth section makes a case for the rationality of predestination; the twenty-seventh section tackles with the issue of ijtihad; the twenty-ninth section rationalizes the existence of angels; and the thirty-third section elaborates on the existence and unity of God.

In the nineteenth section of *Sözler*, Said Nursi declared that Islam's Holy Book, the Quran, was "an eternal translation of the book of great universe." He essentially portrayed the Quran and the universe as the works by the same Author, God. While the former was the product of God's attribute of speech (kelam), the latter was that of God's attribute of power (kudret). As such, the Quran and the universe could not conflict with or contradict one another. Nursi in essence provided a powerful argument defending Islam's compatibility with modern sciences, which were human reason's attempts to discover God's eternal natural laws. This argument was obviously part and parcel of Islamism's broader project of proving Islam's relevance for modern life.

Nursi devoted his scholarly attention to developing arguments that would strengthen individual faith in God and Islam. Yet this was the first stage of a three-stage Islamic revivalism he imagined. In the second stage, his arguments would spread among the masses and strengthen their faith. Only in the final stage, Said Nursi envisioned, would the Islamic Shariah be fully implemented in a society of all pious and faithful Muslims. In a sense, Nursi depoliticized Islamism as the third stage to be realized in some uncertain future and more or less stayed in perfect line with the Directorate.

Starting with the end of the one-party period, Islamism began to make much bolder claims about Islam. Necip Fazıl Kısakürek, one of the most vocal figures who greatly contributed to the rebirth of Islamism in Turkey in the 1950s, declared, for example, "We believe only in Islam" and added, "We believe that the only order that guarantees the internal and external life of humanity and society is, with its depth, eternality, beauty and truthfulness, Islam." Kısakürek further claimed, "We believe that the Islamic Shariah . . . is a whole that does not accept any partition or dispute." Finally, Kısakürek declared, the true/authentic/real view "of the universe," "of the world," "of the humanity," "of economic and social justice," "of positive sciences," "of fine arts," "of gender," "of the state," "of military," "of politics," are "in Islam."[86]

In Kısakürek's poetic statement, reminiscent of Hasan al-Banna's declaration, "the total blessing and solution is Islam." The social justice and equality that socialism and communism sought to realize, the individual well-being and rights that liberalism and capitalism sought to sustain, the most elegant principles for the regulation of freedom of thought and other individual rights that democracy sought to nourish, the highest order and the spiritual unity that Nazism and fascism sought to create, are all in Islam. In short, "the heaven that the West has searched, but could not find in every field is in Islam; the salvation path out of the hell it fell in every field is in Islam, everything is in Islam."[87]

Yet it is critical to add to this discussion that Kısakürek's Islam is not literalist or, in his own wording, that of a pure zealot. He did not see his mission (dava) as deriving some strict rulings from Islam in the imitation of Islamic jurisprudence and implementing them in respective spheres of human life. He saw his mission rather as deriving some guiding moral principles from Islam and with them mobilizing Muslims behind the project of reviving what he called Büyük Doğu (the grand East).

For Kısakürek, the undisputable source of morality is religion, with which no other source, even philosophy, can compete. The foundation of morality in the West, for example, "is only and always Christianity." For Muslims, it was obviously Islam. Yet, Kısakürek believed, the immature and rough medrese people (softa) in old times and the fundamentalist Westernists in the new times destroyed this morality. Moreover, the republic, Kısakürek argued, could construct a new moral perspective and therefore gave birth to what he called "a moral calamity" or "a moral wound that inflicted us from our brain to our toe." Hence, Kısakürek declared, the real mission was to construct a new moral perspective, a perspective that would be comprehensive enough to cover all fields, "scientific, literary, philosophical, legal, political, municipal, health, financial, economic, individual, social, national, military." Needless to reiterate, that perspective has to be derived from Islam.

Islamism in Turkey, it is critical to add, also developed a view of Islam as the name of a once great civilization. Such a view of Islam was definitely present in late Ottoman Islamism. Mehmet Şemsettin Günaltay, for example, stated, "inspired and enlightened by their religion," Muslims once "dominated the world and built a magnificent civilization." Therefore, Islam could "never be a source of backwardness."[88] İskilipli Mehmet Atıf similarly stated, "Islam inaugurated a new era for the development of the useful aspects of progress and created a wonderful civilization." Western civilization had also "good and beneficial aspects," which were in fact imported from Islamic civilization. Yet the West had also a "decadent, immoral, vice-prone and ugly side, . . . such as unbelief [atheism], oppression, prostitution, gambling, drinking alcohol, or dancing." In balance, though, Western civilization was "far from being a model civilization for humanity to adopt, since it does not take an interest in the moral aspects and spiritual happiness of humanity, but focuses only on material gains and encourages mankind's animal instincts."[89]

Another figure of late Ottoman Islamism, Said Nursi, also believed that Western civilization had virtues, such as science and technology, but

numerous vices as well. It rested primarily on brute power and therefore
was aggressive. It preached pursuit of self-interest only and therefore bred
enmity. It regulated social life on the principle of competition and therefore
nurtured societal conflicts. It tied people through ethnicity and therefore
promoted wars. Finally, it encouraged men to satisfy their carnal desires
and hence promoted debauchery and immorality.[90] Islamic civilization
was, on the other hand, the opposite of Western civilization in all these
aspects. It rested on truth, not brute power. It therefore sought justice. It
pursued virtue, not self-interest, and therefore promoted love. It regulated
social life on the principle of cooperation, not competition. It therefore
promoted unity. It guided men to the true path, not to the satisfaction
of their carnal desires.[91]

In the Republican period, Islamism in Turkey continued to espouse
Islam as a name for a distinct and superior civilization. This is obviously
understandable in the context of a restrictive environment created and
sustained by the republic. Necip Fazıl Kısakürek, for example, believed that
there essentially were two opposite civilizations: Western and the Eastern
civilization. While human reason dominated and shaped the West, human
spirit dominated and shaped the East. As God's last revelation, Islam was
the last, and most perfect, addition to the East's historical spirituality.

Islam's major and most valuable contribution to Eastern civilization came at the hands of the Turkish people, who began to convert to
Islam in the ninth century, put their soul and energy at its service, and
established the great Ottoman Empire. The Empire was the most perfect
embodiment of Eastern civilization and its last superiority moment over
the West. Starting in the seventeenth century, the Ottoman Empire and
hence the East declined and eventually fell under the powerful hegemony of the West because of the latter's mobilization of human reason and
subsequent attainment of material power. The West's hegemony over the
East created a parasitical relationship: "the Westerner will produce all
civilizational elements and tools and the Easterner will use these as a mere
stupid consumer, tilling his own lands for the Westerner and putting his
own raw materials under the Westerner's command. In the meantime,
the Easterner's approach to the Westerner is only a will-less admiration
and a shallow imitation under the condition that his rope will be in the
hands of the master."[92]

In Kısakürek's imagination, the East was not equal to Islamic civilization. It covered non-Muslim countries as well, most notably China
and India. Kısakürek seemed to believe that Islam was one, obviously the

last and most perfect one, in the chain of successive spiritual traditions that gave birth to and have shaped the grand Eastern civilization. Sezai Karakoç, another prominent thinker of Islamism in Turkey, was much more explicit and clearly distinguished Islamic civilization from Eastern civilization, which in his imagination included China and India.[93]

Neither Western nor Eastern civilization preached equality between and brotherhood of human beings, both being civilizations of extremes. Islamic civilization did. "We are not Easterner," declared Karakoç, "We are not Westerner either. We are the middle. We are the Middle Easterner. We are Muslim. We are the people of a different world. We are the people of a different civilization. Islam is a message of the Middle East to the whole world and all humanity. It is a message of Truth. It is a message of brotherhood and equality."[94]

Needless to say, Karakoç believed, Islam's origin is divine. Throughout history, in fact, God had sent numerous prophets to humanity, every single one of them marking the birth of a new civilization. Yet all these prophetic civilizations were of the same single civilization: the civilization of Truth (*Hakikat Medeniyeti*). Predicated on oneness/unity of God, this civilization's "only continuator, only legatee is the Islamic civilization."[95] Being divine in origin and the last of its kind, Islamic civilization cannot cease to exist. Yet, with the decline and eventual collapse of the Ottoman Empire, Islamic civilization's last truly great state, Islamic civilization at least de facto ceased to exist. It was incumbent, Karakoç believed, upon Muslims to revive it.

> Muslims have to unify their geographies, histories and through this way arrive at one common culture. Every Muslim is indebted to contribute as much as s/he can to the revival of the Islamic civilization. The ideal of unity of Muslims shall be inerasably placed in every young person's heart. Muslims' running towards political unity is a life-and-death matter. This is the modern ideal of the soldier of revival.[96]

Karakoç believed that achieving political unity was attainable because the Muslim world was territorially compact, divided by superficially and politically drawn borders, and had a shared historical unity. But it was missing cultural unity. Once political and cultural unities were realized, the nation of Islam would be born. "When the nation, the nation of Islam is born, the Islamic civilization, which is the civilization of Truth, will then be realized."[97]

Islamism adopted the concept of civilization in the late Ottoman period to promote a selective modernization, not a total westernization of the state and society. Islamism continued to employ the concept during the Republican period. Like his Ottoman predecessors, Necip Fazıl also believed that Eastern civilization could learn from, and, more specifically adopt, the science and technology of Western civilization. Yet he also added a new meaning to the concept: civilizations were now the main frontiers in the grand civilizational battle of survival and superiority. Countries of the same civilization were supposedly on the same side of the frontier and thus could form stronger alliances and even political units. This new meaning became more pronounced in Sezai Karakoc's employment of the concept. Reviving Islam and Islamic civilization also included realizing the political and cultural unity of Muslims. In other words, the employment of the concept of civilization was intimately linked to another core belief of Islamism: İttihad-ı Islam.

Referring to Islamic civilization was obviously one way of calling for, albeit implicitly, İttihad-ı Islam. Yet Islamism also made quite explicit calls for İttihad-ı Islam during the Republican period. One powerful and unequivocal call came from Mehmet Akif İnan.[98] "Muslims of the earth," İnan declared, "must unite! Against this age, against the age that fights to banish this faith they must unite with unbreakable bonds that extent from hearts to hearts. 'They must firmly hold unto the rope of Allah.'" More provocatively, İnan stated, "the people of unbelief [küfür] are one nation," and added, "so are Muslims . . . when the faithful unite dissolves the hegemony of unbelief, ends the system of exploitation, emancipate enslaved nations, enslaved peoples."[99]

For İnan, the Middle East was a special part of the earth. "This land became the home for the belief in God. On this land are the Prophet's footprints." If the Middle East was the symbol of Godliness, the West, on the other hand, was the symbol of the opposite, godlessness. There lay, İnan believed, the West's eternal enmity toward the Middle East.[100] Throughout history, the West hoped and worked to destroy the unity of the Islamic world, the Crusades being the most spectacular case of the West's efforts.

Having realized the futility of military invasion in subduing and destroying the unity of the Islamic world, the West adopted a new approach and as a part of it spread the idea of ethnic nationalism among Muslims. "It is nothing, but ethnic nationalism that destroyed the Islamic world and dispersed the Ottoman Empire. Not the financial, military, administrative crisis we are in, not our technical incompetency, it is ethnic nationalism that directly demolishes us." İnan argued that the invasion of the Muslim world was made possible thanks to the spread of ethnic nationalistic ideas, especially among the intelligentsia and the ruling strata.[101]

In the First World War, the West could finally destroy the Ottoman Empire and hence realized its eternal aim to bring disunity and disorder to the Middle East.[102] As the Islamic unity dissolved, however, the West rushed to establish its own hegemony over the Muslim world. Thus started "the reign of unbelief in the Muslim world." Depending on the circumstances, İnan argued, the West established direct administration in some Muslim countries and left the others "officially" independent. Yet, in terms of the Western hegemony, there was no difference. The West was fortunate to have found in "officially" independent countries ruling cadres that were Westernists, in fact, more "pro-King than the King himself." As time passed, "officially" non-independent Muslim countries also gained their independence from the West. But the West, İnan believed, left power in the hands of the Westernist cadres. Thus, İnan declared, "in all Muslim countries, the open and intense hegemony of the unbelief gave way to a different period, in other words, the period of hypocrisy."[103]

İnan held that it all started in Turkey. "After [founding] the Republic we built friendships with all Western countries that destroyed the Ottoman Empire. We are still loyal to this friendship." This happened because, İnan believed, "the rulers, intelligentsia of this country have been passionate and irrational lovers [karasevdalı] of the West." And for that love, Turkey cut all its relations with the Middle East. Turkey, İnan further argued, could not even develop "a dry friendship with the Islamic countries" because of "the friendship with" and "assurances given to" the West.[104] İnan held that the formation of this ruling elite and intelligentsia preceded the founding of the republic and was the product of the Ottoman Empire's westerniza-tion efforts to halt the ongoing decline. Over the course of these efforts, the internal and external enemies had purged the faithful from the state and placed in their stead states cadres that were pro-West. It was these pro-West cadres that still prevented the Middle East states from building stronger friendships.[105]

After the destruction of the Islamic unity at the state level, other Muslim countries simply replicated what happened in Turkey. "In the Islamic countries torn apart from the Ottoman Empire as well the West distributed the model [in Turkey] . . . forcing them to implement it." Moreover, the West instilled a source of sedition (fitne) among Muslim countries, thus making them enemies of one another. "The puppeteer constantly produced conflicts among puppets." Turks were taught that Arabs betrayed them in the First World War. On the other side, Arabs were taught that Turks exploited them for centuries and now left religion and became irreligious. "In short, a sedition (fitne) has constantly been pumped to all Muslims, about all Muslim countries."[106]

İnan seemed to believe, however, that after decades of the post-Ottoman disorder in the Middle East, the intelligentsia of the region finally began to realize that the unity of Muslim countries was politically and economically beneficial to all. İnan warned, however, that any future cooperation and rapprochement among Muslim countries should not be based on material interests, but on the Islamic faith. "It is now incumbent upon us . . . to put the Islamic faith, civilization at the foundation. The strength and longevity of our unity is possible only if this foundation, this sincerity, is not left . . . The foundation is the brotherhood of Islam. Now we are at the place to develop this brotherhood."[107] Fortunately, İnan argued, the Muslim countries are a community of countries that had no conflict of interests with one another. As a matter of fact, the world system put them in artificial conflicts and thus created enmity among them. "Even though there are innumerable opportunities for their unification," İnan declared, "Islamic countries are the only community on the face of the earth that cannot unify." "It is the great Islamic unity," İnan believed, "that will save Muslim countries, make them strong, give them agency and pride, help them defend their own rights and rights of every nation, and bring to the world a balance."[108]

İnan celebrated that there was also a powerful wave of Islamic revival that was pushing the Muslim world in that direction. In Iran "a legendary struggle to establish an Islamic state" was ongoing. In Afghanistan Muslims were waging a guerilla war against the pro-Russian regime and demanding an Islamic state. In Pakistan Shariah laws were being introduced. "All these are displays of the Islamic world entering a period of revival. This movement of revival will spread to other Muslim countries." Thus, İnan declared, "Islamic societies are beginning to see that emancipation from exploitation is possible only in 'return to Islam.'" The balance of power in the world was changing. "An 'Islamic world' was de facto emerging. Not just two blocs, but a third power is also emerging and taking its place in our world."[109] In short, with the decolonization, "the unbelief ended." Now, "the hypocricy is coming to an end. What is finally coming is Islam."[110]

What seemed to be underlying İnan's prophecy for the future coming of the Islamic unity was essentially his strong belief in the masses. "Due to their faith, Muslims know all Muslims as brothers with total disregard of differences in language and color. Despite all seditions this feeling of them has never been destroyed."[111] This was to suggest that ethnic nationalism, the prime source of disunity in the Islamic world, had never gained acceptance among the masses. Therefore, "without any exception societies in the Islamic countries are longing for the Islamic unity. They have no interest in ethnic nationalistic and Westernist attitude. Muslim peoples are innocent and suppressed." It was going to be this nature of Muslim people that "will enable the Islamic unity. Because this people are in revival and over time will get the cadres appropriate for themselves."[112]

Mehmet Akif İnan's view on the necessity of [re]building the unity of Muslims, or, as he called it, the Islamic unity, inescapably addressed the question of why Muslims had fallen into disunity in the first place. İnan strongly believed that the West sowed the seeds of disunity among Muslims by instilling foreign ideas, ideas that were harmful to the unity, in the intelligentsia and the ruling strata, which alienated them from the Muslim masses and made them dependent on the West's support to remain in power. As of the late twentieth century, then, the foreign indoctrinated and thus alienated intelligentsia and ruling strata was the prime impediment in front of the unity of Muslims. İnan's portrayal of the modern history of the Muslim world in general and of the Middle East in particular in fact strongly resonates with the much broader and richer interpretative framework Islamism in Turkey had developed in the same century. As discussed before, this interpretative framework had its roots in the late Ottoman period, but truly flourished in the Republican period.

The view of the intelligentsia and the ruling strata becoming more and more irreligious was in part responsible for the birth of Islamism in the late Ottoman period. The same period also gave birth to the idea, popularized by Derviş Vahdeti, that some non-Muslim, or crypto-Jews, were among the intelligentsia and the ruling strata. After witnessing the secularization reforms in the early decades of the republic, the early generation of Islamism, such as Mustafa Sabri and Said Nursi, who witnessed those reforms, became convinced that the intellectual and ruling elites in Turkey were irreligious or even antireligious.

Mustafa Sabri, former Sheikh al-Islam of the Ottoman Empire, called the rulers of the republic "ladini" (nonreligious) and "din düşmanı tağutlar" (idolatrous-enemies of religion) and argued that they "destroyed the Islamic state, the caliphate," and "declared war against and worked to wipe out Islam and its rulings." The rulers of Turkey were, Mustafa Sabri claimed, Muslims in name only, but in essence "secular" who "are harsher towards Islam than other enemies, and more skillful in harming and distorting Islam."[113] Mustafa Sabri also seemed to believe that among the founders of the republic were some non-Muslims, more specifically the Jews. Mustafa Sabri suggested that the founders were simply remnants of the former Unionists. Mustafa Sabri must have definitely heard the rumor that there were Jews among the Unionists, as Derviş Vahdeti and other writers of *Volkan* had made that claim years ago.[114]

Mustafa Sabri left Turkey and eventually settled in Egypt. Said Nursi, on the other hand, remained in Turkey and thus personally faced the changes Turkey had undergone. He was therefore much harsher than Mustafa Sabri in his view of the founders of the republic. He claimed that Mustafa Kemal Atatürk was the awaited Süfyan described in a Prophetic tradition, hadith, as the anti-Christ who would emerge from Muslims. Even though Said Nursi did not specifically name him, his interpretations of the hadiths obviously point to Mustafa Kemal Atatürk. For example, for the hadith that prophesizes, "the formidable man of the end of time will wake up one morning and will find 'this is infidel (kafir)' written on his forehead," Nursi provides the following interpretation: "Süfyan will put the foreigners' hat on his own head and will force all others wear it as well." Obviously, Nursi refers to Atatürk's hat reform in this interpretation. Likewise, Said Nursi interpreted the hadith that prophesizes, 'towards the end of time, there will be no one who will utter Allah Allah," with reference to the closure of madrasahs (higher religious schools) in 1924 and Sufi dervish lodges in 1925, and the translation of Adhan and Iqamah (calls to prayer) into Turkish.[115] Yet, in an epistle, which had been kept in secrecy and only recently made public, Said Nursi allegedly called Mustafa Kemal as one of the anti-Christs who would appear at the end of the time. More critically, however, he explicitly said he was a Jew, or, more specifically, "the worst of the Jews."[116] Such an attribution should not be surprising because Nursi was a columnist of *Volkan* and therefore must have been familiar with Derviş Vahdeti's views.

Mustafa Sabri's and Said Nursi's main contention was that the Republican political elites were essentially irreligious and even antireligious. With their extensive writings, other figures such as Eşref Edib and Necip Fazıl Kısakürek helped consolidate the same idea.[117] Kısakürek also helped with the formation of an Islamist victimology, or an anthology of victims of the republic, telling and retelling the personal hardships some religious figures had experienced during the early years of the republic. The whole point was again and again to show how irreligious or antireligious the republic was.[118]

Mustafa Sabri's and Said Nursi's attribution of Jewishness to the Republican elites on the other hand was incidental, not central in their writings. The idea that Jews or crypto-Jews were conspiring against Islam and Muslims entered Islamism in Turkey thanks to Cevat Rıfat Atilhan, an eccentric figure who became rather infamous for his anti-Semitic writings. In 1933 he even visited Germany, met Nazi officials, and more critically brought back to Turkey anti-Semitic literature, including the notorious Protocols of the Elders of Zion. Atilhan in fact began to publish excerpts from the Protocols in *Milli İnkılap* journal until the journal's closure a few months later. For the rest of his life, Atilhan continued to publish articles and books, propagating the view that the Jews were about to take over the world and to this end conspiring to undertake every step. Some of the titles of his books might be illustrative: *The Threat that Pervades Islam and Zionism*; *How did FreeMasons Work to Destroy Islam and Turkishness?*; *The Secret State and the Sinister Program*; *Islam and Sons of Israel*; *FreeMasonry: The Cancer of Humanity*; *How are the Jews Invading the World*; and *World Revolutionaries: Israel*.[119] More importantly, of course, starting in the late 1940s, Atilhan regularly penned columns in two journals, *Sebilürreşad* and *Büyük Doğu*, published respectively by Eşref Edib and Necip Fazıl Kısakürek, two figures who played critical roles in the rebirth and revival of Islamism in Turkey.

In addition to providing a venue in his journal to Atilhan, Necip Fazıl made his own contribution to the spread of anti-Semitic ideas in Turkey and helped them become deeply ingrained in Islamism in Turkey. In 1946, for example, Necip Fazıl published excerpts from the Protocols, introducing them as "the official and obvious document of the real truth about the objectives of the Jews," the ultimate one being "the establishment of world hegemony."[120] Necip Fazıl made his own summary of the Protocols in twenty-three articles, citing among them, for example, moral degeneration of the youth, the destruction of family life, undermining respect for religious values, waging a smear campaign against religious leaders, et cetera.

The Jew, Necip Fazıl stated, "is an entirely new species, born out of both the spiritual and the racial evolution of an ethnicity, named the sons of Israel." That evolution, Necip Fazıl believed, started with the betrayal of "their own prophets" and continued with the development of an evil spirit and evil attitudes (which the Jews seemed to have already, but latently). He became "the enemy of religion, of nation and of the concept of nationality, of pure faith and creed, with one word of spirit and sublime human." He became "the destroyer, dissolver and corrosive everywhere of all standing values," all to "establish his bloody empire behind human poverty, regression and profiteering. This is the Jew."[121]

It was, for example, the Jew who "corrupted the true religion of the Prophet Jesus from within," "disseminated hypocrisy and deceit within Islam," "established and fostered all of the mystical sects," "played the greatest role behind the scenes in the French Revolution [all for the "hope of simply destroying France]," and "the 1917 Communist Revolution," and "on one hand have established any and all sects or movements [capitalism, communism et cetera] throughout the world, and on the other destroyed them," so that humanity could not attain "any sort of unity and solidarity."[122]

Necip Fazıl claimed that after being dispersed by the Romans, the Jews spread all over the world, but were "ejected from every place in which they . . . sucked the blood of [their hosts]." Likewise ejected from Spain, Necip Fazıl narrated, they found refuge and safe haven among Turks, "insinuating their way into our midst by virtue of the kindness and mercy of . . . Sultan Suleiman." They soon "came to dominate Turkish economic life" and had brought the Janissaries, once formidable military force of the Ottoman Empire, "to ruin by employing the teaching of 'currency devaluation—printing more money.'"[123]

Since the Tanzimat (a set of reforms introduced in 1839), the Jews had also become influential over "all our transformation and reforms." Until the Tanzimat, Necip Fazıl claimed, the Jews had just "gnawed us inside," yet respected "our national and state integrity." In the Tanzimat period, however, the period during which Western imperialism and capitalism fully encircled Turkey, the Jews set out to "seize the castle inside," infiltrating masonry and cosmopolitan ideas and destroying "our financial and economic life." More critically, the Jews were the guiding and administrative force in the [second] constitutional period or the force behind the Young Turks: the Jew thus "opened that epoch of defeat and collapse of ours."[124] It is worth recalling that it was the Young Turks who brought down Abdülhamid II, the Ottoman sultan who objected to and successfully thwarted the Jews' plans to establish a state in Palestine. "The Jew," Necip Fazıl asserted, "succeeded in arranging the deposition of Abdülhamid II because he viewed him as the orchestrator of the moral and religious bulwark that protects us."[125]

Finally, Necip Fazıl believed, the Jew also played a critical role in shaping the republic. More specifically, Necip Fazıl seemed to have believed,

Turkey's implementation of secularization reforms was a Jewish plot. In return for this "sacrifice of religion," the Jew helped Turkey secure an "artificial sovereignty" in the treaty of Lausanne, the treaty that ended the First World War and the War of Independence for Turkey and essentially recognized much of the current borders and sovereignty of modern Turkey. Necip Fazıl argued that the former chief Rabbi of Istanbul, Hayim Naum, was tasked to realize this Jewish plot. Having toured in the United States and Britain, Naum then attended the Lausanne meetings and was able to persuade both the British representative, Lord Curzon, himself a Jew, and the Turkish representative, İsmet İnönü, to implement the plan. Necip Fazıl also believed that Hayim Naum also had access to Mustafa Kemal Atatürk, who agreed to the plan. The West thus recognized Turkey as a sovereign state in Lausanne; Turkey, in return, promised to implement reforms that sacrificed religion and religious representation, meaning the caliphate. Necip Fazıl further argued that recognition of Turkey as a sovereign state raised opposition in the British House of Commons. In response to the criticisms, Lord Curzon stated, "In fact after now Turks will never regain their former awesome power and pride. Because we killed them in their otherworldly and spiritual fronts." Necip Fazıl put this statement in his own wording: "in other words, the decision Mustafa Kemal and Ismet made is the decision to kill the Turkish nation from the perspective of Islam and religion."[126]

Necip Fazıl thus helped create an image of an eternal enemy of Islam and of Muslims, or the Jew, essentially completing what Derviş Vahdeti started. In this eternal enmity the Jew also found support from the Sabataists of Turkey, who were Muslims in name only, but essentially crypto-Jews. Like the Jews, the Sabataists had also constantly worked to undermine Islam in the Ottoman Empire and partnered with the Jews in the overthrow of Abdülhamid II and the subsequent corrosion of "the national Turkish unity, morality and tradition."[127] In their cause, the Jews also received support of the Masons, who were not Jews themselves, but still put themselves in their services. Under the cover of humanity and brotherhood, the Masons, Necip Fazıl claimed, were in fact protecting "the Jewish capitalism, defending "secret Jewish interests," damaging "the religious and national unities," and seeking to take their places.[128] In another piece, Necip Fazıl, claimed Masonry was "absolute Godlessness," "assassin of the state and national unity," "an absolute Jewish institution" and "absolute internationalism and cosmopolitanism." More than the Jews and the Sabataists or crypto-Jews, in fact, Necip Fazıl claimed, the Masons were influential among the Unionists, to say the least, two of the triumvirate, Talat and Cemal Pashas, being themselves Masons.[129] Needless to add, the Unionists were the raw power that ignited the constitutional revolution and hence overthrew Abdülhamid II. Necip Fazıl declared many other prominent figures as Masons and rhetorically asked, "and who knows, which Masons we could not diagnose are now our heads [governing us]?" And he asked, "hey, Turkish youth, who do you think rule the world?"[130]

Necip Fazıl essentially laid out an interpretive framework, which as discussed before had already been developing since the early twentieth century. This framework is in fact a simple construct, which assumes the existence of external and internal enemies, which were continuously and tireless working against Islam. Unquestioningly attached to Islamism thanks to the high standing and prestige of its proponents, this framework was later enriched with new details and anecdotes brought up by other figures of Islamism, all to confirm, not to undermine the framework's empirical validity.[131]

It is critical to note that what became Islamism's interpretive framework perfectly resonated with the more official interpretive framework, generally associated with which came to be famously called the Sèvres Syndrome. Named after the infamous treaty of Sèvres,[132] this syndrome, Fatma Müge Göcek describes, "refers to those individuals, groups or institutions in Turkey who interpret all public interactions—domestic and foreign—through a framework of fear and anxiety over the possible annihilation, abandonment or betrayal of the Turkish state by the West."[133] Both frameworks, in short, assumed the existence of external enemies collaborating with internal enemies in the pursuit of a common objective of domination. Both frameworks differed only in terms of who the external and enemies were and in the subject of domination: for Islamism, the world powers, controlled by the international Jewry, were external enemies; the local Jews, crypto-Jews, and the seculars were internal enemies; Islam and Muslims were to be dominated.[134]

Necip Fazıl Kısakürek and other figures of Islamism have focused their attention predominantly on the Ottoman/Republican Turkey, only occasionally extending this interpretive framework to the developments in the Middle East. Yet it would not require a stretch of imagination to interpret the history of the region in a similar way. In fact, as already discussed, Mehmet Akif İnan's explanation of the disunity in the Muslim world and the Middle East perfectly fit into that interpretive framework. Not surprisingly, in fact, İnan's view of the Jews was not different. The

Jews, İnan argued, were "Islam's greatest enemy" and through all powers under their control "spread enmity of Islam across the world" and "keep Islamic countries in constant unrest." The Jews were so powerful in world politics that they could make the United Nations offer the Jews a state of their own after the Second World War. The Jews were not just a nation of a few millions, but an awesome force that "gives direction to world culture, industry, capital and propaganda." The Jews "caused the eruption of the First World War" and "mobilized powers that destroyed the Ottoman Empire," for they knew that had the Empire not been destroyed; they could not settle in Palestine. To defeat the Jews and expel them from Palestine, İnan argued, one had to confront and defeat "the Western world, especially America." In every war the Jews made with the Arabs, İnan claimed, "it was America that was actually fighting. Muslims are fighting America's infinite money and weapons." Only by developing internal solidarity and putting together all their strength, İnan declared, Muslims could protect their rights, for "the infidels only respect power."[135]

Ahmet Davutoğlu: Islamism's Foray into International Relations

Our discussion on Islamism started with Ahmet Davutoğlu and should end with him. As a well-read intellectual/academic and a prolific writer, Davutoğlu has not in fact introduced radically novel ideas and perspectives into Islamism. He certainly wrote much more sophisticatedly than other figures of Islamism in Turkey. Unfortunately, perhaps, his writings make for difficult reads, both in English and Turkish. They are marred by verbosity, opaqueness, overuse of academic jargon, and unnecessarily complex and long sentences. Yet they are still richer in philosophical, theological, and historical material, which must be due to his superior educational achievements. Nonetheless, the claims Davutoğlu made and conclusions he drew in his writings are not radical deviations from, but more or less reiterations of, Islamism's core beliefs and interpretive framework. Davutoğlu is, however, still a critical figure to visit in this study because he served as the prime conduit between Islamist ideology and foreign policy, greatly influencing Turkey's foreign policy both before and during the Arab Spring as the chief foreign policy advisor to Turkey's prime minister from 2002 to 2009, minister of foreign affairs from 2009 to 2014, and prime minister from 2014 to 2015.[136]

Ahmet Davutoğlu belonged to a rather minor, but highly intellectual, group within Islamism called Medeniyetçiler or the Civilizationalists. As discussed above, almost from the very beginning, in fact, Islamism treated Islam not merely as a religion, but also as a civilization. Because Islam was superior as a civilization to the rival and dominant Western civilization, Islamism advocated that modernization must be limited in scope or that importation from the West must not be wholesale. Only technology and science were acceptable, but not civilizational elements, such as values, institutions, and laws. It was not unusual for early generation of Islamism to express nostalgia for the past times, or the so-called Golden Ages of Islam. Mehmet Akif (1873–1936), for example, recited:

> *That Buhara, that blessed, that stupendous land*
> *Immersed in, sleeping in the bosom of desolation*
> *That climate which had given birth to Ibn-i Sina in hundreds,*
> *Does not give a single child to the arms of science, fruitless.*[137]

The view of Islam as a civilization has survived during the Republican period thanks to figures such as Necip Fazıl Kısakürek, Sezai Karakoç, and Mehmet Akif İnan. Ahmet Davutoğlu embraced this view of Islam more enthusiastically than his predecessors and portrayed the Islamic and Western civilizations as two starkly distinct, incompatible, and even conflicting civilizations. What distinguishes them, according to Davutoğlu, are their philosophical-theological bases, or, more specifically, views of God's relationship with man and nature. Davutoğlu elaborates his view in great detail in his dissertation-turned-book *Alternative Paradigm*s.[138]

For Davutoğlu, Islam's most distinguishing feature concerns its view of God. The Arabic phrase *La Ilaha illallah* (literally, there is no God, but Allah) best features this view. This statement, Davutoğlu explains, has two parts: the first and negative part of the statement, *la ilaha* (there is no God), unequivocally denies divinity or divine quality to any being, and the second and positive part introduces the sole exception, which is Allah. Islam's Holy Book, the Quran, repeatedly confirms this view of God, known as in Islamic terminology as *tawhid*.[139]

A verse quoted by Davutoğlu, for example, states, "He is Allah, than whom there is no other God (59:22)." The same section in the Quran attributes to Islam's God many other features. He is also, for example, "the Knower ['Alim] of the invisible and the visible. He is the Beneficient [Rahman], the Merciful [Rahim] . . . the Sovereign Lord [Malik], the

Holy One [Quddus], Peace [Salam], the Keeper of Faith [Mu'min], the Guardian [Muhaimin], the Majestic ['Aziz], the Compeller [Jabbar], the Superb [Mutakabbir] . . . the Creator [Khaliq], the Shaper out of naught [Bari'], and the Fashioner [Musawwir] . . . the Mighty, the Wise [Hakim] (59:22–24)."[140]

In addition to these, Islam attributes other features and names to God. As a matter of fact, one prophetic tradition states, "there are ninety-nine names of Allah." Given that some, if not all, of these features can also be found in humans, Islam further specifies that God's features expressed in His names and attributes are unique in the sense that they are not comparable in any way with those of humans. God's names and features are, Davutoğlu argues, "ultimate-absolute" and "impenetrable by the limited intellectual capacity of human beings." In addition, Islam sets forth a principle known as *tanzih* with which God is exempted from any defect from which other beings suffer.[141] Thus all features and attributes attributed to Allah are a pure and perfect part of His very Essence.

Islam thus builds an image of God that is all-powerful, all-knowing, all-sovereign, and so forth. Furthermore Islam's God, Allah, is also an extremely active and interventionist God, not only creating, but also sustaining the universe and all beings in it at every moment. And He is not dependent on any Being, human or non-human, in undertaking His Godly duties, receiving no help from any other Being: as a matter of fact, He is not in need of any such help.

By portraying God as such, or, in Davutoğlu's own words, as a "highly concentrated ontological trancendency and absoluteness," Islam brought about "a semantic and imaginative revolution in the understanding of Allah."[142] It did so first in the particular context of Makkah, the birthplace of Islam. Pre-Islam Arabs of this city had a high God, in fact named Allah. But they also believed in the existence of other Gods as associates of Allah. Furthermore, these lesser Gods were believed to be more active in people's lives such that Allah was more like *deus otiosus* (idle God) in the universe of Meccan Gods. Islam in other words dethroned these lesser Gods and installed Allah as the sole God in their places in the imagination of Arabs of this city.

Islam's reimagination of God was revolutionary not only in the particular context of Mekkah but also in the broader geographical context. Islam's monotheism was stronger even than those of other monotheistic religions, such as Judaism and Christianity. Hence, Eliade asserts, quoted by Davutoğlu, "from the viewpoint of religious morphology, Muhammad's message, such as it is formulated in the Qur'an, represents the purest expression of absolute monotheism."[143] Other monotheistic religions essentially compromised on the absoluteness of the oneness of God.

Davutoğlu discusses how a short surah (section), *al-Ikhlas*, best illustrates Islam's difference from all other religions, including monotheistic ones. "Say," the surah states, "He is Allah, the One! Allah, the Eternally Besought of All [Samad]! He begets not nor was begotten. And there is none comparable unto Him." This short surah, Davutoğlu claims, unequivocally rejects Arab polytheists' belief that their lesser Gods were Allah's kindred, Jews' belief that Uzayr (Ezra) was God's son, and Christians' belief that Jesus was God's son.[144]

Other religions preach what Davutoğlu calls "ontological proximity" between the creator (God) and the created. Ancient beliefs about God, for example, are of this kind: quoted by Davutoğlu, James G. Frazer describes them as "the supernatural agents are not regarded as greatly, if at all, superior to man, for they may be frightened and coerced by him into doing his will . . . the world is viewed as a great democracy; all beings in it, whether natural or supernatural, are supposed to stand on a footing of tolerable equity."[145] No matter how diverse they might be, Davutoğlu claims, other religions imagined God pretty much in the same way, establishing "ontological proximity" between God and the rest "either through the deification of any part of the relative being or through the incarnation of the absolute in the form of relative beings."[146] Davutoğlu details how this peculiar view of God has remained constant across ages in the European world: "from the perspective of this 'ontological proximity,'" Davutoğlu asserts, "there is an essential, continual link between ancient mythology, ancient philosophy, Christian theology, and modern philosophy."[147]

In stark contrast to all other religions, therefore, Islam uncompromisingly asserts "an absolute ontological hierarchy" between God and His creatures, man and all other beings in the universe. This assertion is not only what makes Islam distinct from other religions, but also what keeps Islam's otherwise different schools of thought at least paradigmatically united. "This absolute ontological hierarchy and transcendency in the Qur'anic theocentric system," asserted Davutoğlu, "became the essence of the paradigmatic unity among several Muslim schools in the history of Islamic thought. In a very general sense, the members of *kalam, falsafah,* and *tasawwuf*—as fundamental divisions of Islamic thought—aimed to show and systematize several aspects of this fundamental truth using different methodologies and nomenclatures."[148]

Islam's ontological hierarchy and others' ontological proximity constitute two alternative paradigms, or Weltanschauungs, each of which in turn has different political consequences, generating different theories, imaginations, cultures, and images.[149] For example, the Western paradigm justifies a sociopolitical system on the basis of its origin, elaborated in state of nature and social contract theories, and of its aims, utilitarian in essence, that basically prioritizes worldly happiness. The Islamic paradigm, on the other hand, views a sociopolitical system that is essentially a contract between man and man as an extension of the original contract made between God and man through God's declaration that man is his vicegerent on earth, and in that capacity divinely tasked to establish a just community. In judging the legitimacy of political authority, the Western paradigm emphasizes conformity with the established mechanisms of decision-making or procedures. The Islamic paradigm, by contrast, pays attention not to the procedures, but to the content, or conformity with a set of normative values that are set in divine law prior to political decision-making. More interestingly, the Western paradigm eventually produced the nation-state, which in turn is the constitutive unit of the whole international system. The Islamic paradigm, on the other hand, produced ummah as its ultimate political unit, the members of which are believers. "Those who believe in the unity of Allah," states Davutoğlu, "accept to be a member of Muslim socio-political society," and thus discard not "only their old ethnic identity but also all possible alternate identities."[150] Davutoğlu claims that as man has a special divine mission, so does the ummah as stated in the verse (3:103–4): "And there may spring from you an ummah who invite to goodness, and enjoin right conduct and forbid indecency." Furthermore, Davutoğlu argues, the ummah is one as stated in the verse (21:92) "the ummah of yours is one ummah," which is in Davutoğlu's view intimately linked to Islam's belief in the absolute unity of Allah. As the ummah is one, so is its leader, called caliph. Yet, as history attests, the caliph might not have all the state power concentrated in his hands. Individual power holders might arise from time to time, but could not claim representation of the whole ummah and thus undermine its unity.[151]

It is critical to add that Islamic and Western civilizations, Davutoğlu argues, have in the end developed such different political theories, images, cultures, and institutions and hence become irreconcilable. But, he emphasizes, the root cause of the end outcome, irreconcilability, and even conflict between the two civilizations lies in their irreconcilable belief about what Davutoğlu calls "ontological consciousness" or views of

God's relationship with man and nature: ontological hierarchy produced the Islamic civilization and ontological proximity the Western civilization.

Because of the said irreconcilability of the two civilizations, Davutoğlu argues, any attempt at adaptation from one civilization to the other is inevitably going to fail. In fact, in the very first sentence of his *Alternative Paradigms*, Davutoğlu writes: "many scholars and politicians were convinced that the existing Western style of life, thought, and political institutions could easily be adapted to Muslim societies by bringing them into line with Islamic belief systems and rules. But after some experiences they were surprised when they saw that even those intellectuals who had Western academic training remained deeply attached to Islamic belief system, doctrine, civilization, history, and culture."[152]

This was obviously what Muslim reformists, modernizers, and/or westernizers had been attempting to accomplish since the early nineteenth century in order to confront the Western civilization's total assault, which pushed the Islamic civilization into a civilizational crisis. Davutoğlu in fact provides a quite standard historical account of the period: colonization, reforms in the Ottoman Empire, anticolonial reactions elsewhere, decolonization, formation of nation-states, modernization attempts, and Islamic revivalism.

For Davutoğlu, the First World War, the collapse of the Ottoman Empire and more critically the abolition of caliphate in 1924 effectively put into total confusion or disorientation the traditional world imagination Muslims had been living with. They knew that the one ummah had gone and the concept of Dar al-Islam (abode of Islam) did not apply to the reality on the ground. There was a new reality: the West-imposed nation-state system. Yet this new system faced "a comprehensive problem of political legitimacy." Part of the problem was that the new ruling elites were totally westernized: in the Ottoman Empire, they were educated in the state's own school system, which was founded on the assumption that some Western institutions could be reconciled with Islam. Elsewhere in the Muslim world, the new elites were educated in the very hands of the Western colonizers and assumed the administration of their countries upon decolonization and subsequent independence.[153]

The new ruling elites worked to make their peoples accept "a new understanding of state," which was a "sovereign element within the international system." But, Davutoğlu emphasizes, this system was no longer imagined to be a "political instrument for the ethics-legal ideals of the Islamic belief system." More critically, Davutoğlu claims, the new state was to be imagined as "an element of the international system which was established by and based on the interests of the colonial powers."[154] To recall, according to Davutoğlu, the nation-state system was essentially an artifact of an alien civilization and thus incompatible with Islamic civilization's world imagination.

Even though Davutoğlu believes the new political reality would not be wholeheartedly accepted by Muslims, he still claims that the imposition of the nation-state and subsequent developments had long-lasting consequences for the Muslim world. All in all, Muslims had lost their living space, or Lebensraum in Davutoğlu's formulation, where they could have realized their ethico-legal ideals as they had done throughout history. It was just matter of time before this deprivation and consequent tension between traditional culture and "westernized elites" on the one hand and "international system" on the other set in motion counterreactions from the Muslim masses.[155] Davutoğlu suggests that the Islamic revivalism of the later decades in fact constituted such reactions aiming to correct the internal inconsistencies and contradictions between the ontological consciousness of Muslims and the political conditions in which they lived. To quote at some length:

> the leaders of Islamic communities such as Ikhwan al-Muslimin or Jama'at-i-Islami which were established in the post-caliphate era aimed at re-establishing the links between ontological and political images. The definitions of 'the indispensable Islamic state as a pre-requisite of man's subservience to Allah' . . . and 'the universal and all-embracing Islamic state as an ideological state' . . . are the versions of modern rhetoric for this readjustment of the imaginative and theoretical connection between Weltanschauung and political culture. The widespread impact of Qutb's Milestones is a consequence of its significance to reinterpret Islamic concept of tawhid as a foundation of social dynamism. Ali Shariati's influence during the Iranian revolution originated from his impressive theory related to the historical dialectic determined by the Islamic theological and social imaginative connections against the tyrannical suppression. So, the socio-political dynamism in this era was directly influenced by the political rhetoric which aimed at establishing a new theoretical consistency between Weltanschauung and political ideals.[156]

Davutoğlu argues that this religious revivalism eventually impacted politics across the Muslim world, increasing demands for political participation. Within the broader context of societal, economic, and political changes, popular demand increased for both democratization and Islamization, thus aggravating an increasing tension between the secular elites and Islamic forces.[157]

Davutoğlu draws from his civilization theory critical conclusions for Turkey's foreign policy. In his popular book *Stratejik Derinlik* (Strategic Depth),[158] Davutoğlu cites history, geography, population, culture, economy, the military, and technology as elements of national power. But, he adds, strategic mindset, strategic planning, and the political are multipliers of these elements and turn them into active national power.[159] According to Davutoğlu, Turkey's major weakness in foreign policy making is, as far as our discussion is concerned, its deficient strategic mindset. More specifically, Davutoğlu claims, political elites, bureaucratic establishment, and ordinary citizens have inconsistent views on Turkey's sources of power. While some, for example, see Turkey's history and culture as valuable foundations on which Turkish foreign policy should be built, others see them as serious obstacles for Turkey. Likewise, Turkey's geography is also a matter of disagreement in Turkey. While some advocate for Turkey's integration with its immediate neighbors, some others advocate for integration with beyond-region elements.[160]

In explaining why these and similar disagreements exist, Davutoğlu draws from psychology and suggests that Turkey is like an individual who has a divided self or is a country estranged from its own history and place in the world and has developed a false self. Historically, Davutoğlu suggests, this process started with the declaration of the Tanzimat and was completed with the foundation of the republic during the course of which the Ottoman/Republican Turkey worked to detach itself from Islamic civilization and attached itself to Western civilization. All in all, the Ottoman/Republican modernization dislocated Turkey from the central position it once occupied in Islamic civilization and placed it on the periphery of Western civilization. Turkey's new peripheral location became most obviously manifest in its adoption by the founders of the republic of a pacifist foreign policy and rejection of the Ottoman past with all of its ideals and institutions.[161]

With this civilizational move, Davutoğlu claims, Turkey has become estranged not only from its own history and place in the world, but also from the Middle East.[162] For Davutoğlu, the Middle East is a special and unique region because of its historical depth and peculiar cultural features. It is in this region that the most radical cultural, religious, and intellectual movements are born and then influenced human history. It is also in this region where Islamic civilization was born and flourished. Despite its historical and modern cultural, religious, and ethnic diversity, the Middle East, in Davutoğlu's eyes, had always been one geocultural space. With the collapse of the Ottoman Empire, however, this geocultural space has fragmented as ethnic and religious differences transformed into political identities. Even before the collapse, Davutoğlu argues, imperial powers and missionary activities had been increasingly involved in this region, thus making it vulnerable to outside influence. After the Empire collapsed, the colonial administrations instituted such educational systems and put in place such cultural policies that were to culturally alienate the elites from the masses. The establishment of the Jewish State of Israel and the Christian-dominated Lebanon and the foundation of new nation-states further fragmented the geoculture of the Middle East. Davutoğlu believes that geocultural fragmentation makes the region more conducive to political, religious, and ethnic polarization and manipulation by outside powers. "Bringing a lasting peace to the Middle East," Davutoğlu declares, "depends on minimizing political risks that this geo-cultural fragmentation can give birth to."[163]

Turkey's alienation from the region is therefore part of the broader regional trend. However, Turkey can act differently. It is the heir to the Ottoman Empire, which had kept the Middle East in political order for five centuries without endangering the region's cultural richness. Turkey can use this heritage strategically and help create a just and lasting order in the region. By contributing to the geocultural fragmentation of the region, Turkey cannot benefit from its Ottoman heritage. Only by using this heritage can Turkey move up its place in the international system from the periphery to the center.

Ingrained in Davutoğlu's otherwise quite elaborate narratives are several critical elements of Islamist ideology. Davutoğlu espouses, for example, a typical Islamist claim that rests on its binary view of Christianity and Islam: while the former was apt for secularization, the latter was not. Assuming that Muslims are deeply and strongly attached to Islam, Davutoğlu strongly believes that any top-down attempt or "pyramidal institutional secularization in Muslim societies"[164] will fail to change or penetrate the masses' beliefs and values. The outcome is predictable: culturally and ideologically polarized societies. Hence, Davutoğlu views the post-Ottoman ruling strata in Muslim societies as political elites who are culturally and ideologically alienated from their peoples. Furthermore, he believes, these elites see their own political futures as resting on the continuation of the nation-state system, a system that was forcefully imposed on the Muslim world by Western civilization. Artificially dividing the Muslim world, to recall, the nation-state system is not compatible with the Islamic core belief, absolute unity of God, from which the ideal of one ummah follows. It would be unjust to Davutoğlu, however, if we do not add that, unlike the popular Islamist interpretive narrative, Davutoğlu carefully avoids assigning any significant role to the Jews and their usual suspect allies, local or international.

By the time Turkey entered the twenty-first century, Islamism had already been a mature ideology and even generated successive political parties under the leadership of Necmettin Erbakan. The JDP hailed from this tradition and came to power in 2002. Yet, in order to pursue a foreign policy in line with Islamism, it had to wait for an opportune moment. That moment came and died with the Arab Spring.

CONCLUSION

Reflections on the So-called Turkish Model

Ideology and idealism often go hand in hand. Turkey's Islamists are no exception with their ambitious religious vision and project of Muslim unity. Their idealism stems from a sense of historic mission. It is also grounded in a sense of Turkish Islamic exceptionalism with the belief that Turkey is a strong state with an imperial and religious legacy that should protect and strive to unite Muslims all around the word.[1] In a sense,if there is one country in the Muslim world that has the history, vision, and power to provide such leadership, they believe, it is Turkey and the model it provides for the Muslim world. Westerners have also often praised Turkey as a model, but often for reasons having more to do with modernization and democratization than with Islamic greatness.

One such Westerner was none other than George W. Bush, the forty-third president of the United States. "This land has always been important for its geography—here at the meeting place of Europe, Asia, and the Middle East," Bush declared in a speech delivered in 2004 at the NATO summit held in Istanbul, adding, "Now Turkey has assumed even greater historical importance, because of your character as a nation. Turkey is a strong, secular democracy, a majority Muslim society, and a close ally of free nations. Your country, with 150 years of democratic and social reform, stands as a model to others, and as Europe's bridge to the wider world. Your success is vital to a future of progress and peace in Europe and in the broader Middle East—and the Republic of Turkey can depend on the support and friendship of the United States of America."[2]

George W. Bush was neither the first nor the last to present Turkey "as a model to others." The idea can be traced back to the late Ottoman period as various Ottoman statesmen and intellectuals developed their own Orientalism toward the Empire's subject populations,[3] imagining and portraying themselves as modernized, progressive, and enlightened Muslims and hence entitled and even obliged (by some divine destiny) to lead other Muslim nations, especially those Ottoman subject populations, toward modernity. The idea survived the Republic and became even more deeply entrenched into Turkish popular culture. Popularly seen and believed to be the best of the Muslim world, many internalized the belief that Turkey can serve as a model for the Muslim world.

Turkey has been portrayed as a model again and again throughout the twentieth century.[4] By the time the JDP came to power, Turkey was once again a model, now representing an even better combination: a secular, Muslim, democratic, pro-West, pro-Israel state, where a conservative-pious political party, which had just renounced its Islamist past and embraced liberal democracy, was in power.[5] Yet as the JDP consolidated its power and pacified the power of the Kemalist establishment, Turkey's image in the United States and the EU noticeably worsened. It is all the more remarkable how quickly Turkey's worsening image spectacularly recovered as the Arab Spring began to shake the core of the Arab world. Instead of asking "Who lost Turkey?" or complaining about the Islamization of Turkish foreign policy, Western as well as non-Western analysts, sometime the same ones who criticized Turkey, began to ask whether the post-authoritarian regimes in the Arab world will be lucky enough to follow the "Turkish model."[6] As the most democratic and secular Muslim country in the region, Turkey has come to be seen in a much more positive light. Turkey's call for democratic change in Egypt and Syria, as well as its support—after initial reluctance—for the NATO military effort in Libya have also contributed to the perception that Ankara is playing a constructive role in promoting democratic change in the Middle East. Even the Arab media began commenting on the Turkish model: one of the most discussed questions was whether Islamic movements in Egypt, Tunisia, Yemen, Libya, Syria, and other Arab states will be able to generate political parties that are as moderate as Erdoğan's JDP.

This rapid turnaround in public debate, from talk of a "lost" state to one worthy of emulation, showed the confusion surrounding what the Turkish model was and whether it was indeed transferable to an Arab world in transformation. How relevant was the Turkish model for the Arab world? The answer to this question depends on what we mean by the Turkish model. There seem to be two different Turkish models. As far

US policy makers and analysts are concerned, the most familiar aspect of the debate is the focus on political Islam, with the underlying question of whether the Muslim Brotherhood in Egypt and other Arab states will consider Turkey's JDP as a model. In that sense, as it is often repeated, Turkey is a model of "moderate" or "reformist" Islam.[7]

Yet there is a second dimension of the Turkish model that is equally relevant: the role of the Turkish military in shaping the political system. Because in both Egypt and Tunisia the army was playing a crucial role in the transition to postauthoritarianism during the Arab Spring, it should not be a surprise that whenever the military becomes the most important factor shaping the domestic political environment, people often think of Turkey. After all, the Turkish military played a crucial role in the formation of the Republic and became the self-declared guardian of the Kemalist regime in Turkey after 1923. There seemed to be an interesting paradox in this duality of the Turkish model. How can Turkey be a model for an activist military as well as for a moderate Islamic movement?

The answer to this question requires a deeper look at some historical characteristics of the Turkish political system and the more recent dynamics of democratization in Turkey. The Turkish state has a tradition of political supremacy over Islam that goes back to Ottoman times. In many ways, the Ottoman state was based on political supremacy over Islam. A body of law, known as "kanuns," promulgated by the sultan were enacted outside the realm of Shariah and had no direct Islamic justification. The sultan made these laws based on rational rather than religious principles. These laws applied to the spheres of public, administrative, and criminal law as well as state finance.[8] Whenever there was a clash between a "*raison d'état*" and Islamic law, the former emerged victorious. In other words, politics had primacy over religion.

After the emergence of the modern Turkish Republic under Atatürk, the staunchly secularist military continued this tradition of political supremacy over Islam.[9] Political Islam, in its Turkish form, had to respect the red lines of Turkish secularism or suffer the consequences. In that sense, the moderation of Turkish political Islam was partly dictated by the presence of a strong secular state and an interventionist military. The JDP was the fourth reincarnation of political Islam in Turkey. As we studied in previous chapters, its predecessors have been shut down either by military interventions or by the Constitutional Court. Interestingly, this pattern has not caused radicalization within the Islamic movement. On the contrary, the trend has been one of moderation. The JDP, for instance, has followed a very pragmatic and moderately conservative agenda compared with the Welfare Party. Similarly, the Welfare Party was much more moderate during the 1990s than its predecessor, the National Salvation Party, which was banned after the 1980 coup. Compared to their Arab counterparts, who dream about a caliphate under Shariah law, the JDP and its cohorts had much less ambitious agendas, such as ending the ban on headscarves in public universities.

Yet as the military was sidelined between 2007 and 2011, Turkey's domestic context of radical secularism was altered, and the road was paved for a more vocal expression of Islamist leanings. In other words, once the military was emasculated, Islamists now had the space and opportunity to speak more loudly about the JDP's Islamist-leaning foreign policy objectives. It is in this context that the hard-core Islamist supporters of the JDP began to portray Erdoğan in a more religious role, often repeating the now famous slogan, "you [in reference to Erdoğan] are this ummah's dream come true."[10] It is hard to imagine such a discourse being permitted during the late 1990s when the army reigned supreme over Islamists. Context therefore greatly mattered for political Islam to gain such voice and visibility.

Despite the importance of a deeply rooted Turkish state tradition, all credit should not go to the military and the red lines of militant secularism in terms of moderating Turkish political Islam. After all, militaristic political dynamics could have easily radicalized Islamists by pushing them underground, as has often happened in the Arab world. This is why, in analyzing the pragmatism and moderation of Turkish political Islam, an equally important part of the story is the presence of a democratic system in the country. Turkey's transition to multiparty democracy with free and fair elections in 1950 was a crucial turning point. Democracy is often the best antidote against radical political Islam. In the absence of freedom of expression, freedom of the press, free political parties, and free elections, the mosques and Islam are the only outlets for political dissent. Islam, in such authoritarian contexts, becomes a powerful symbol of resistance against tyranny. The emergence of the myth that somehow an Islamic political system would solve all problems is rooted in such authoritarian contexts. Unsurprisingly, "Islam is the solution" is the motto of the Muslim Brotherhood, the most powerful Islamic movement in the Arab world.

Turkey has managed to avoid this vicious cycle with the transition to multiparty democracy in the 1950s and the participation of conservative Muslims in the political system. As Islamists entered the political competition, they developed a more pragmatic and realistic outlook. Yet one point is now obvious: if democratic politics contributed to the moderation and democratization of political Islam in Turkey, it is only normal that the opposite—the deterioration of democracy in Turkey after 2013—had the reverse effect. In other words, JDP's Islamism became much more resentful, radical, and counterproductive at home and abroad as Turkish politics moved away from democracy closer to one-man rule under Erdoğan.

It is also crucial to remember that without EU membership prospects, Turkey would have been deprived of a very significant driver both of modernization and of democratization. By 2013 the JDP turned increasingly autocratic at home, greatly reducing Turkey's prospects of EU membership. Even strong supporters of Erdoğan in the EU during its first decade have turned against Turkey. From civil-military relations, to the Kurdish question, and from judicial independence to gender rights, the drive for EU membership has been a great incentive for structural reforms in Turkey. There would be no Turkish model to emulate without this external anchor of Turkish foreign policy. As a result, as in the role of other factors that contributed to a more moderate and reformist Islam in Turkey, the absence of the EU had the same effect of contributing to Islamization and authoritarianism within JDP circles. One can add to this list the return of repressive and strictly security-oriented measures on the Kurdish issue as a contributing factor of Islamization in Turkish foreign policy, particularly in the context of Syrian Kurds, where Ankara partnered up with Jihadist forces in the country.

It should come as no surprise that none of the political, economic, and cultural elements that define the Turkish model are easily "transferable" to the Arab world. But in the absence of the factors that made Turkey an exception in terms of political Islam, Turkish Islamists began looking more like their Middle Eastern counterparts. To be sure, the Arab world is not a monolith. Arab states have different histories, class structures, political regimes, and economic systems. Given the sui generis nature of Turkey and the diversity of the Arab world, the concept of a country serving as a model will always be an intellectual exercise in abstraction with a great level of uncertainty. But one thing is likely to remain constant: there will always be some aspects of the Turkish model that Turkish Islamists and Kemalist secularists will project to the Arab world as the "right path" to emulate in accordance with ideological predispositions. And once again, it will be the interplay between identity and foreign policy that will determine their narratives.

Today, the Turkish model that the West praised as a much-needed example of Muslim, democratic, secular identity is no more. Sadly, the country has turned increasingly autocratic, nationalistic, and conspiratorial under the same leader who received so much praise during his first decade in power. Many analysts now speak of Erdoğan as an incorrigible Islamist dictator. Because the West once saw in Erdoğan the compatibility of Islam with democracy, it is only logical that the same circles now interpret Turkey's descent into authoritarianism in symmetrical terms: as a clash between Islam and democracy or a conflict between Islam and secularism. In other words, the problem is conceptualized around Islam, religion, and secularism.

In reality, however, the end of the Turkish model has more to do with failed governance, rampant illiberalism, and populist nationalism. In other words, more than an Islamist dictator determined to bury Atatürk's secular legacy, Erdoğan has turned into an illiberal populist who has the support of ultranationalists and even some of ultrasecularist pro-Russia Eurasianist circles within the Kemalist establishment. In fact, the most striking development in Turkish politics over the last few years—and particularly in the wake of the failed coup attempt in July 2016—has been the convergence of secular nationalism, represented by the top brass in the military, and religious nationalism represented by Erdoğan. These twin faces of Turkish nationalism share the same enemies: Western liberal democracy, Kurdish ethnic demands, the Gülen movement, the United States, and the European Union. This is why religious nationalism and the deeply rooted Turkish-Islamic synthesis of the last fifty years are perhaps a better guide to explore the peculiarities of the so-called Turkish model. This is also why history will certainly remember the JDP's Islamist policies during the Arab Spring as a period when the pendulum between the nation and the ummah swung too far in the direction of the latter.

NOTES

Introduction

1. The Arab Spring refers to a series of street protests that first erupted in Tunisia in late 2010 and the spread to Bahrain, Egypt, Libya, Syria, and Yemen.

2. On Turkey's foreign policy during the Arab Spring, see Birol Başkan, "Ankara Torn Apart: Arab Spring Turns into Turkey's Autumn," *Turkish Yearbook of International Relations*, no. 42 (2011): 1–25; Philip Robins, "Turkey's 'Double Gravity' Predicament: The Foreign Policy of a Newly Activist Power," *International Affairs* 89, no. 2 (March 2013): 381–97; Ziya Öniş, "Turkey and the Arab Revolutions: Boundaries of Regional Power Influence in a Turbulent Middle East," *Mediterranean Politics* 19, no. 2 (June 2014): 203–19; Aaron Stein, *Turkey's New Foreign Policy: Davutoğlu, the AKP, and the Pursuit of Regional Order* (London: Routledge, 2015); Birol Başkan, *Turkey and Qatar in the Tangled Geopolitics of the Middle East* (New York: Palgrave, 2016).

3. For an overview of Turkish foreign policy under the JDP in the 2000s, see Philip Robins, "Turkish Foreign Policy since 2002: Between a "Post-Islamist" Government and a Kemalist State," *International Affairs* 83, no. 2 (March 2007): 289–304; Meliha Altunışık and Lenore G. Martin, "Making Sense of Turkish Foreign Policy in the Middle East under AKP," *Turkish Studies* 12, no. 4 (December 2011): 569–87. For a much detailed analysis, see Kerem Öktem, Ayşe Kadıoğlu, and Mehmet Karlı, *Another Empire? A Decade of Turkey's Foreign Policy under the Justice and Development Party* (Istanbul: Istanbul Bilgi University Press, 2012).

4. For an alternative interpretation of Turkey's Syrian policy during the Arab Spring, see İmran Demir, *Overconfidence and Risk Taking in Foreign Policy Decision Making: The Case of Turkey's Syria Policy* (New York: Palgrave Macmillan, 2017).

5. David McLellan, *Ideology*, 2nd ed. (Minneapolis: University of Minnesota Press, 1995), 1.

6. We found the following studies useful in pinning down our definition and tracing the history of the concept: Terry Eagleton, *Ideology: An Introduction*

(London: Verso, 1991); Teun A. Van Dijk, *Ideology: A Multidisciplinary Approach* (London: Sage Publications, 1998); Michael Freeden, *Ideology: A Very Short Introduction* (Oxford: Oxford University Press, 2003).

7. It was Napoleon Bonaparte who first employed the concept pejoratively. He even "claimed to have invented the derogatory term 'ideologue' himself." With this term, he aimed to demote de Tracy and his colleagues at Institute de France "from scientists and *savants* to sectarians and subversives. Tracy and his kind," Napoleon complained, "were 'windbags' and dreamers." See Eagleton, *Ideology*, 67.

8. Alvin W. Gouldner, *The Dialectic of Ideology and Technology: The Origins, Grammar and Future of Ideology* (London: MacMillan, 1976), 3.

9. Ibid., p. 4.

10. Hans J. Morgenthau, *Politics among Nations: The Struggle for Power and Peace* (New York: Alfred A. Knopf, 1948), 13.

11. Ibid., 16–17.

12. Kenneth N. Waltz, *A Theory of International Politics* (Reading: Addison-Wesley, 1979), 65.

13. Kenneth N. Waltz, "A Response to My Critics," in *Neorealism and Its Critiques*, ed. Robert Keohane (New York: Columbia University Press, 1986), 329.

14. Waltz, *A Theory of International Politics*, 173.

15. Another doyen of Realism, George Kenan, is not different. Kennan for example argues that Marxism deeply shaped the Soviet leaders' perception of the world. "The political personality of Soviet power," Kennan says, "is the product of ideology and circumstances." See X [George F. Kennan], "Sources of Soviet Conduct," *Foreign Affairs* 25, no. 4 (July 1947): 566–82. Kennan's realism lies in his rejection of an ideologically driven foreign policy.

16. Stephen D. Krasner, *Defending the National Interest: Raw Materials Investments and U.S. Foreign Policy* (Princeton: Princeton University Press, 1978).

17. Stephen M. Walt, *The Origins of Alliances* (Ithaca: Cornell University Press, 1987).

18. Stephen M. Walt, *Revolution and War* (Ithaca: Cornell University Press, 1996).

19. John J. Mearsheimer, *The Tragedy of Great Power Politics* (New York: W. W. Norton, 2001).

20. Robert O. Keohane, *After Hegemony: Cooperation and Discord in the World Political Economy* (Princeton: Princeton University Press, 1984), 22.

21. According to Karl Marx and Friedrich Engels, creating "false consciousness." or masking the undesirable conditions of the existing system is precisely what ideology does.

22. Keohane, *After Hegemony*, 45.

23. Religions as belief systems are obviously among the ideational factors Constructivists point to and are likewise overlooked by international relations theories. For a detailed discussion, see Nükhet A. Sandal and Jonathan Fox,

Religion in International Relations Theory: Interactions and Possibilities (London: Routledge, 2013). Also see Jonathan Fox and Shmuel Sandler, *Bringing Religion into International Relations* (New York: Palgrave Macmillan, 2004).

24. For a critical review, see Fred Halliday, *The Middle East in International Relations: Power, Politics and Ideology* (Cambridge: Cambridge University Press, 2005).

25. Alexander Wendt, *Social Theory of International Relations* (New York: Cambridge University Press, 1999).

26. Friedrich V. Kratochwil, *Rules, Norms and Decisions: On the Conditions of Practical and Legal Reasoning in International Relations and Domestic Affairs* (New York: Cambridge University Press, 1989); Peter J. Katzenstein, *Cultural Norms and National Security: Police and Military in Postwar Japan* (Ithaca: Cornell University Press, 1996); see also Peter J. Katzenstein, *The Culture of National Security: Norms and Identity in World Politics* (New York: Columbia University Press, 1996).

27. Foreign policy analysis shares with international relations theories such as realism and liberalism, or what Kenneth Waltz calls "the first and second image theories." While also taking into consideration the systemic factors, foreign policy analysis aims to explain a particular state's or a group of states' actual foreign policies, not patterns of interactions or plausible outcomes of those interactions among two or more states. For a comprehensive introduction, see Valerie M. Hudson and Benjamin S. Day, *Foreign Policy Analysis: Classic and Contemporary Theory*, 3rd ed. (Lanham: Rowman & Littlefield, 2020). For extensive reviews of these two fields, see Valerie M. Hudson, "Foreign Policy Analysis: Actor-Specific Theory and the Ground of International Relations," *Foreign Policy Analysis* 1, no. 1 (March 2005): 1–30.

28. Ibid., 20–21.

29. For an illustrative review, see Benjamin Martill, "International Ideologies: Paradigms of Ideological Analysis and World Politics," *Journal of Political Ideologies* 23, no. 3 (June 2017): 236–55.

30. A notable exception is William Hale, *Turkish Foreign Policy since 1774* (London: Routledge, 2000). For a succinct critique of studies that take ideology as a factor in Turkish foreign policy, see Nicholas Danforth, "Ideology and Pragmatism in Turkish Foreign Policy: From Atatürk to the AKP," *Turkish Policy Quarterly* 7, no. 3 (fall 2008): 83–95.

31. Mustafa Aydın, "Determinants of Turkish Foreign Policy: Historical Framework and Traditional Inputs," *Middle Eastern Studies* 35, no. 4 (October 1999): 171.

32. For an illustration, see Bülent Aras, "Turkish Foreign Policy Towards Iran: Ideology and Foreign Policy in Flux," *Journal of Third World Studies* 18, no. 1 (spring 2001): 105–24.

33. Philip Robins, *Suits and Uniforms: Turkish Foreign Policy Since the Cold War* (London: Hurst & Company, 1991), 139. Also see Şaban H. Çalış, *Turkey's*

Cold War: Foreign Policy and Western Alignment in the Modern Republic (London: I.B. Tauris, 2017).

34. Yücel Bozdağlıoğlu, *Turkish Foreign Policy and Turkish Identity: A Constructivist Approach* (New York: Routledge, 2003), 4.

35. Hasan Kösebalan, *Turkish Foreign Policy: Islam, Nationalism, and Globalization* (New York: Palgrave MacMillan, 2011), 18. Kösebalaban is not alone in adopting this line of research. Also see Ümit Uzer, *Identity and Turkish Foreign Policy* (New York: Palgrave Macmillan, 2011); Ramazan Kılınç, "İdeoloji ve Dış Politika: Türkiye'de Kemalist (1930–1939) ve İslamcı (2011–2015) Dış Politikaların Karşılaştırmalı Bir Analizi," *Uluslararası İlişkiler* 13, no. 52 (December 2016): 67–88; Lisel Hintz, *Identity Politics Inside Out: National Identity Contestation and Foreign Policy in Turkey* (New York: Oxford University Press, 2018). For a critical review, see Doğan Gürpınar, "Foreign Policy as a Contested Front of the Cultural Wars in Turkey: The Middle East and Turkey in the Era of the AKP," *Uluslararası İlişkiler* 17, no. 65 (March 2020): 3–21.

36. There are a number of insightful studies that take ideology seriously in their analyses of foreign policy or international relations. See, for example, Michael H. Hunt, *Ideology and U.S. Foreign Policy* (New Haven: Yale University Press, 1987); Alan Cassels, *Ideology and International Relations in the Modern World* (London: Routledge, 1996); Halliday, *The Middle East in International Relations*; Mark L. Haas, *The Clash of Ideologies: Middle Eastern Politics and American Security* (New York: Oxford University Press, 2012).

37. There are other ways ideology can surely influence foreign policy making. For example, ideology can grant legitimacy to or serve as justification for foreign policy actions. As a classical example, see William A. Williams, *The Tragedy of American Diplomacy* (Cleveland: World Publishing Company, 1959). Çalış, *Turkey's Cold War*, also seems to suggest that Kemalism eventually served the military to keep its influence over politics. In another way, ideology can fill in what Kalevi J. Holsti calls "national role conception" of decision-makers. On the concept, see K. J. Holsti, "National Role Conceptions in the Study of Foreign Policy," *International Studies Quarterly* 14, no. 3 (September 1970): 233–309. For an application of this concept, see Bülent Aras and Aylin Görener, "National Role Conceptions and Foreign Policy Orientation: The Ideational Bases of the Justice and Development Party's Foreign Policy Activism in the Middle East," *Journal of Balkan and Near Eastern Studies* 12, no. 1 (March 2010): 73–93.

38. Ours is of course not the only line of inquiry into the origins and evolutions of ideologies, ideas, beliefs, perceptions, and imaginations that have influenced Turkey's foreign policy. Burcu Sunar, *Adalet ve Kalkınma Partisi'nin Dış Politika Söyleminin Biçimlenmesinde Bir Etken Olarak Siyasi İlahiyat* (Ankara: İmaj Yayıncılık, 2014); and Hakan Yavuz, *Nostalgia for the Empire: The Politics of Neo-Ottomanism* (New York: Oxford University Press, 2020) are two noteworthy attempts. There are also several noteworthy dissertations: Seçil Özyanık, "Adalet

ve Kalkınma Partisi'nin Doğu-Batı Eksenli Dış Politika Yaklaşımında Din Unsuru," unpublished doctoral Dissertation, Hacettepe University, 2015; Emirhan Yorulmazlar, "The Role of Ideas in Turkish Foreign Policy: The JDP-Davutoğlu Paradigm and Its Role After 2002," unpublished doctoral dissertation, Boğaziçi University, 2015; Gamze Helvacıköylü, "The Effect of Neo-Ottomanism in Turkish Foreign Policy for the Balkans and Africa in Davutoğlu Period (2009–2014)," unpublished doctoral dissertation, Yeditepe University, 2019; Coşkun Soysal, "The Stillborn Neo-Ottomanist Foreign Policy Aspiration of the Özal Era," unpublished doctoral dissertation, Middle East Technical University, 2020.

39. Even the list of Turkey-based international relations scholars who have made a high academic impact on the field is quite extensive. See Ali Balcı, Filiz Cicioğlu, and Duygu Kalkan, "Türkiye'de Uluslararası İlişkiler Akademisyenleri ve Bölümlerinin Akademik Etkilerinin *Google Scholar* Verilerinden Hareketle İncelenmesi," *Uluslararası İlişkiler* 16, no. 64 (December 2019): 57–75.

40. For a critical review, see Faruk Yalvaç, "Approaches to Turkish Foreign Policy: A Critical Realist Analysis," *Turkish Studies* 15, no. 1 (March 2014): 117–38.

41. Available in English, Hale, *Turkish Foreign Policy Since 1774* is quite an extensive account of the pre-JDP period. For a more recent attempt, see Bill Park, *Modern Turkey: People, State and Foreign Policy in a Globalized World* (London: Routledge, 2012); Öktem, Kadıoğlu, and Karlı, *Another Empire?*

42. In addition to those cited in footnote 2, see Ziya Öniş, "Turkey and the Arab Spring: Between Ethics and Self-Interest," *Insight Turkey* 14, no. 3 (summer 2012): 45–63; Burak Bilgehan Özpek and Yelda Demirağ, "Turkish Foreign Policy After The 'Arab Spring': From Agenda-Setter State To Agenda-Entrepreneur State," *Israel Affairs* 20, no. 3 (June 2014): 328–45. Furthermore, Bülent Aras and Fuat Keyman, *Turkey, the Arab Spring and Beyond* (New York: Routledge, 2017). In this volume, Aras and Keyman brought together a variety of articles on the topic.

43. The following are particularly useful for the Arab Spring period: Burhanettin Duran, Kemal İnat, and Ali Resul Usul, eds., *Türk Dış Politikası Yıllığı 2011* (Ankara: SETA, 2012); Burhanettin Duran, Kemal İnat, and Ufuk Ulutaş, eds., *Türk Dış Politikası Yıllığı 2012* (Ankara: SETA, 2013); Burhanettin Duran, Kemal İnat, and Ali Balcı, eds., *Türk Dış Politikası Yıllığı 2013* (Ankara: SETA, 2014).

44. See, for example, Banu Eligür, *The Mobilization of Political Islam* (New York: Cambridge University Press, 2010); Jenny B. White, *Islamist Mobilization in Turkey: A Study in Vernacular Politics* (Seattle: University of Washington Press, 2011).

45. A notable exception is Hakan Yavuz, *Islamic Political Identity in Turkey* (New York: Oxford University Press, 2003).

46. The project's website is https://idp.org.tr/. The project organizes an annual conference on Islamist journals and supports academic research on Islamism. See, for example, Lütfi Sunar, *"İslam'ı Uyandırmak": Meşrutiyet'ten Cumhuriyet'e İslamcı Düşünce ve Dergiler* (two volumes) (Istanbul: İLEM, 2018).

Chapter 1

1. For a detailed overview of the period between 1991 and 2002 with all the political, economic, and foreign policy factors that created the "lost decade," see Kerem Öktem, *Angry Nation: Turkey since 1989* (London: Zed Books, 2011), 84–121. For an extensive coverage of the period, see Gencer Özcan and Şule Kut, *En Uzun Onyıl: Türkiye'nin Ulusal Güvenlik ve Dış Politika Gündeminde Doksanlı Yıllar* (Istanbul: Büke Yayınları, 2000).

2. Conservative democracy, which the JDP claims as its official identity, was developed by Erdoğan advisor Yalçın Akdoğan, who explains the meaning and utility of the concept in Yalçın Akdoğan, "The Meaning of Conservative Democratic Identity," in *The Emergence of a New Turkey: Democracy and the AK Party*, ed. Hakan Yavuz (Salt Lake City: University of Utah Press, 2006).

3. For an "official" explanation of the strategy by the person who coined the concept, see Ahmet Davutoğlu, "Turkey's Zero-Problems Foreign Policy," *Foreign Policy*, May 20, 2010.

4. Piotr Zalewski, "How Turkey Went from Zero-Problems to Zero Friends," *Foreign Policy*, August 22, 2013.

5. For one of the many discussions on whether Turkey provided a political model for democratization and Islamism, see Ömer Taşpınar, "Turkey: The New Model?," in *The Islamists Are Coming: Who They Really Are*, ed. Robin Wright (Washington, DC: Woodrow Wilson Center Press, 2012).

6. Michael Reynolds, "Echoes of Empire: Turkey's Crisis of Kemalism and the Search for an Alternative Foreign Policy," Brookings Institute Saban Center Paper No. 26, June 2012.

7. The strategic reorientation of Turkey known as neo-Ottomanism was first articulated in the early 1990s by Turgut Özal's adviser and prominent journalist Cengiz Çandar in reference to the mindset and vision of the late Turkish leader. See Hakan Yavuz, "Turkish Identity and Foreign Policy in Flux: The Rise of Neo-Ottomanism," *Critique: Critical Middle Eastern Studies* 7, no. 12 (spring 1998): 19–41. Also see Yavuz's most recent book, *Nostalgia for the Empire*.

8. For a succinct and balanced historical overview of the role of domestic and international context as well as ideology, see Danforth, "Ideology and Pragmatism in Turkish Foreign Policy: From Atatürk to the AKP."

9. Robins, *Suits and Uniforms*.

10. For a historical overview of the interplay between Kemalism and the Kurdish question, see Ömer Taşpınar, *Kurdish Nationalism and Political Islam: Kemalist Identity in Transition* (New York: Routledge, 2005).

11. For more on Atatürk, see Ali Kazancıgil and Ergun Özbudun, eds., *Atatürk: Founder of a Modern State* (London: C. Hurst, 1981); Jacob M. Landau, ed., *Ataturk and the Modernization of Turkey* (Boulder: Westview Press, 1984);

Şükrü Hanioğlu, *Atatürk: An Intellectual Biography* (Princeton: Princeton University Press, 2013).

12. Ümit Cizre Sakallıoğlu, "The Anatomy of the Turkish Military's Autonomy," *Comparative Politics* 9, no. 4 (January 1997): 153.

13. See Robert Olson, *The Emergence of Kurdish Nationalism and the Sheikh Said Rebellion (1880–1925)* (Austin: University of Texas Press, 1989); Henri J. Barkey and Graham E. Fuller, *Turkey's Kurdish Question* (Lanham: Rowman & Littlefield, 1998); Taşpınar, *Kurdish Nationalism and Political Islam in Turkey*.

14. Erik Jan Zürcher, "The Vocabulary of Muslim Nationalism," *International Journal of the Sociology of Language* 137 (1999): 81–92.

15. Niyazi Berkes, *The Development of Secularism in Turkey* (Montreal: McGill University Press, 1964). For more modern treatments, see Ahmet Kuru, *Secularism and State Policies toward Religion: The United States, France, and Turkey* (New York: Cambridge University Press, 2012); Birol Başkan, *From Religious Empires to Secular States: State Secularization in Turkey, Iran, and Russia* (London: Routledge, 2014); Ceren Lord, *Religious Politics in Turkey: From the Birth of the Republic to the AKP* (Cambridge: Cambridge University Press, 2018).

16. Çağatay Okutan, *Tek Parti Döneminde Azınlık Politikaları* (Istanbul: Bilgi Üniversitesi Yayınları, 2004).

17. According to the 24th article (a) the state is the only institution to carry out religious education; (b) religious education and ethics courses are compulsory in elementary and high schools. İştar B. Tarhanlı, *Müslüman Toplum, "Laik" Devlet: Türkiye'de Diyanet İşleri Başkanlığı* (Istanbul: AFA, 1993), 57.

18. Bahattin Akşit, "Islamic Education in Turkey: Medrese Reform in Late Ottoman times and Imam-Hatip Schools in the Republic," in *Islam in Modern Turkey*, ed. Richard Tapper (London: I.B. Tauris, 1991), 160–62.

19. Behlül Özkan, "The Cold War–Era Origins of Islamism in Turkey and Its Rise to Power," *Current Trends in Islamist Ideology* 22 (November 2017): 41–57.

20. Robins, *Suits and Uniforms*. Also see Özgür Mutlu Ulus, *The Army and the Radical Left in Turkey: Military Coups, Socialist Revolution and Kemalism* (London: I.B. Tauris, 2011).

21. Despite the absence of reliable data on the Kurdish population, it is generally accepted that there are 12 to 15 million Kurds in Turkey, 4 million in Iraq, 5 to 6 million, in Iran and 1 million in Syria. David McDowall, *A Modern History of the Kurds* (London: I.B. Tauris, 1996).

22. For an excellent analysis of this legacy, see Dietrich Jung, "The Sèvres Syndrome: Turkish Foreign Policy and its Historical Legacies," *American Diplomacy*, August, 2003, http://americandiplomacy.web.unc.edu/2003/08/the-sevres-syndrome/.

23. See Fiona Hill and Ömer Taşpınar, "Turkey and Russia: Axis of the Excluded," *Survival: Global Politics and Strategy* 48, no. 1 (March 2006): 81–92;

and Ömer Taşpınar, "The Sultan and the Tsar: Turkey's Flirtation with Russia Has a Long History," *Syndication Bureau*, August 16, 2019, https://syndicationbureau.com/en/the-sultan-and-the-tsarturkeys-flirtation-with-russia-has-a-long-history-2/.

24. Michael Reynolds captures this elegantly in Michael Reynolds, "The Key to the Future Lies in the Past: The World View of Erdoğan and Davutoğlu," *Current Trends in Islamist Ideology* 19 (September 2015): 5–38.

25. For a detailed study of British intentions regarding the Kurds of Iraq, see Olson, *The Emergence of Kurdish Nationalism and the Sheikh Said Rebellion*.

26. See Robert Olson, *The Kurdish Question and the Turkish-Iranian Relations: From World War I to 1998* (Costa Mesa: Mazda Publishers, 1998), 24–25.

27. See Abbas Vali, "The Making of the Kurdish Identity in Iran," *Critique: Critical Middle Eastern Studies* 4, no. 7 (fall 1995): 10.

28. For a detailed history of the Kurdish Republic of Mahabad, see William Eagleton, *The Kurdish Republic of 1946* (London: Oxford University Press, 1963).

29. Philip Robins, *Turkey and the Middle East* (New York: Council on Foreign Relations Press, 1991), 23–24.

30. Ömer Kürkçüoğlu, *Turkiye'nin Arap Orta-Doğusuna Karşı Politikası: 1945–1970* (Ankara: Siyasal Bilgiler Fakültesi, 1972), 87.

31. Andrew Mango, "Turkish Policy in the Middle East," in *Turkish Foreign Policy: New Prospects*, ed. Clement H. Dodd (Huntington: Eothen Press, 1992), 62.

32. For the 1964 crisis and the Johnson letter, see Süha Bölükbaşı, *Turkish-American Relations and Cyprus* (Lanham: University Press of America, 1988), 60–81.

33. Republic of Turkey State Institute of Statistics, *Foreign Trade Statistics* (Ankara: State Institute of Statistics, 1981).

34. Mahmut Bali Aykan, *Turkey's Role in the Organization of the Islamic Conference: 1960–1992: The Nature of Deviation from the Kemalist Heritage* (New York: Vantage Press, 1994), 75–76.

35. Süha Bölükbaşı, "Turkey Challenges Iraq and Syria: The Euphrates Dispute," *Journal of South Asia and Middle Eastern Studies* 16, no. 4 (summer 1993): 13.

36. Tuğba Evrim Maden and Seyfi Kılıç, "Irak'ta Su Kaynakları Sorunu ve Yönetimi," *Ortadoğu Analiz* 4, no. 43 (July 2012): 90.

37. This section relies on Taşpınar, *Kurdish Nationalism and Political Islam*. Also see Kemal Kirişçi and Gareth M. Winrow, *The Kurdish Question and Turkey: An Example of a Trans-state Ethnic Conflict* (New York: RoutledgeCurzon, 1997).

38. Ben Lombardi, "The Return of the Reluctant Generals?," *Political Science Quarterly* 112, no. 2 (summer 1997): 196.

39. Mehmet Ali Birand, *The Generals' Coup in Turkey* (New York: Brassey's Defense Publisher, 1987), 173–89.

40. Already in 1979, Bülent Ulusu, commander of the naval forces and one of the architects of the 1980 coup, declared in his own words: "the East is boiling;

the Kurds and communists are in complete cooperation there." He complained, in the same interview, that when the army went on maneuvers in the southeast, it was met with slogans calling for its expulsion. Cüneyt Arcayürek, *Müdahalenin Ayak Sesleri* (Istanbul: Bilgi Yayinevi, 1985), 272.

41. Interview with Sezgin Tanrıkulu, then president of the Diyarbakır Bar Association. Diyarbakır, August 15, 1996. Also see Hasan Cemal, *Kürtler* (Istanbul: İletişim, 2003).

42. According to Abdülmelik Fırat, Sheikh Said's grandson and parliamentary deputy, the state's repressive policies in the eastern parts of the country proved more influential than the PKK in strengthening Kurdish ethnic consciousness. Interview with Abdülmelik Fırat, *Aktüel*, December 11, 1991, p. 28.

43. Ahmet Kuru, "The Rise and Fall of Military Tutelage in Turkey: Fears of Islamism, Kurdism, and Communism," *Insight Turkey* 14, no. 2 (spring 2012): 37–57.

44. Ümit Cizre Sakallıoğlu, "The Anatomy of the Turkish Military's Autonomy," *Comparative Politics* 9, no. 4 (January 1997): 153.

45. Doğan Duman, *Demokrasi Sürecinde Turkiye'de Islamcılık* (İzmir: Dokuz Eylül Yayınları, 1999), 162.

46. In 1979–1980, the DRA employed 39,544 preachers. Their number rose to 51,533 by the end of the military regime in 1983. Ibid., 20.

47. Kenan Evren, *Kenan Evren'in Anıları*, vol. 4 (Ankara: Milliyet Yayinları, 1991), 301.

48. Ümit Cizre Sakallıoğlu, "Parameters and Strategies of Islam-State Interaction in Turkey," 242.

49. According to the 24th article, (a) the state is the only institution to carry out religious education; (b) religious education and ethics courses are compulsory in elementary and high schools. See Tarhanlı, *Müslüman Toplum, "Laik" Devlet*, 57.

50. See the Decision 1982/614 of Higher Military Court (Askeri Yargitay) in Mustafa Tuncel, *163.Madde Hakkinda Kesinleşmiş Kararlar* (Istanbul: Yeni Asya Yayınları, 1983), 13. In the preparation of the article 24 in the Consultative Assembly, the framers of the constitution justified compulsory teaching as a means of offering a "standardized knowledge on Islam" and "a source of national culture, which is the primary task of the state." See *Danışma Meclisi Tutanak Dergisi*, B:140, January 9, 1982, pp. 278–81.

51. Etienne Copeaux, *Türk Tarih Tezinden Türk İslam Sentezine 1931–1993* (Istanbul: Tarih Vakfı Yurt Yayınları, 1998), 107.

52. The Heart of the Enlightened was founded in 1970 by a group of nationalist Turkish academicians such as Mümtaz Turhan, Nihat Tarlan, İbrahim Kafesoğlu, and Nihat Sami Banarlı who were alarmed by the rise of left-wing ideologies in Turkey, especially in the universities. The founding charter of organization stated the goal of protecting the Turkish soul and body against ethnic, sectarian, and ideological enemies. Because Turkey was overwhelmingly Muslim, the association believed there was a natural need to reassert a strong place for

Islam in the secular culture of the Turkish republic. Although the association's third article prohibited any engagement in politics, the Hearth has been the main force shaping the official ideology of the Turkish political elite since the late 1970s. See *Aydınlar Ocağı Derneği Tüzüğü* (Istanbul: Aydınlar Ocağı Yayınları, 1989), 7.

53. Mustafa Erkal, "21. Yüzyıla Doğru Milli Kültürlerin Geleceği ve Bazı Çelişkiler," in *Islamiyet, Millet Gercegi ve Laiklik* (Istanbul: Aydınlar Ocağı Yayınları, 1994), 51.

54. In fact, two key members of the Constitutional Preparation Committee (Şener Akyol and Yılmaz Altuğ) were members of the Heart of the Enlightened. Moreover, the military regime, which sought to engineer a depoliticized Turkish society, prepared the well-known National Culture Report with the help of the association. This report based its Turkish-Islamic synthesis on the pillars of family, the mosque, and the military. See *Milli Kültür Raporu* (Ankara: The State Planning Organization, 1983), 505, 536–54.

55. Richard Tapper, "Introduction," in *Islam in Modern Turkey*, ed. Richard Tapper (London: I.B. Tauris, 1991), 16.

56. "Yükseköğretim Kanunu," *Resmi Gazete*, November 4, 1981.

57. Walter Weiker, "Constitution-Making for Turkey's Third Republic," in *Turkic Culture: Continuity and Change*, ed. Sabri M. Akural (Bloomington: Indiana University Press, 1987), 31.

58. Ziya Öniş, "The Evolution of Privatization in Turkey: The Institutional Context of Public-Enterprise Reform," *International Journal of Middle East Studies* 13, no. 2 (May 1991): 164.

59. Birand, *The Generals' Coup in Turkey*, 123.

60. Üstün Ergüder, "The Motherland Party, 1982–1989," in *The Political Parties and Democracy in Turkey*, ed. Meter Heper and Jacob M. Landau (London: Tauris & Co Ltd, 1991), 155.

61. For instance, Özal's minister of education, Vehbi Dinçerler, was a well-known Nakşibendi disciple. He prepared a curriculum that advised all public schools to use the Nakşibendi magazine *İslam* in their courses on religion. See Tarhanlı, *Müslüman Toplum, "Laik" Devlet*, 62.

62. The number of İmam-Hatip schools and Kuran courses continued to increase under the Motherland Party governments from 1983 to 1991. The number of Quran courses reached 5,000 in 1991 from 3,246 in 1983. Within the same period, the number of İmam-Hatip schools reached 416 from 329. One of the signs of the increasing Islamicization of the governing elite was the introduction and institutionalization of the *iftar* (break-fast) dinners during the month of fasting (Ramadan). The *iftar* dinners became, in the fashion of the national prayer breakfast in Washington, a spectacle to acknowledge and bestow prestige on a more pious elite at the center of government. Özal was also the first prime minister to make the pilgrimage to Mecca and Medina. Duman, *Demokrasi Sürecinde Türkiye'de İslamcılık*, 188–89.

63. One of the first policy decrees of the Özal government concerned the regulation of private financial institutions in December 1983. This decree provided a legal ground for petro-dollars to be poured into Turkey in newly established financial institutions such as the Faisal Finance, Al-Baraka, and Kuwait-Turk Finance. Nurcu groups helped form the Faisal Finance Co. in August 1984. Korkut Özal, the prime minister's brother and a prominent Nakşibendi follower, and Eymen Topbaş, the brother of the Nakşhibendi sheikh Musa Topbaş, founded Al-Baraka Trust. These institutions also benefited from the tax reform laws of the Özal government that exempted institutions working under non-interest Islamic principles. See Vural Arıkan, "Vergi Paketiyle İslam Bankacılığı Teşvik Ediliyor," *Yeni Gündem*, November 1–14, 1985.

64. As a consequence, the national debt grew from $13.5 billion in 1980 to $40 billion in 1989. By the end of the decade, yearly repayment amounted to $7 billion, about 60 percent of export earnings. See *Statistical Yearbook of Turkey* (Ankara: State Institute of Statistics, 1992), 321–24.

65. For more details, see Rüştü Saraçoğlu, "Liberalization of the Turkish Economy," in *Politics in the Third Republic*, ed. Metin Heper and Ahmet Evin (Boulder: Westview Press, 1994), 65–78.

66. Ziya Öniş, "The Political Economy of Islamic Resurgence in Turkey: The Rise of the Welfare Party in Perspective," *Third World Quarterly* 18, no. 4 (September 1997): 757–60.

67. The *tarikat* (sect) leaders try hard to give primacy to person-to-person relations, however brief and temporary their encounters with their followers may be. At the same time, their networks are wide, diverse, and productive. The tarikats and Islamic groups develop networks, the boundaries of which extend far beyond the immediate local and even national community. As previously noted, the brotherhoods often have links in the Middle East, in the new Central Asian republics, and with the Turkish migrant-worker communities in Western Europe. Like Freemasonry, these organizations facilitate the economic and social mobility of their members by creating parallel opportunity structures. For the historical roots and social analysis of the Nakşibendis, see Şerif Mardin, "The Nakshibendi Order in Turkish History," in Tapper, *Islam in Modern Turkey*, 121–45.

68. Cemal, *Kürtler*.

69. Berdal Aral, "Dispensing with Tradition? Turkish Politics and International Society during the Özal decade, 1983–93," *Middle Eastern Studies* 37, no. 1 (January 2001): 72–88.

70. For instance, the WP strongly cooperated with Tansu Çiller in shelving the so-called Susurluk scandal, in which Çiller and some her closest political aides were accused of close links with Mafia crimes.

71. Gencer Özcan, "Yalan Dünyaya Sanal Politikalar," in *Onbir Aylık Saltanat: Siyaset, Ekonomi ve Dış Politikada Refahyol Dönemi*, ed. Gencer Özcan (Istanbul: Boyut Yayınları, 1998), 191–93.

72. Hakan Yavuz, "Turkish-Israeli Relations Through the Lens of the Turkish Identity Debate," *Journal of Palestine Studies* XXXVII, no. 1 (autumn 1997): 32.

73. Ibid., 33.

74. Kemali Saybaşılı, "Siyasal Sistem Bunalımı," in *Onbir Aylik Saltanat*, ed. Özcan, 88.

75. "RP'li Başkan Zorda," *Milliyet*, November 12, 1996.

76. Saybaşılı, "Siyasal Sistem Bunalımı," 89.

77. Hikmet Çicek, *İrticaya Karşı Genelkurmay Belgeleri* (Istanbul: Kaynak Yayınları, 1998), 29–32.

78. As Heath Lowry argues: "The absence of a public outcry over the interference of the military in the country's political life has led in the past two years (1998–1999) to a de-facto dual government, in which many of the nation's real policy objectives are being generated by the Turkish General Staff and its various working groups and task forces. . . . Recommendations are passed to the military wing of the NSC and fed to the elected officials for implementation." Heath Lowry, "Betwixt and Between: Turkey's Political Structure on the Cups of the Twenty-First Century," in *Turkey's Transformation and American Policy*, ed. Morton Abramowitz (New York: The Century Foundation Press, 2000), 42–43.

79. Jeremy Salt, "Turkey's Military Democracy," *Current History* 98, no. 625 (February 1999): 75–76.

80. Çiçek, *İrticaya Karşı Genelkurmay Belgeleri*, 93–94.

81. Ibid., 95–97.

82. Ibid., 22–23.

83. "Tehdidin Adı İrtica," *Milliyet*, April 30, 1997.

84. Çiçek, *İrticaya Karşı Genelkurmay Belgeleri*, 35–37.

85. "Çiller Lays the Cards on the Table," *Briefing* 1122, December 23, 1996, p. 3.

86. Dan Arbell, "The U.S.-Turkey-Israel Triangle," Brookings Institution Analysis Paper No. 34, October 2014.

Chapter 2

1. Ümit Cizre Sakallıoğlu and Menderes Çınar, "Turkey 2002: Kemalism, Islamism, and Politics in the Light of the February 28 Process," *South Atlantic Quarterly* 102, no. 2/3 (spring/summer 2003): 309–322.

2. Ersin Kalaycıoğlu, "Turkish Democracy: Patronage versus Governance," *Turkish Studies* 2, no. 1 (spring 2001): 54–70.

3. A. Erinç Yeldan and Burcu Ünüvar, "An Assessment of the Turkish Economy in the AKP Era," *Research and Policy on Turkey* 1, no. 1 (February 2016): 11–28.

4. In terms of Turkish lira, the lowest salary paid by the Turkish state was approximately 392 million TL in December 2002. See Anonymous, "En düşük memur maaşı kaç YTL olacak?," *Anadolu Ajansı*, December 5, 2007. The figure jumped to 1,299 YTL (in 2005, six zeros were dropped from the currency) in July 2010. See Anonymous, "Maliye zamlı memur maaşlarını açıkladı," *Anadolu Ajansı*, July 5, 2010.

5. "Renault sales edge higher," *BBC News Business*, January 3, 2002.

6. "Renault-Pars News Letter," February 2005.

7. Ayşe Buğra and Osman Savaşkan, *New Capitalism in Turkey: The Relationship between Politics, Religion and Business* (Cheltenham: Edward Elgar Publishing, 2014).

8. Dexter Filkins, "Turkey Turns to Moderate in Islamic Party as New Premier," *New York Times*, November 17, 2002.

9. Luigi Narbone and Natalie Tocci, "Running in Circles? The Cyclical Relationship between Turkey and the European Union," *Journal of Southern Europe and the Balkans* 9, no. 3 (December 2007): 233–46.

10. For a symptomatic example of the genre, see Halil Nebiler, *Emperyalizm ve Ilımlı İslam* (Istanbul: Toplumsal Dönüşüm Yayınları, 2010).

11. Ömer Taşpınar, "The Old Turks' Revolt: When Radical Secularism Endangers Democracy," *Foreign Affairs* (November/December 2007): 114–30.

12. "We are ready to pay the price, says Erdogan," *Hürriyet*, February 12, 2008.

13. İhsan Dağı, "Turkey's AKP in Power," *Journal of Democracy* 19, no. 3 (July 2008): 25–30.

14. Ziya Öniş, "Turkey-EU Relations: Beyond the Current Stalemate," *Insight Turkey* 10, no. 4 (fall 2008): 35–50.

15. Menderes Çınar, "The Justice and Development and the Kemalist Establishment," in *Secular and Islamic Politics in Turkey: The Making of the Justice and Development Party*, ed. Ümit Cizre (New York: Routledge, 2008), 109–27.

16. Alexander Murinson, "The Strategic Depth Doctrine of Turkish Foreign Policy," *Middle Eastern Studies* 42, no. 6 (2006): 945–64.

17. For an earlier article of Davutoğlu where he criticizes Erbakan, see Ahmet Davutoğlu, "The Clash of Interests: An Explanation of the World (Dis)Order," *Perceptions: Journal of International Affairs* 2, no. 4 (December 1997), n.p.

18. Graham Fuller, *The New Turkish Republic: Turkey as a Pivotal State in the Islamic World* (Washington, DC: United States Institute of Peace, 2008), 68–72.

19. Reynolds, "Echoes of Empire."

20. Ömer Taşpınar, "Turkey's Middle East Policies: Between Neo-Ottomanism and Kemalism," Carnegie Endowment for International Peace Paper, October 2008.

21. Cenk Saraçoğlu and Özhan Demirkol, "Nationalism and Foreign Policy Discourse in Turkey under the AKP Rule: Geography, History and National Identity," *British Journal of Middle Eastern Studies* 42, no. 3 (2015): 301–19.

22. For a leading name of the genre, see Michael Rubin, "Turkey from Ally to Enemy," *Commentary* (July/August 2010).

23. Gönül Tol, "Turkey's End Game in Syria," *Foreign Affairs*, October 9, 2019.

24. For a summary of Turkish-American relations during this era, see Philip H. Gordon and Ömer Taşpınar, *Winning Turkey: How America, Europe, and Turkey Can Revive a Fading Partnership* (Washington, DC: Brookings Institution Press, 2008).

25. On Turkish Gaullism, see Ömer Taşpınar, "The Rise of Turkish Gaullism: Getting Turkish-American Relations Right," *Insight Turkey* 13, no. 1 (winter 2011): 11–17.

26. Igor Tobakov, "Neo-Ottomanism versus Neo-Eurasianism?: Nationalism and Symbolic Geography in Postimperial Turkey and Russia," *Mediterranean Quarterly* 28, no. 2 (June 2017): 125–45.

27. Stephen J. Flanagan et al., *Turkey's Nationalist Course: Implications for the U.S.-Turkish Strategic Partnership and the U.S. Army* (Santa Monica: RAND Corporation, 2020).

28. Gönül Tol and Ömer Taşpınar, "Erdoğan's Turn to the Kemalists," *Foreign Affairs*, October 27, 2016.

29. Robins, *Suits and Uniforms*.

30. Davutoğlu, "Turkey's Zero-Problems Foreign Policy."

31. For a good overview of this period, see Murat Yetkin, *Tezkere: Irak Krizinin Gerçek Öyküsü* (Istanbul: Remzi Kitabevi, 2004).

32. Meliha Altunışık, "Turkey's Iraq Policy: The War and Beyond," *Journal of Contemporary European Studies* 14, no. 2 (August 2006): 183–96.

33. Marina E. Henke, "The Rotten Carrot: US-Turkish Bargaining Failure over Iraq in 2003 and the Pitfalls of Social Embeddedness," *Security Studies* 27, no. 1 (August 2017): 120–47.

34. Soni Effron, "Defense Chief Reflects on Invasion Regrets," *Los Angeles Times*, March 21, 2005. Also see Donald Rumsfeld, *Known and Unknown: A Memoir* (London: Penguin, 2011), 520.

35. Michael Howard, "US Arrest of Soldiers Infuriates Turkey," *The Guardian*, July 7, 2003.

36. Aliza Marcus, *Blood and Belief: The PKK and the Kurdish Fight for Independence* (New York: New York University Press, 2007).

37. Mesut Yeğen, "The Kurdish Peace Process in Turkey: Genesis, Evolution, and Prospects," Istituto Affari Internazionali Working Paper no. 11, May 2015.

38. Hugh Pope, "Pax Ottomana: The Mixed Success of Turkey's New Foreign Policy," *Foreign Affairs,* November/December 2010.

39. See Bülent Aras and Rabia Karakaya Polat, "From Conflict to Cooperation: Desecuritization of Turkey's Relations with Syria and Iran," *Security Dialogue* 39, no. 5 (October 2008): 495–515; Meliha Benli Altunışık and Özlem Tür, "From Distant Neighbors to Partners? Changing Syrian-Turkish Relations,"

Security Dialogue 37, no. 2 (June 2006): 229–48; Raymond Hinnebusch and Özlem Tür, *Turkey Syria Relations: Between Enmity and Amity* (London: Ashgate Publishing Limited, 2013).

40. Ö. Zeynep Oktay Alantar, "The October 1998 Crisis: The Change of Heart of Turkish Foreign Policy towards Syria?," *CEMOTI: Cahiers D'Etudes Sur La Mediterranee Orientale et Le Monde Turco-Iranien*, no. 31 (January–June 2001): 142–61.

41. Shaimaa Magued, "Turkey's Economic Rapprochement towards Syria and the Territorial Conflict over Hatay," *Mediterranean Politics* 24, no. 1 (2019): 20–39.

42. Ömer Taşpınar, "Turkey's Strategic Vision and Syria," *Washington Quarterly*, Summer 2012.

43. Arbell, "The U.S-Turkey-Israel Triangle." Also see Tarık Oğuzlu, "The Changing Dynamics of Turkey-Israel Relations: A Structural Realist Account," *Mediterranean Politics* 15, no. 2 (June 2010): 273–88; Ali Balcı and Tuncay Kardaş, "The Changing Dynamics of Turkey's Relations with Israel: An Analysis of 'Securitization,'" *Insight Turkey* 14, no. 2 (spring 2012): 99–120.

44. Michael B. Bishku, "Turkish-Syrian Relations: A Checkered History," *Middle East Policy* 19, no. 3 (fall 2012): 36–53.

45. See Aras and Polat, "From Conflict to Cooperation: Desecuritization of Turkey's Relations with Syria and Iran"; Nihat Ali Özcan and Özgür Özdamar, "Uneasy Neighbors: Turkish-Iranian Relations since the 1979 Islamic Revolution," *Middle East Policy* 17, no. 3 (fall 2010): 101–17; Bayram Sinkaya, "Rationalization of Turkey-Iran Relations: Prospects and Limits," *Insight Turkey* 14, no. 2 (spring 2012): 137–56.

46. For more on the D-8 see Berdal Aral, "An Inquiry into the D-8 Experiment: An Incipient Model of an Islamic Common Market?," *Alternatives: Turkish Journal of International Relations* 4, no. 1–2 (spring–summer 2005):. 89–107.

47. Bayram Sinkaya, "The Kurdish Question in Iran and Its Effects on Iran-Turkey Relations," *British Journal of Middle Eastern Studies* 45, no. 5 (2018): 840–59.

48. Alireza Nader and Stephen Larrabee, "Turkish-Iranian Relations in a Changing Middle East," Rand Corporation Research Report, 2013.

49. "Defying U.S., Turkey to Sign Gas Deal in Iran," *New York Times*, August 11, 1996.

50. Mevlüt Katık, "Turkey to Negotiate Energy Deal with Iran," Center for Security Studies Eidgenössische Technische Hochschule Zürich, 2020.

51. Omid Shokri Kalehsar, "Energy Factor in Iran-Turkey Relations," *Energy & Environment* 26, no. 5 (2015): 777–87.

52. Nader and Larrabee, "Turkish-Iranian Relations in a Changing Middle East."

53. The reference is to Kemal Kirişci, "The Transformation of Turkish Foreign Policy: The Rise of the Trading State," *New Perspectives on Turkey* 40 (spring 2009): 29–56.

Chapter 3

1. This was not the first time Turkey seemed to entertain the idea of using the Muslim Brotherhood as a foreign policy tool. See Behlül Özkan, "1980 ve 1990'larda Türkiye ve Suriye arasındaki İlişkiler: Siyasi İslam, Müslüman Kardeşler ve İstihbarat Savaşları," *Uluslararası İlişkiler* 16, no. 62 (June 2019): 5–25.

2. "Erdogan Calls for a Secular Egypt," *Egypt Independent*, September 13, 2011.

3. "Erdogan, in Cairo, Touts Turkey as a Model for the Arab World," *Haaretz*, September 14, 2011.

4. For a more critical treatment of the same period, see İlhan Uzgel and Bülent Duru, eds., *AKP Kitabı: Bir Dönüşümün Bilançosu* (Ankara: Phoenix, 2009).

5. Marcie J. Patton, "AKP Reform Fatigue in Turkey: What Has Happened to the EU Process?," *Mediterranean Politics* 12, no. 3 (2007): 339–58.

6. Ziya Öniş, "The Triumph of Conservative Globalism: The Political Economy of the AKP Era," *Turkish Studies* 13, no. 2 (June 2012): 135–52.

7. Murat Ucer, "Turkey's Economy: Now for the Hard Part," *Foreign Policy*, August 12, 2014.

8. Şakir Dinçşahin, "A Symptomatic Analysis of the Justice and Development Party's Populism in Turkey, 2007–2010," *Government and Opposition* 47, no. 4 (2012): 618–40.

9. Kirişçi, "The Transformation of Turkish Foreign Policy."

10. Independent Commission on Turkey, "Turkey in Europe: More Than a Promise," in *Report of the Independent Commission on Turkey* (Brussels: British Council and Open Society Institute, 2004).

11. Josh Rogin, "Obama Names His World Leader Best Buddies!," *Foreign Policy*, January 19, 2012.

12. Yeğen, "The Kurdish Peace Process in Turkey."

13. Ersel Aydınlı, Nihat Ali Özcan, and Doğan Akyaz, "The Turkish Military's March Toward Europe," *Foreign Affairs* 85, no. 1 (January/February 2006).

14. Ayhan Kaya, "Islamisation of Turkey under the AKP Rule: Empowering Family, Faith and Charity," *South European Society and Politics* 20, no. 1 (2015): 47–69.

15. Aslı Aydıntaşbaş, "The Good, The Bad and the Gülenists: The Role of the Gülen Movement in Turkey's Coup Attempt," European Council on Foreign Relations Essay, September 2016.

16. Dexter Filkins, "The Deep State," *The New Yorker*, March 4, 2012.

17. Sakallıoğlu and Çınar, "Turkey 2002."

18. Berna Turam, "The Politics of Engagement between Islam and the Secular State: Ambivalences of 'Civil Society,'" *British Journal of Sociology* 55, no. 2 (June 2004): 259–81.

19. Demet Lüküslü, "Creating a Pious Generation: Youth and Education Policies of the AKP in Turkey," *Southeast European and Black Sea Studies* 16, no. 4 (October 2016): 637–49.

20. Taşpınar, "The Old Turks' Revolt."

21. Ergun Özbudun, "Turkey's Judiciary and the Drift toward Competitive Authoritarianism," *International Spectator* 50, no. 2 (June 2015): 42–55.

22. Simon Waldman and Emre Çalışkan, *The New Turkey and Its Discontents* (New York: Oxford University Press, 2017), 34–45.

23. Kuru, "The Rise and Fall of Military Tutelage in Turkey."

24. Kaya Genç, "Erdogan's Way: The Rise and Rule of Turkey's Islamist Shapeshifter," *Foreign Affairs*, September/October 2019.

25. Graham Fuller, *Turkey and the Arab Spring* (N.P: Bozorg Press, 2014), 345–86.

26. On the Arab Spring, see Jason Brownlee, Tarek Masoud, and Andrew Reynolds, *The Arab Spring: Pathways of Repression and Reform* (London: Oxford University Press, 2015); Asef Bayat, *Revolution without Revolutionaries: Making Sense of the Arab Spring* (Stanford: Stanford University Press, 2017); Mark L. Haas and David W. Lesch, eds., *The Arab Spring: The Hope and Reality of the Uprisings* (New York: Routledge, 2018); For a critical review of approaches to the Arab Spring, see Ali Acar and Habib Aydın, "Arap Baharı Üzerine Oryantalist ve Marksist Değerlendirmeler," *Süleyman Demirel Üniversitesi İktisadi ve İdari Bilimler Fakültesi Dergisi* 22, no. 2 (April 2017): 514–24.

27. Steven Cook, "Arab Spring; Turkish Fall," *Foreign Policy*, May 5, 2011.

28. Thomas Friedman, "Letter from Istanbul," *New York Times*, June 15, 2010.

29. For the following discussion, see Birol Başkan, "Islamism and Turkey's Foreign Policy during the Arab Spring," in *Islamism, Populism, and Turkish Foreign Policy*, ed. Burak Bilgehan Özpek and Bill Park (New York: Routledge, 2020).

30. The full text of Erdoğan's speech can be found at http://www.akparti.org.tr/site/haberler/basbakan-erdoganin-ak-parti-grup-toplantisinda-yaptigi-konusmanin-tam-metni/7006#1 (The link is unfortunately no longer functional).

31. TC Dışişleri Bakanlığı, "Bahreyn'de Meydana Gelen Olaylar Hk," Statement No. 72, March 17, 2011.

32. "NATO, "nun Libya'da ne işi var," *NTV*, February 28, 2011.

33. "Turkish Assembly Backs Joining NATO Naval Operation," *Reuters*, March 24, 2011.

34. "Turkey and Syria to Stage Joint Military Exercise," *Anadolu Ajansı*, April 26, 2009.

35. "Turkish Army to Train Syrian Army," *Anadolu Ajansı*, January 31, 2011.

36. F. Gregory Gause III called it "the new Middle East Cold War." See his "Beyond Sectarianism: The New Middle East Cold War," Brookings Doha Center Analysis Paper, Number 11, July 2014. Malcolm Kerr originally coined the term the Arab Cold War to describe the rivalry that raged in the 1950s and the 1960s pitting Egypt against a number of other Arab countries, such as Iraq, Syria, and Saudi Arabia. See Malcolm Kerr, *The Arab Cold War: Gamal 'Abd al-Nasir and His Rivals, 1958–1970* (London: Oxford University Press, 1971).

37. See Frederic Wehrey, Theodore W. Karasik, Alireza Nader, Jeremy Ghez, Lydia Hansell, and Robert A. Guffey, *Saudi-Iranian Relations since the Fall of Saddam: Rivalry, Cooperation and Implications for U.S. Policy* (Pittsburgh: RAND Cooperation, 2009).

38. See Başkan, *Turkey and Qatar in the Tangled Geopolitics of the Middle East.*

39. Gürkan Zengin, *Kavga: Arap Baharı'nda Türk Dış Politikası* (Istanbul: İnkilap, 2013), 124.

40. The speech is available at http://www.akparti.org.tr/site/pdf/ak-parti-grup-toplantisinda-konustu/16252.

41. It was not lost on Erdoğan's critics in the West that a Turkish sense of urgency and love for freedom and democracy was clearly absent when Erdoğan refused to comment on Iran's Green Movement in 2009. See Eric S. Edelman, Svante E. Cornell, and Michael Makovsky, "The Roots of Turkish Conduct: Understanding the Evolution of Turkish Policy in the Middle East," Bipartisan Policy Center Report, December 2013.

42. See Semih İdiz, "Erdoğan'in 'laiklik' çıkışının önemi," *Milliyet*, September 17, 2001.

43. See Edelman, Cornell, Lobel, and Makovsky, "The Roots of Turkish Conduct."

44. Also see the discussion in Birol Başkan, "Turkey's Pan-Islamist Foreign Policy," *Cairo Review of Global Affairs*, spring 2019.

45. Ibid.

46. Anthony Shadid, "Turkey Predicts Alliance with Egypt as Regional Anchors," *New York Times*, September 18, 2011.

47. David Lev, "Turkey, Egypt Hold Naval Exercises," *Israel National News*, December 15, 2011.

48. David D. Kirkpatrick and May El Sheik, "Morsi Spurned Deals, Seeing Military as Tamed," *New York Times*, July 6, 2013.

49. R4BIA is a stylized version of the word rabia expressing solidarity with anticoup protesters in the Rabia Square in Cairo. The word rabia literally means "fourth," which is why the four-fingered hand gesture is used.

50. "Kerry Says Egypt's Military Was 'Restoring Democracy' in Ousting Morsi," *New York Times*, August 1, 2013.

51. Soner Cağaptay, "Erdogan's Failure on the Nile," *Cairo Review of Global Affairs*, spring 2019.

52. For a comprehensive treatment, see the special issue of *Uluslararası İlişkiler* on Syria edited by Gencer Özcan and Salih Bıçakçı: Uluslarası İlişkiler 16, no. 62 (June 2019).

53. Charles Lister, "The Free Syrian Army: A Decentralized Insurgent Brand," The Brookings Project on US Relations with the Islamic World, Analysis Paper, No. 26, November 2016, 7.

54. Lister names eighty different groups affiliated with the FSA. The total number of FSA groups is most likely higher than this number. See the list in ibid., 34–38.

55. See, for example, Elizabeth Dickinson, "The Case Against Qatar," *Foreign Policy*, September 30, 2014; Ceylan Yeginsu, "ISIS Draws a Steady Stream of Recruits from Turkey," *New York Times*, September 15, 2014.

56. See, for example, Doğu Eroğlu, "Jihadist Clinic on Turkey's Syrian Border," September 22, 2014, http://dogueroglu.com/jihadist-clinicon-turkeys-syrian-border/.

57. Lina Sinjab, "Syria: How a New Rebel Unity Is Making Headway against the Regime," *BBC News*, May 1, 2015.

58. On the reasons behind Turkey's shooting down of a Russian jet, see Gencer Özcan, "Rusya'nın Suriye Bunalımına Müdahalesi ve Türkiye," in *Kuşku ile Komşuluk: Türkiye Rusya İlişkilerinin Değişen Dinamiği*, ed. Gencer Özcan, Evren Balta, and Burç Beşgül (Istanbul: İletişim, 2017), 269–98.

59. Krishnadev Calamur, "Turkey and Russia Reconcile," *The Atlantic*, June 27, 2016.

60. Serhat Erkmen, "6 Ay Sonra Zeytin Dalı Operasyonu ve Afrin," *Ortadoğu Analiz* 9, no. 84 (October–November 2018): 61–62; Necdet Özçelik and Can Acun, "Terörle Mücadelede Yeni Safha: Zeytin Dalı Harekatı," SETA Rapor, 2018.

61. "Turkey: Preparations 'Complete' for Syria Military Action," *Al Jazeera*, October 8, 2019.

62. Gönül Tol, "Turkey's Endgame in Syria," *Foreign Affairs*, October 9, 2019.

63. Halil Karaveli, "Erdogan's Journey: Conservatism and Authoritarianism in Turkey," *Foreign Affairs* 95, no. 6 (November/December 2016): 121–31.

64. Funda Gençoğlu Onbaşı, "Gezi Park Protests in Turkey: From 'Enough Is Enough' to Counter-Hegemony?," *Turkish Studies* 17, no. 2 (March 2016): 272–94.

65. Ayla Göl, "Turkey's Clash of Islamists: Erdogan vs Gülen," *Open Democracy*, August 3, 2016.

66. Ömer Taşpınar, "The Conflict within Turkey's Islamic Camp," Istituto Affari Internazionali Research Report, November 2014.

67. Ryan Gingeras, "Is Turkey Turning into a Mafia-State?," *Foreign Affairs*, November 30, 2017.

68. Gönül Tol and Ömer Taşpınar, "Erdogan's Turn to the Kemalists," *Foreign Affairs*, October 27, 2016.

69. Berk Esen and Şebnem Gümüşçü, "Rising Competitive Authoritarianism in Turkey," *Third World Quarterly* 37, no. 9 (2016): 1581–1606.

Chapter 4

1. This statement was made in a memorable and powerful speech delivered by Erdoğan to his party group in the parliament on February 1, 2011. "Erdogan to Mubarak: 'Listen to the Egyptians,'" February 1, 2011, https://www.setav.org/en/erdogan-to-mubarak-listen-to-the-egyptians-2/.

2. "Gazze davasını yalnız bırakmayacağız," *Al Jazeera Turk*, July 20, 2014.

3. The following excerpts are taken from Ministry of Foreign Affairs, "Dışişleri Bakanı Ahmet Davutoğlu'nun 'Arap Uyanışı ve Ortadoğu'da Barış: Müslüman ve Hristiyan Perspektifler' Konferansı Kapsamında Yaptıkları Konuşma," September 7, 2012.

4. Ahmet Davutoğlu's view of history is Hegelian in the sense that Middle East history is God's own doing. Davutoğlu possibly would not disagree that world history is also God's own doing. But his association of civilization and revelation seem to be borrowed from Sezai Karakoç. Ahmet Davutoğlu admits the influence of Sezai Karakoç on his thinking. For a discussion of how similar and dissimilar the two are, see Nurullah Ardıç, "Modernite, Kimlik, Siyaset: Ahmet Davutoğlu'nun Medeniyet Söylemi," in *Stratejik Zihniyet: Kuramdan Eyleme Ahmet Davutoğlu ve Stratejik Derinlik*, ed. Talha Köse, Ahmet Okumuş, and Burhanettin Duran (Istanbul: Küre Yayınları, 2014), 47–87.

5. "Al Jazeera Forum: Ahmet Davutoğlu," *Al Jazeera*, March 13, 2011.

6. Ibid.

7. Ibid.

8. The interview was aired on May 24, 2011 in TRT Haber.

9. Ministry of Foreign Affairs, "Dışişleri Bakanı Sayın Ahmet Davutoğlu'nun Diyarbakır Dicle Üniversitesinde Verdiği 'Büyük Restorasyon: Kadim'den Küreselleşmeye Yeni Siyaset Anlayışımız' Konulu Konferans," March 15, 2013.

10. "Al Jazeera Forum: Ahmet Davutoğlu."

11. Ministry of Foreign Affairs, "Dışişleri Bakanı Sayın Ahmet Davutoğlu'nun Türk Ocakları'nın Kuruluşunun 100. Yılını Kutlama Etkinlikleri Kapsamında Düzenlenen 'Büyük Türkiye'ye Doğru' Sempozyumunda Yaptığı Konuşma," March 26, 2011.

12. "Al Jazeera Forum: Ahmet Davutoğlu."

13. Ministry of Foreign Affairs, "Dışişleri Bakanı Sayın Ahmet Davutoğlu'nun Diyarbakır Dicle Üniversitesinde Verdiği 'Büyük Restorasyon: Kadim'den Küreselleşmeye Yeni Siyaset Anlayışımız' Konulu Konferans."

14. Ministry of Foreign Affairs, "Dışişleri Bakanı Sayın Ahmet Davutoğlu'nun Türk Ocakları'nın Kuruluşunun 100. Yılını Kutlama Etkinlikleri Kapsamında Düzenlenen "Büyük Türkiye'ye Doğru" Sempozyumunda Yaptığı Konuşma."

15. Ministry of Foreign Affairs, "Dışişleri Bakanı Sayın Ahmet Davutoğlu'nun Fas Dışişleri Bakanı Saad Eddine El Othmani ile Birlikte Katıldıkları 'Demokratik Dönüşüm ve Ortak Bölgesel Vizyon' Konulu Seta Panelinde Yaptığı Konuşma," March 19, 2012.

16. "Davutoğlu: Arap baharı Türk baharıdır da," *Haber 7*, March 25, 2011.

17. Davutoğlu, "Medeniyetlerin Ben-idraki," *Divan: Disiplinlerarası Çalışmalar Dergisi*, no. 1 (1997): 1–53.

18. Davutoğlu, *Stratejik Derinlik*.

19. See, for example, David R. Blanks and Michael Frassetto, eds., *Western Views of Islam in Medieval and Early Modern Europe: Perception of Other* (New York: St. Martin's Press, 1999).

20. Ernest Renan, *Islam and Science*, 2nd ed., trans. Sally P. Ragep (Montreal: McGill University, 2011), 3.

21. These reforms are narrated in great detail in a number of studies. Two classical ones are Bernard Lewis, *The Emergence of Modern Turkey* (London: Oxford University Press, 1961); Berkes, *The Development of Secularism in Turkey*. For a simpler account, see Birol Baskan, *From Religious Empires to Secular States: State Secularization in Turkey, Iran, and Russia* (New York: Routledge, 2014).

22. Hanioğlu, *Atatürk*, 49

23. Ahmet Şeyhun, *Islamist Thinkers in the Late Ottoman Empire and Early Turkish Republic* (Leiden: Brill, 2015), 46.

24. Ibid., 153.

25. Ibid., 154.

26. Ibid., 20, 68.

27. Ibid., 38. Also see ibid., 60.

28. Ibid., 20–21.

29. Ibid., 38.

30. Ibid., 29.

31. Ibid., 66–67. On Islam's compatibility with science and promotion of progress, see Namık Kemal, *Renan Müdafaanamesı: İslamiyet ve Maarif* (Ankara: Güven Matbaası, 1962) [originally published in Istanbul by Mahmud Bey Matbaasi in 1910]. To clarify, Namik Kemal was a prominent member of Young Ottoman movement and claimed to have made intellectual contributions to very diverse schools of thoughts in Turkey. For his contribution to Islamism, see Mümtaz'er Türköne, "Siyasi İdeoloji Olarak İslamcılığın Doğuşu (1867–1873)," unpublished doctoral dissertation, Ankara University, 1990.

32. Şeyhun, *Islamist Thinkers*, 46. Also see ibid., 74.

33. Ibid., 38.

34. For the most detailed and recent biography of Said Nursi, see Cemalettin Canlı and Yusuf Kenan Beysülen, *Zaman İçinde Bediüzzaman* (Istanbul: İletişim Yayınları, 2010).

35. For the broader context within which Said Nursi was born and raised, see Şerif Mardin, *Bediüzzaman Said Nursi Olayı* (Istanbul: İletişim Yayınları, 1991).

36. Bediüzzaman Said Nursi, *Eski Said Dönemi Eserleri* (Istanbul: Yeni Asya Neşriyatı, 2010), 383.

37. Said Nursi and his contemporaries were not aware of Max Weber's more specific discussion on the relationship between Islam and economic development. Weber's argument would be introduced to Turkish intellectual circles by Sabri F. Ülgener, *İktisadi İnhitat Tarihimizin Ahlak ve Zihniyet Meseleleri* (Istanbul: Akgün Matbaası, 1951).

38. Nursi, *Eski Said Dönemi Eserleri*, 334–36.

39. To be fair to Said Nursi, he attributed the decline of the Muslim world to a host of other factors, such as despair, untruthfulness in social and political life, love of enmity, lack of knowledge of the bonds binding the faithful together, despotism, egocentrism. idleness, illiteracy, and prevailing bad morality, some of which are directly related to nonobservance of Islam. See the discussion in Nursi, *Eski Said Dönemi Eserleri*, 29–41, 150–57.

40. Nursi, *Eski Said Dönemi Eserleri*, 327. To be fair to Said Nursi, he attributed the material superiority of Europe not just to the weakening of Christianity, but also to a host of other factors, including the physical features of Europe, such as its geography and climate. See Nursi, *Eski Said Dönemi Eserleri*, 384–85, 337.

41. Ibid., 665.

42. Ibid., 326–34.

43. Said Nursi, *Hakikat Çekirdekleri*, Articles 1–2, https://sorularlarisale.com/risale-i-nur-kulliyati/mektubat/hakikat-cekirdekleri/663.

44. Wilfred Madelung, *The Succession to Muhammad: A Story of the Early Caliphate* (Cambridge: Cambridge University Press, 1997), chap. 1.

45. On how to reconcile God's wrath and God's mercy, see Gabriel Said Reynolds, "Divine Mercy in the Qur'an," in *Finding Beauty in the Other: Theological Reflections Across Religious Traditions*, ed. Peter Casarella and Mun'im Sirry (New York: The Crossroad Publishing Company, 2019).

46. The following is a standard account and can be found in any text on the period. See, for example, Madelung, *The Succession to Muhammad*; Ira M. Lapidus, *A History of Islamic Societies*, 2nd ed. (Cambridge: Cambridge University Press, 2002).

47. For more on the topic, see Ann K. S. Lambton, *State and Government in Medieval Islam* (London: Routledge Curzon, 1981).

48. For a detailed account, see Kemal Karpat, *Politization of Islam: Reconstructing Identity, State, Faith, and Community in the Late Ottoman State* (Oxford: Oxford University Press, 2001).

49. A sermon published in Sıratı Müstakim shows awareness of these pan-movements. See "Hutbe-i Arafat ve İttihad-ı İslam," *Sıratı Müstakim*, no. 119, December 15, 1910, in M. Ertuğrul Düzdağ, *Sebilürreşad*, vol. 9 (Istanbul: Bağcılar Belediye Başkanlığı, 2015).

50. Karpat, *The Politicization of Islam*, 121.

51. Quoted in Türköne, "Siyasi İdeoloji Olarak İslamcılığın Doğuşu (1867–1873)," 155.

52. For a discussion of various articles, see ibid., Part IV.

53. See ibid., 173.

54. For a biography of Esad Efendi, see Hamdi Özdiş, "Yeni Osmanlıcılıktan İttihatçılığa Bir Portre: 'Esad Efendi' (1842–1901)," *kebikeç* 26 (2008): 7–36.

55. For a detailed discussion of this pamphlet, see Hasan Barlak, "Esad Efendi'nin 'İttihad-ı İslam' Risalesinde İslam Birliği ve Osmanlı Halifesine Bağlılık Düşüncesi," *Uluslararası Sosyal Araştırmalar Dergisi* 9, no. 43 (April 2016): 598–615.

56. See Jacob M. Landau, *The Politics of Pan-Islam: Ideology and Organization* (Oxford: Clarendon Press, 1990).

57. Mehmet Akif, "Mev'iza: … Beyazıd Kürsüsünde," *Sebilürreşad*, no. 230, February 6, 1913, in M. Ertuğrul Düzdağ, *Sebilürreşad*, vol. 9 (Istanbul: Bağcılar Belediye Başkanlığı, 2017).

58. Seyhun, *Islamist Thinkers*, 60.

59. Quoted in Landau, *The Politics of Pan-Islam*, 336.

60. Said Halim Paşa, *Buhranlarımız* (n.p: Tercüman 1001 Temel Eser, 1970), 228.

61. Muhammed Hamidullah, İslam Peygamberi Hayatı ve Faaliyeti (I), trans. Salih Tuğ (Ankara: YeniŞafak Gazetesi, 2003), 543–616.

62. David Nirenberg, *Anti-Judaism: The Western Tradition* (New York: W.W. Norton, 2013), 148.

63. See Bernard Lewis, *The Jews of Islam* (Princeton: Princeton University Press, 1984), 103. Also see Nirenberg, *Anti-Judaism*, 172–75.

64. See Lewis, *The Jews of Islam*, chap. 4

65. Quoted in Landau, *The Politics of Pan-Islam*, 336.

66. Ibid., 338.

67. Ibid., 339.

68. For a detail discussion, see Landau, *The Politics of Pan-Islam*, chap. 1. Also see Azmi Özcan, *Pan-Islamism: Indian Muslims, the Ottomans and Britain, 1877–1924* (Leiden: Brill, 1997); Selim Deringil, *The Well-Protected Domains: Ideology and the Legitimation of Power in the Ottoman Empire, 1876–1909* (London: I.B. Tauris, 1998); Kemal Karpat, *Politization of Islam*.

69. See Mehmet Salih Arı and İbrahim Halil Ozan, "Sırat-ı Müstakim ve Volkan'a Göre 31 Mart Vakası," in "*İslam'ı Uyandırmak*," ed. Sunar.

70. See Marc David Baer, *The Dönme: Jewish Converts, Muslim Revolutionaries, and Secular Turks* (Stanford: Stanford University Press, 2010), chap. 4.

71. See Mustafa Ünal, "Volkan ve Mecmua-yı Ebu'z-Ziya Dergilerindeki Yahudilik ve Masonlukla İlgili Yazıların Dinler tarihi Açısından Değerlendirilmesi," in n.a., *Bütün Yönleriyle Yahudilik Uluslararası Sempozyum* (Ankara: Türkiye Dinler Tarihi Derneği, 2012).

72. Ibid., 739.

73. See the discussion in Baer, *The Dönme*, chap. 4. Also see Marc David Baer, "An Enemy Old and New: The Dönme, Anti-Semitism, and Conspiracy Theories in the Ottoman Empire and Turkish Republic," *The Jewish Quarterly Review* 103, no. 4 (fall 2013): 523–55.

74. As to the sources of Dervis Vahdeti's ideas about the CUP, Freemasons, and crypto-Jews, there are two suggestions: it is plausible, as Marc David Baer

seems to believe, that Vahdeti's ideas were simply public information. It is also the case, however, that the British Embassy in Istanbul, its chief dragoman in particular, Gerald Grey Fitzmaurice, held similar ideas. Fitzmaurice called the CUP "the Jews Committee of Union and Progress." See Elie Kedourie, "Young Turks, Freemasons and Jews," *Middle Eastern Studies* 7, no. 1 (January 1971): 90.

75. These reforms are well-known and well-studied. Two classic works are Lewis, *The Emergence of Modern Turkey*; Berkes, *The Development of Secularism in Turkey.*

76. Quoted in Bernard Lewis, *Middle East Mosaic: Fragments of Life, Letters, and History* (New York: Random House, 2000), pp. 257–258.

77. See Başkan, *From Religious Empires to Secular States.*

78. Mustafa Kemal Atatürk, "Kastamonu'da İkinci Konuşma," [the speech is delivered in 1925], https://www.atam.gov.tr/ataturkun-soylev-ve-demecleri/kastamonuda-ikinci-konusma.

79. William Hale, *Turkish Politics and the Military* (London: Routledge, 1994), 80. Hale also notes that the military became a school that spread the ideals of the republic among the young men who served in the military. It is critical to remember that military service has been and still is mandatory for males in Turkey.

80. Also see Umut Azak, *Islam and Secularism in Turkey: Kemalism, Religion and the Nation State* (London: I.B. Tauris, 2010).

81. Süleyman Hayri Bolay, "Akseki, Ahmet Hamdi," *İslam Ansiklopedisi*, vol. 2 (Ankara: Türkiye Diyanet Vakfı, 1989), 293–95.

82. The text of the recommendation letter was printed on the first page of the copy I have. The author also stated that the book was primarily written for preachers and prayer leaders. See A. Hamdi Akseki, *Islam Dini: İtikat, İbadet ve Ahlak*, 20th ed. (Ankara: Güzel Sanatlar Matbaası, 1969).

83. Ibid., 8.

84. Ibid., 10.

85. Ibid., 19–22.

86. Necip Fazıl Kısakürek, "Islam, Neye İnanıyoruz?," in *İdeolocya Örgüsü* (Istanbul: Büyük Doğu Yayınları, N.D) [originally published in 1959]. Kısakürek discusses each topic from the perspective of Islam in the succeeding pages of his book.

87. Necip Fazıl Kısakürek, "İslam ve Herşey," in *İdeolocya Örgüsü.*

88. See Seyhun, *Islamist Thinkers*, 74.

89. Ibid., 43.

90. Nursi, *Eski Said Dönemi Eserleri*, 672–73.

91. Ibid., 673.

92. Our discussion depends on Kısakürek, *İdeolocya Örgüsü.*

93. We owe this comparative insight to Hilal Barın, "Sezai Karakoç'ta ve Necip Fazıl Kısakürek'te Medeniyet Anlayışı: Karşılaştırmalı Bir İnceleme," *Muhafazakar Düşünce*, 12 (45–46) (July–December 2015): 145–76. Also see Cemil Aydın and Burhanettin Duran, "Arnold J. Toynbee and Islamism in Cold War-Era Turkey:

Civilizationalism in the Writings of Sezai Karakoç," *Comparative Studies of South Asia, Africa and the Middle East* 35, no. 2 (August 2015): 310–23; Burhanettin Duran, "Türkiye İslamcılığında Medeniyet Söylemi ve Sezai Karakoç'un Düşüncesi," in *Türkiye'de İslamcılık Düşüncesi ve Hareketi Sempozyum Tebliğleri*, ed. İsmail Kara and Asım Öz (Istanbul: Zeytinburnu Belediyesi Kültür Yayınları, 2013).

94. Cited in Barın, "Sezai Karakoç'ta ve Necip Fazıl Kısakürek'te Medeniyet Anlayışı," 163.

95. Cited in ibid., 162.

96. Sezai Karakoç, *Diriliş Neslinin Amentüsü*, 30th ed. (Istanbul: Diriliş Yayınları, 2015), 63.

97. Ibid., 63–64.

98. The following discussion is based on Mehmet Akif İnan's columns published in *Yeni Devir* between 1977 and 1985, which are collected in Mehmet Akif İnan, *İslam Dünyası ve Ortadoğu* (Ankara: Eğitim-Bir-Sen, 2016).

99. Ibid., 31.

100. Ibid., 32–33.

101. Ibid., 69–71.

102. Ibid., 32–33.

103. Ibid., 72–74. Also see ibid., 34–36.

104. Ibid., 46–48.

105. Ibid., 49–51.

106. Ibid., 107–9.

107. Ibid., 37–39.

108. Ibid., 66–68.

109. Ibid., 89–91.

110. Ibid., 72–74.

111. Ibid., 120–22.

112. Ibid., 69–71.

113. Sabri Efendi, *Hilafetin İlgasının Arka Planı* (Istanbul: İnsan Yayınları, 2016), 43–44. Mustafa Sabri repeats similar accusations throughout the text.

114. See Baer, *The Dönme*; Baer, "An Enemy Old and New."

115. Nursi, "5. Şua," in *Şualar*, http://risaleoku.com/oku/sualar/578.

116. Said Nursi, *Sırr-ı İnna A'tayna Risalesi* (Istanbul: Derin Tarih, 2016).

117. See Eşref Edib, *Kara Kitap: Milleti Nasıl Aldattılar? Mukaddesatına Nasıl Saldırdılar?* (Istanbul: Beyan Yayıncılık, 2000).

118. A classic in this genre is Necip Fazıl Kısakürek, *Son Devrin Din Mazlumları* (Istanbul: Büyük Doğu Yayınları, 2008).

119. For an extensive study on Cevat Rifat Atilhan, Mustafa Murat Çay, "Cevat Rifat Atilhan: Askeri, Siyasi ve Fikri Yönleriyle," unpublished doctoral dissertation, Selçuk University, 2013.

120. Necip Fazıl's writings on the topic were published in his journal *Büyük Doğu*, but collected in a volume: Necip Fazıl Kısakürek, *Yahudilik, Masonluk ve Dönmelik*, 2nd ed. (Istanbul: Büyük Doğu Yayınları, 2008).

121. Ibid., 38–39.

122. Cited in Rifat N. Bali, *A Scapegoat for All Seasons: The Dönmes or Crypto-Jews of Turkey*, trans. Paul Bessemer (Istanbul: The ISIS Press, 2008), 374–77.

123. Bali, *A Scapegoat for All Seasons*, 375.

124. Kısakürek, *Yahudilik, Masonluk ve Dönmelik*, 52.

125. Cited in Doğan Gürpınar, *Conspiracy Theories in Turkey: Conspiracy Nation* (London: Routledge, 2020), 29.

126. Necip Fazıl published this article under a pen name. See Dedektif X Bir, "İsmet Paşa ve (Lozan)ın İç Yüzü," *Büyük Doğu* 5, no. 29 (October 6, 1950): 10–11.

127. Kısakürek, *Yahudilik, Masonluk ve Dönmelik*, 198.

128. Ibid., 129–42.

129. Ibid., 121.

130. Ibid., 124.

131. Rıfat N. Bali, *Musa'nın Evlatları, Cumhuriyet'in Yurttaşları* (Istanbul: İletişim Yayınları, 2001). Also see Bali, *A Scapegoat for All Seasons*.

132. This treaty was the peace treaty signed in 1920 and imposed upon the Ottoman Empire after the First World War. The treaty divided the Empire's territories among the Western powers and left in the hands of Turks a small piece of territory in Northern Anatolia.

133. Fatma Müge Göcek, *The Transformation of Turkey: Redefining State and Society from the Ottoman Empire to the Modern Era* (London: I.B. Tauris, 2011), 99. Göcek traces the origin and development of this syndrome in this book. Also see Dietrich Jung and Wolfango Piccoli, *Turkey at the Crossroads: Ottoman Legacies and a Greater Middle East* (London: Zed Books, 2001).

134. For a comparative analysis, see Gürpınar, *Conspiracy Theories in Turkey*.

135. İnan, *İslam Dünyası ve Ortadoğu*, 154–56.

136. For Davutoğlu's contribution to Turkey's foreign policy, see Bülent Aras, "The Davutoğlu Era in Turkish Foreign Policy," *Insight Turkey* 11, no. 3 (summer 2009): 127–42; Bülent Aras, "Davutoğlu Era in Turkish Foreign Policy Revisited," *Journal of Balkan and Near Eastern Studies* 16, no. 4 (July 2014): 404–18.

137. Mehmet Akif Ersoy, "Süleymaniye Kürsüsünde," Safahat, https://safahat.diyanet.gov.tr/PoemList.aspx?bID=7.

138. Ahmet Davutoğlu, *Alternative Paradigms: The Impact of Islamic and Western Weltanschauungs on Political Theory* (Lanham: University Press of America, 1994).

139. Ibid., 47–48.

140. Cited in ibid., 50.

141. Ibid., 50.

142. Ibid., 50–51.

143. Ibid., 51.

144. Ibid., 52.

145. Cited in ibid., 5.

146. Ibid., 48.
147. Ibid., 11.
148. Ibid., 56.
149. Ibid., chap. 4–7.
150. Ibid., 181.
151. Ibid., 180–86.
152. Ibid., 1.
153. Ibid., 201–2.
154. Ibid., 193–94.
155. Ibid., 194.
156. Ibid., 202.
157. Davutoğlu elaborates this history in more detail in his "İslam Dünyasının siyasi dönüşümü: Dönemlendirme ve projeksiyon," *Divan: Disiplinlerarası Çalışmalar Dergisi* 7, no. 12 (2002–11): 1–50.
158. Ahmet Davutoğlu, *Stratejik Derinlik: Türkiye'nin Uluslararası Konumu* (Istanbul: Küre Yayınları, 2001).
159. See ibid., Part I, chap. 1.
160. Ibid., Part I, chap. 2.
161. Ibid., Part I, chap. 3.
162. The following discussion depends on ibid., Part III, chap. 3.
163. Ibid., 331.
164. Davutoğlu, *Alternative Paradigms*, 196.

Conclusion

1. For a sophisticated historical analysis of such exceptionalism, see Şerif Mardin, "Turkish Islamic Exceptionalism Yesterday and Today: Continuity, Rupture and Reconstruction in Operational Codes," *Turkish Studies* 6, no. 2 (June 2005): 145–65.
2. George W. Bush, *Public Papers of the Presidents of the United States* (Washington, DC: United States Government Printing Office, 2007), 1152.
3. Ussama Makdisi, "Ottoman Orientalism," *American Historical Review* 107, no. 3 (June 2002): 768–96.
4. See Anita Sengupta, *Myth and Rhetoric of the Turkish Model: Exploring Development Alternatives* (New Delhi: Springer, 2014).
5. Meliha B. Altunışık, "The Turkish Model and Democratization in the Middle East," *Arab Studies Quarterly* 27, no. 1/2 (winter/spring 2005): 45–63.
6. Alper Y. Dede, "The Arab Uprisings: Debating the 'Turkish Model,'" *Insight Turkey* 13, no. 2 (spring 2011): 23–32.
7. Burhanettin Duran and Nuh Yılmaz, "Whose Model? Which Turkey?," *Foreign Policy*, February 8, 2011.

8. Halil İnalcik, "The Meaning of Legacy: The Ottoman Case," in *Imperial Legacy: The Ottoman Imprint on the Balkans and the Middle East*, ed. L. Carl Brown (New York, Columbia University Press, 1996), 17–29.

9. Şükrü Hanioğlu, "The Historical Roots of Kemalism," in *Democracy, Islam and Secularism in Turkey*, by Ahmet Kuru and Alfred Stepan (New York: Columbia University Press, 2012), 32–56.

10. Başkan "Turkey's Pan-Islamist Foreign Policy."

BIBLIOGRAPHY

Magazine and Journal Articles

"Al Jazeera Forum: Ahmet Davutoğlu," *Al Jazeera*, March 13, 2011.

"Çiller Lays the Cards on the Table," *Briefing* 1122, December 23, 1996.

"Davutoğlu: Arap baharı Türk baharıdır da," *Haber 7*, March 25, 2011.

"Defying U.S., Turkey to Sign Gas Deal in Iran," *New York Times*, August 11, 1996.

"En düşük memur maaşı kaç YTL olacak?," *Anadolu Ajansı*, December 5, 2007.

"Erdogan Calls for a Secular Egypt," *Egypt Independent*, September 13, 2011.

"Erdogan, in Cairo, Touts Turkey as a Model for the Arab World," *Haaretz*, September 14, 2011.

"Erdogan to Mubarak: 'Listen to the Egyptians,'" *SETAV*, February 1, 2011.

"Gazze davasını yalnız bırakmayacağız," *Al Jazeera Turk*, July 20, 2014.

"Kerry Says Egypt's Military Was 'Restoring Democracy' in Ousting Morsi" *New York Times*, August 1, 2013.

"Maliye zamlı memur maaşlarını açıkladı," *Anadolu Ajansı*, July 5, 2010.

"NATO'nun Libya'da ne işi var," *NTV*, February 28, 2011.

"Renault-Pars News Letter," February 2005.

"Renault sales edge higher," *BBC News Business*, January 3, 2002.

"RP'li Başkan Zorda," *Milliyet*, November 12, 1996.

"Tehdidin Adı İrtica," *Milliyet,* April 30, 1997.

"The Turkish 2000–2001 Banking Crisis: Economic Report," *RaboBank*, September 4, 2013.

"Turkey: Preparations 'complete' for Syria military action," *Al Jazeera*, October 8, 2019.

"Turkey and Syria to stage joint military exercise.," *Anadolu Ajansı*, April 26, 2009.

"Turkish army to train Syrian army," *Anadolu Ajansı*, January 31, 2011.

"Turkish assembly backs joining NATO naval operation," *Reuters*, March 24, 2011.

"We are ready to pay the price, says Erdogan," *Hürriyet*, February 12, 2008.

"Yükseköğretim Kanunu," *Resmi Gazete*, November 4, 1981.

Primary Sources

"Hutbe-i Arafat ve İttihad-ı İslam," *Sıratı Müstakim*, no. 119, December 15, 1910 in M. Ertuğrul Düzdağ, *Sebilürreşad*, v. 9 (Istanbul: Bağcılar Belediye Başkanlığı, 2015).

Acar, Ali, and Habib Aydın, "Arap Baharı Üzerine Oryantalist ve Marksist Değerlendirmeler," *Süleyman Demirel Üniversitesi İktisadi ve İdari Bilimler Fakültesi Dergisi*, v. 22, no. 2 (April, 2017), pp. 514–524.

Akdoğan, Yalçın, "The Meaning of Conservative Democratic Identity" in Hakan Yavuz ed., *The Emergence of a New Turkey: Democracy and the AK Party* (Salt Lake: the University of Utah Press, 2006).

Akif, Mehmet, "Mev'iza: . . . Beyazıd Kürsüsünde," *Sebilürreşad*, no. 230, February 6, 1913, in M. Ertuğrul Düzdağ, *Sebilürreşad*, v. 9 (Istanbul: Bağcılar Belediye Başkanlığı, 2017).

Akseki, A. Hamdi, *Islam Dini: İtikat, İbadet ve Ahlak*, 20th ed. (Ankara: Güzel Sanatlar Matbaası, 1969).

Akşit, Bahattin, "Islamic Education in Turkey: Medrese Reform in Late Ottoman times and Imam-Hatip shools in the Republic" in Richard Tapper ed., *Islam in Modern Turkey* (London: I.B. Tauris, 1991).

Alantar, Ö. Zeynep Oktay, "The October 1998 Crisis: The Change of Heart of Turkish Foreign Policy towards Syria?," *CEMOTI: Cahiers D'Etudes Sur La Mediterranee Orientale et Le Monde Turco-Iranien*, no. 31 (January–June, 2001), pp. 142–161.

Altunışık, Meliha B., "The Turkish Model and Democratization in the Middle East," *Arab Studies Quarterly*, Vol. 27, No. 1 & 2 (Winter/Spring, 2005), pp. 45–63.

Altunışık, Meliha, "Turkey's Iraq Policy: The War and Beyond," *Journal of Contemporary European Studies*, v. 14, no. 2 (August, 2006), pp. 183–196.

Altunışık, Meliha Benli, and Özlem Tür, "From Distant Neighbors to Partners? Changing Syrian-Turkish Relations," *Security Dialogue*, v. 37, no. 2 (June, 2006), pp. 229–248.

Altunışık, Meliha and Lenore G. Martin, "Making sense of Turkish foreign policy in the Middle East under AKP," *Turkish Studies*, v. 12, no. 4 (December, 2011), pp. 569–587.

Aral, Berdal, "Dispensing with Tradition? Turkish Politics and International Society during the Özal decade, 1983–93," *Middle Eastern Studies*, v. 37, no. 1 (January 2001), pp. 72–88.

Aral, Berdal, "An Inquiry into the D-8 Experiment: An Incipient Model of an Islamic Common Market?," *Alternatives:Turkish Journal of International Relations*, v. 4, no. 1 & 2 (Spring–Summer, 2005), pp. 89–107.

Aras, Bülent, "Turkish Foreign Policy Towards Iran: Ideology and Foreign Policy in Flux," *Journal of Third World Studies*, v. 18, no. 1 (Spring, 2001), pp. 105–124.

Aras, Bülent, "The Davutoğlu Era in Turkish Foreign Policy," *Insight Turkey*, v. 11, no. 3 (Summer, 2009), pp. 127–142.

Aras, Bülent, "Davutoğlu Era in Turkish Foreign Policy Revisited," *Journal of Balkan and Near Eastern Studies*, v. 16, no. 4 (July, 2014), pp. 404–418.

Aras, Bülent and Aylin Görener, "National role conceptions and foreign policy orientation: the ideational bases of the Justice and Development Party's foreign policy activism in the Middle East," *Journal of Balkan and Near Eastern Studies*, Vol. 12, No. 1 (March, 2010), pp. 73–93.

Aras, Bülent, and Fuat Keyman, *Turkey, the Arab Spring and Beyond* (New York: Routledge, 2017).

Aras, Bülent, and Rabia Karakaya Polat, "From conflict to cooperation: Desecuritization of Turkey's relations with Syria and Iran," *Security Dialogue*, v. 39, no. 5 (October, 2008), pp. 495–515.

Arbell, Dan, "The U.S.-Turkey-Israel Triangle," Brookings Institution Analysis Paper Number 34, October, 2014.

Arcayürek, Cüneyt, *Müdahalenin Ayak Sesleri* (Istanbul: Bilgi Yayinevi, 1985).

Ardıç, Nurullah, "Modernite, Kimlik, Siyaset: Ahmet Davutoğlu'nun Medeniyet Söylemi," in Talha Köse, Ahmet Okumuş and Burhanettin Duran eds., *Stratejik Zihniyet: Kuramdan Eyleme: Ahmet Davutoğlu ve Stratejik Derinlik* (Istanbul: Küre Yayınları, 2014), p. 47–87.

Arı, Mehmet Salih and İbrahim Halil Ozan, "Sırat-ı Müstakim ve Volkan'a Göre 31 Mart Vakası," in Lütfi Sunar, *"İslam'ı Uyandırmak": Meşrutiyet'ten Cumhuriyet'e İslamcı Düşünce ve Dergiler* (two volumes) (Istanbul: İLEM, 2018).

Arıkan, Vural, "Vergi Paketiyle İslam Bankacılığı Teşvik Ediliyor," *Yeni Gündem*, November 1–14, 1985.

Atatürk, Mustafa Kemal, "Kastamonu'da İkinci Konuşma," Atam.gov.tr, ND [the speech is delivered in 1925].

Aydın, Mustafa, "Determinants of Turkish Foreign Policy: Historical Framework and Traditional Inputs," *Middle Eastern Studies*, v. 35, no. 4 (October, 1999), p. 152–186.

Aydın, Cemil and Burhanettin Duran, "Arnold J. Toynbee and Islamism in cold war-era Turkey: civilizationalism in the writings of Sezai Karakoç," *Comparative Studies of South Asia, Africa and the Middle East*, v. 35, no. 2 (August, 2015), pp. 310–323.

Aydınlar Ocağı Derneği, *Aydınlar Ocağı Derneği Tüzüğü* (Istanbul: Aydınlar Ocağı Yayınları, 1989)

Aydınlı, Ersel, Nihat Ali Özcan and Doğan Akyaz, "The Turkish Military's March Toward Europe," *Foreign Affairs*, vol. 85, no. 1 (January/February, 2006).

Aydıntaşbaş, Aslı, "The Good, The Bad and the Gülenists: The Role of the Gülen Movement in Turkey's Coup Attempt," European Council on Foreign Relations Essay, September 2016.

Aykan, Mahmut Bali, *Turkey's Role in the Organization of the Islamic Conference:1960–1992: The Nature of Deviation from the Kemalist Heritage* (New York: Vantage Press, 1994).

Azak, Umut, *Islam and Secularism in Turkey: Kemalism, Religion and the Nation State* (London: I.B. Tauris, 2010).

Baer, Marc David, *The Dönme: Jewish Converts, Muslim Revolutionaries, and Secular Turks* (Stanford: Stanford University Press, 2010).

Baer, Marc David, "An Enemy Old and New: The Dönme, Anti-Semitism, and Conspiracy Theories in the Ottoman Empire and Turkish Republic," *The Jewish Quarterly Review*, v. 103, no. 4 (Fall, 2013), pp. 523–555.

Balcı, Ali, Filiz Cicioğlu and Duygu Kalkan, "Türkiye'de Uluslararası İlişkiler Akademisyenleri ve Bölümlerinin Akademik Etkilerinin *Google Scholar* Verilerinden Hareketle İncelenmesi," *Uluslararası İlişkiler*, v. 16, no. 64 (December, 2019), pp. 57–75.

Balcı, Ali and Tuncay Kardaş "The Changing Dynamics of Turkey's Relations with Israel: An Analysis of 'Securitization,'" *Insight Turkey*, v. 14, no. 2 (Spring, 2012), pp. 99–120.

Bali, Rıfat N., *Musa'nın Evlatları, Cumhuriyet'in Yurttaşları* (Istanbul: İletişim Yayınları, 2001).

Bali, Rifat N., *A Scapegoat for All Seasons: The Dönmes or Cyrpto-Jews of Turkey*, translated by Paul Bessemer (Istanbul: The ISIS Press, 2008).

Barın, Hilal, "Sezai Karakoç'ta ve Necip Fazıl Kısakürek'te Medeniyet Anlayışı: Karşılaştırmalı Bir İnceleme," *Muhafazakar Düşünce*, 12(45–46) (July–December, 2015), pp. 145–176.

Barkey, Henri J., and Graham E. Fuller, *Turkey's Kurdish Question* (Lanham: Rowman & Littlefield, 1998).

Barlak, Hasan, "Esad Efendi'nin 'İttihad-ı İslam' Risalesinde İslam Birliği ve Osmanlı Halifesine Bağlılık Düşüncesi," *Uluslararası Sosyal Araştırmalar Dergisi*, v. 9, no. 43 (April, 2016), pp. 598–615.

Başkan, Birol, "Ankara Torn Apart: Arab Spring Turns into Turkey's Autumn," *Turkish Yearbook of International Relations*, no. 42 (2011), pp. 1–25.

Başkan, Birol, *From Religious Empires to Secular States: State Secularization in Turkey, Iran, and Russia* (London: Routledge, 2014).

Başkan, Birol, *Turkey and Qatar in the Tangled Geopolitics of the Middle East* (New York: Palgrave, 2016).

Başkan, Birol, "Turkey's Pan-Islamist Foreign Policy" *Cairo Review of Global Affairs* (Spring, 2019).

Başkan, Birol, "Islamism and Turkey's foreign policy during the Arab Spring," in Burak Bilgehan Özpek and Bill Park, eds., *Islamism, Populism, and Turkish Foreign Policy* (New York: Routledge, 2020).

Bayat, Asef, *Revolution without Revolutionaries: Making Sense of the Arab Spring* (Stanford: Stanford University Press, 2017).

Berkes, Niyazi, *The Development of Secularism in Turkey* (Montreal: McGill University Press, 1964).

Bir, Dedektif X [Necip Fazıl Kısakürek], "İsmet Paşa ve (Lozan)ın İç Yüzü," *Büyük Doğu*, v. 5, no. 29, October 6, 1950, pp. 10–11.

Birand, Mehmet Ali, *The Generals' Coup in Turkey* (New York: Brassey's Defense Publisher, 1987).

Bishku, Michael B., "Turkish-Syrian Relations: A Checkered History," *Middle East Policy*, v. 19, no. 3 (Fall, 2012), pp. 36–53.

Blanks, David R., and Michael Frassetto, eds., *Western Views of Islam in Medieval and Early Modern Europe: Perception of Other* (New York: St. Martin's Press, 1999).

Brownlee, Jason, Tarek Masoud and Andrew Reynolds, *The Arab Spring: Pathways of Repression and Reform* (London: Oxford University Press, 2015).

Bolay, Süleyman Hayri, "Akseki, Ahmet Hamdi," *İslam Ansiklopedisi*, vol. 2 (Ankara: Türkiye Diyanet Vakfi, 1989), pp. 293–295.

Bozdağlıoğlu, Yücel, *Turkish Foreign Policy and Turkish Identity: A Constructivist Approach* (New York: Routledge, 2003).

Bölükbaşı, Süha, *Turkish-American Relations and Cyprus* (Lanham: University Press of America, 1988).

Bölükbaşı, Süha, "Turkey challenges Iraq and Syria: The Euphrates Dispute," *Journal of South Asia and Middle Eastern Studies*, v. 16, no. 4 (Summer 1993), pp. 9–32.

Buğra, Ayşe, and Osman Savaşkan, *New Capitalism in Turkey: The Relationship between Politics, Religion and Business* (Cheltenham: Edward Elgar Publishing, 2014).

Bush, George W., *Public Papers of the Presidents of the United States* (Washington DC: United States Government Printing Office, 2007).

Calamur, Krishnadev, "Turkey and Russia Reconcile," *The Atlantic*, June 27, 2016.

Canlı, Cemalettin, and Yusuf Kenan Beysülen, *Zaman İçinde Bediüzzaman* (Istanbul: İletişim Yayınları, 2010).

Cassels, Alan, *Ideology and International Relations in the Modern World* (London: Routledge, 1996).

Cemal, Hasan, *Kürtler* (Istanbul: İletişim, 2003).

Cook, Steven, "Arab Spring; Turkish Fall," *Foreign Policy*, May 5, 2011.

Copeaux, Etienne, *Türk Tarih Tezinden Türk İslam Sentezine 1931–1993* (Istanbul: Tarih Vakfı Yurt Yayınları, 1998).

Cağaptay, Soner, "Erdogan's Failure on the Nile," *Cairo Review of Global Affairs*, Spring 2019.

Çalış, Şaban H., *Turkey's Cold War: Foreign Policy and Western Alignment in the Modern Republic* (London: I.B. Tauris, 2017).

Çay, Mustafa Murat, "Cevat Rifat Atilhan: Askeri, Siyasi ve Fikri Yönleriyle," Unpublished Doctoral Dissertation, Selçuk University, 2013.

Çınar, Menderes, "The Justice and Development and the Kemalist Establishment" in Ümit Cizre ed., *Secular and Islamic Politics in Turkey: The Making of the Justice and Development Party* (New York:Routledge, 2008).

Çicek, Hikmet, *İrticaya Karşı Genelkurmay Belgeleri* (Istanbul: Kaynak Yayınları, 1998).

Dağı, İhsan, "Turkey's AKP in Power," *Journal of Democracy*, v. 19, no. 3 (July, 2008), pp. 25–30.

Danforth, Nicholas, "Ideology and Pragmatism in Turkish Foreign Policy: From Atatürk to the AKP," *Turkish Policy Quarterly*, v. 7, no. 3 (Fall, 2008), pp. 83–95.

Davutoğlu, Ahmet, *Alternative Paradigms: The Impact of Islamic and Western Weltanschauungs on Political Theory* (Lanham: University Press of America, 1994).

Davutoğlu, Ahmet, "Medeniyetlerin Ben-idraki," *Divan: Disiplinlerarası Çalışmalar Dergisi*, no. 1 (1997), pp. 1–53.

Davutoğlu, Ahmet, "The Clash of Interests: An Explanation of the World (Dis) Order," *Perceptions: Journal of International Affairs*, v. 2, no. 4 (December, 1997), n.p.

Davutoğlu, Ahmet, *Stratejik Derinlik: Türkiye'nin Uluslararası Konumu* (Istanbul: Küre Yayınları, 2001).

Davutoğlu, Ahmet, "İslam Dünyasının siyasi dönüşümü: Dönemlendirme ve projeksiyon," *Divan: Disiplinlerarası Çalışmalar Dergisi*, v. 7, no. 12 (2002–1), pp. 1–50.

Davutoğlu, Ahmet, "Turkey's Zero-Problems Foreign Policy," *Foreign Policy*, May 20, 2010.

Dede, Alper Y., "The Arab Uprisings: Debating the 'Turkish Model,'" *Insight Turkey*, Vol. 13, No. 2 (Spring, 2011), pp. 23–32.

Demir, İmran, *Overconfidence and Risk Taking in Foreign Policy Decision Making: The Case of Turkey's Syria Policy* (New York: Palgrave Macmillan, 2017).

Deringil, Selim, *The Well-Protected Domains: Ideology and the Legitimation of Power in the Ottoman Empire, 1876–1909* (London: I. B. Tauris, 1998).

Dickinson, Elizabeth, "The Case Against Qatar," *Foreign Policy*, September 30, 2014.

Dinçşahin, Şakir, "A Symptomatic Analysis of the Justice and Development Party's Populism in Turkey, 2007–2010," *Government and Opposition*, v. 47, no. 4 (2012), pp. 618–640.

Duman, Doğan, *Demokrasi Sürecinde Turkiye'de Islamcılık* (İzmir: Dokuz Eylül Yayınları, 1999).

Duran, Burhanettin, "Türkiye İslamcılığında Medeniyet Söylemi ve Sezai Karakoç'un Düşüncesi," in İsmail Kara and Asım Öz, eds., *Türkiye'de İslamcılık Düşüncesi ve Hareketi Sempozyum Tebliğleri* (Istanbul: Zeytinburnu Belediyesi Kültür Yayınları, 2013).

Duran, Burhanettin, Kemal İnat and Ali Resul Usul (eds.), *Türk Dış Politikası Yıllığı 2011* (Ankara: SETA, 2012).

Duran, Burhanettin, Kemal İnat and Ufuk Ulutaş (eds.), *Türk Dış Politikası Yıllığı 2012* (Ankara: SETA, 2013).

Duran, Burhanettin, Kemal İnat and Ali Balcı (eds.), *Türk Dış Politikası Yıllığı 2013* (Ankara: SETA, 2014).

Duran, Burhanettin, and Nuh Yılmaz, "Whose model? Which Turkey?," *Foreign Policy,* February 8, 2011.

Eagleton, Terry, *Ideology: An Introduction* (London: Verso, 1991).

Eagleton, William, *The Kurdish Republic of 1946* (London: Oxford University Press, 1963).

Edelman, Eric S., Svante E.Cornell, Aaron Lobel and Michael Makovsky, "The Roots of Turkish Conduct: Understanding the Evolution of Turkish Policy in the Middle East," Bipartisan Policy Center Report, December 2013.

Edib, Eşref, *Kara Kitap: Milleti Nasıl Aldattılar? Mukaddesatına Nasıl Saldırdılar?* (Istanbul: Beyan Yayıncılık, 2000).

Effron, Soni, "Defense Chief Reflects on Invasion Regrets," *Los Angeles Times,* March 21, 2005.

Eligür, Banu, *The Mobilization of Political Islam* (New York: Cambridge University Press, 2010).

Ergüder, Üstün, "The Motherland Party, 1982–1989" in Meter Heper and Jacob M. Landau, eds. *The Political Parties and Democracy in Turkey* (London: Tauris & Co Ltd, 1991).

Erkal, Mustafa, "21. Yüzyıla Doğru Milli Kültürlerin Geleceği ve Bazı Çelişkiler," in I*slamiyet, Millet Gercegi ve Laiklik* (Istanbul: Aydınlar Ocağı Yayınları, 1994).

Erkmen, Serhat, "6 Ay Sonra Zeytin Dalı Operasyonu ve Afrin," *Ortadoğu Analiz,* v. 9, no. 84 (October-November, 2018), pp. 60–61.

Eroğlu, Doğu, "Jihadist Clinic on Turkey's Syrian Border," *Dogueroglu.com,* 22 September 2014.

Ersoy, Mehmet Akif Ersoy, *Safahat*: https://safahat.diyanet.gov.tr/.

Esen, Berk, and Sebnem Gümüşçü, "Rising Competitive Authoritarianism in Turkey," *Third World Quarterly,* v. 37, no. 9 (2016), pp. 1581–1606.

Evren, Kenan, *Kenan Evren'in Anıları,* v. 4 (Ankara: Milliyet Yayinlari, 1991).

Filkins, Dexter, "Turkey Turns to Moderate in Islamic Party As New Premier," *New York Times,* November 17, 2002.

Filkins, Dexter, "The Deep State," *The New Yorker,* March 4, 2012.

Flanagan, Stephen J., et al., *Turkey's Nationalist Course: Implications for the U.S.-Turkish Strategic Partnership and the U.S. Army* (Santa Monica: RAND Corporation, 2020).

Fox, Jonathan and Shmuel Sandler, *Bringing Religion into International Relations* (New York: Palgrave Macmillan, 2004).

Freeden, Michael, *Ideology: A Very Short Introduction* (Oxford: Oxford University Press, 2003).

Friedman, Thomas, "Letter from Istanbul," *New York Times*, June 15, 2010.

Fuller, Graham, *The New Turkish Republic: Turkey as a Pivotal State in the Islamic World* (Washington DC: United States Institute of Peace, 2008).

Fuller, Graham, *Turkey and the Arab Spring* (N.P: Bozorg Press, 2014).

Gause III, F. Gregory, "Beyond Sectarianism: The New Middle East Cold War," Brookings Doha Center Analysis Paper, Number 11, July 2014.

Genç, Kaya, "Erdogan's Way: The Rise and Rule of Turkey's Islamist Shapeshifter," *Foreign Affairs,* September/October, 2019.

Gingeras, Ryan, "Is Turkey turning into a Mafia-State?," *Foreign Affairs*, November 30, 2017.

Gordon, Philip H., and Ömer Taşpınar, *Winning Turkey: How America, Europe, and Turkey Can Revive a Fading Partnership* (Washington, D.C.: Brookings Institution Press, 2008).

Gouldner, Alvin W., *The dialectic of ideology and technology: The Origins, Grammar and Future of Ideology* (London: MacMillan, 1976).

Göcek, Fatma Müge, *The Transformation of Turkey: Redefining State and Society from the Ottoman Empire to the Modern Era* (London: I.B. Tauris, 2011).

Göl, Ayla, "Turkey's clash of Islamists: Erdogan vs Gülen," *Open Democracy*, August 3, 2016.

Gürpınar, Doğan, *Conspiracy Theories in Turkey: Conspiracy Nation* (London: Routledge, 2020).

Gürpınar, Doğan, "Foreign Policy as a Contested Front of the Cultural Wars in Turkey: The Middle East and Turkey in the Era of the AKP," *Uluslararası İlişkiler*, v. 17, no. 65 (March, 2020), pp. 3–21.

Haas, Mark L., *The Clash of Ideologies: Middle Eastern Politics and American Security* (New York: Oxford University Press, 2012).

Haas, Mark L., and David W. Lesch, eds., *The Arab Spring: The Hope and Reality of the Uprisings* (New York: Routledge, 2018).

Hale, William, *Turkish Politics and the Military* (London: Routledge, 1994).

Hale, William, *Turkish Foreign Policy since 1774* (London: Routledge, 2000).

Halliday, Fred, T*he Middle East in International Relations: Power, Politics and Ideology* (Cambridge: Cambridge University Press, 2005).

Hamidullah, Muhammed, *İslam Peygamberi Hayatı ve Faaliyeti (I)*, trans. by Salih Tuğ (Ankara: YeniŞafak Gazetesi, 2003).

Hanioğlu, Şükrü, "The Historical Roots of Kemalism" in Ahmet Kuru and Alfred Stepan, *Democracy, Islam and Secularism in Turkey* (New York: Columbia University Press, 2012).

Hanioğlu, Şükrü, *Atatürk: An Intellectual Biography* (Princeton: Princeton University Press, 2013).

Helvacıköylü, Gamze, "The Effect of Neo-Ottomanism in Turkish Foreign Policy for the Balkans and Africa in Davutoğlu Period (2009–2014)," Unpublished Doctoral Dissertation, Yeditepe University, 2019.

Henke, Marina E., "The Rotten Carrot: US-Turkish Bargaining Failure over Iraq in 2003 and the Pitfalls of Social Embeddedness," *Security Studies*, v. 27, no. 1 (August, 2017), pp. 120–147.

Hill, Fiona and Ömer Taşpınar, "Turkey and Russia: Axis of the Excluded," *Survival: Global Politics and Strategy*, v. 48, no. 1 (March, 2006), pp. 81–92.

Hinnebusch, Raymond, and Özlem Tür, *Turkey Syria Relations: Between Enmity and Amity* (London: Ashgate Publishing Limited, 2013).

Hintz, Lisel, *Identity Politics Inside Out: National Identity Contestation and Foreign Policy in Turkey* (New York: Oxford University Press, 2018).

Holsti, K. J., "National Role Conceptions in the Study of Foreign Policy," *International Studies Quarterly*, v. 14, no. 3 (September, 1970), pp. 233–309.

Howard, Michael, "US arrest of soldiers infuriates Turkey," *The Guardian*, July 7, 2003.

Hudson, Valerie M., "Foreign Policy Analysis: Actor-Specific Theory and the Ground of International Relations," *Foreign Policy Analysis*, v. 1, no. 1 (March, 2005), pp. 1–30.

Hudson, Valerie M. and Benjamin S. Day, *Foreign Policy Analysis: Classic and Contemporary Theory*, 3rd Ed. (Lanham: Rowman & Littlefield, 2020).

Hunt, Michael H., *Ideology and U.S. Foreign Policy* (New Haven: Yale University Press, 1987).

İdiz, Semih, "Erdoğan'in 'laiklik' çıkışının önemi," *Milliyet*, September 17, 2001.

İnalcik, Halil, "The Meaning of Legacy: The Ottoman Case" in L. Carl Brown ed., *Imperial Legacy: The Ottoman Imprint on the Balkans and the Middle East* (New York, Columbia University Press, 1996).

İnan, Mehmet Akif, *İslam Dünyası ve Ortadoğu* (Ankara: Eğitim-Bir-Sen, 2016).

Independent Commission on Turkey, "Turkey in Europe: More than a Promise," in *Report of the Independent Commission on Turkey* (Brussels: the British Council and the Open Society Institute, 2004).

Jung, Dietrich, and Wolfango Piccoli, *Turkey at the Crossroads: Ottoman Legacies and a Greater Middle East* (London: Zed Books, 2001).

Jung, Dietrich, "The Sèvres Syndrome: Turkish Foreign Policy and its Historical Legacies," *American Diplomacy* (August, 2003).

Kalaycıoğlu, Ersin, "Turkish Democracy: Patronage versus Governance," *Turkish Studies*, v. 2, no. 1 (Spring, 2001), pp. 54–70.

Kalehsar, Omid Shokri, "Energy Factor in Iran-Turkey Relations," *Energy & Environment*, v. 26, no. 5, 2015, pp. 777–787.

Karakoç, Sezai, *Diriliş Neslinin Amentüsü*, 30th ed. (Istanbul: Diriliş Yayınları, 2015).

Karaveli, Halil, "Erdogan's Journey: Conservatism and Authoritarianism in Turkey," *Foreign Affairs*, v. 95, no. 6 (November/December, 2016), pp. 121–131.

Karpat, Kemal, *Politization of Islam: Reconstructing Identity, State, Faith, and Community in the Late Ottoman State* (Oxford: Oxford University Press, 2001).

Katık, Mevlüt, "Turkey to Negotiate Energy Deal with Iran," Center for Security Studies Eidgenössische Technische Hochschule Zürich, 2020.

Katzenstein, Peter J., *Cultural Norms and National Security: Police and Military in Postwar Japan* (Ithaca: Cornell University Press, 1996).

Katzenstein, Peter J., *The Culture of National Security: Norms and Identity in World Politics* (New York: Columbia University Press, 1996).

Kaya, Ayhan, "Islamisation of Turkey under the AKP Rule: Empowering Family, Faith and Charity," *South European Society and Politics*, v. 20, no. 1 (2015), pp. 47–69.

Kazancıgil, Ali, and Ergun Özbudun, eds., *Atatürk: Founder of a Modern State* (London: C. Hurst, 1981).

Kedourie, Elie, "Young Turks, Freemasons and Jews," *Middle Eastern Studies*, v. 7, no. 1 (January, 1971), pp. 89–104.

Kemal, Namık, *Renan Müdafaanamesı: İslamiyet ve Maarif* (Ankara: Güven Matbaası, 1962) [originally published in Istanbul by Mahmud Bey Matbaasi in 1910].

Keohane, Robert O., *After Hegemony: Cooperation and Discord in the World Political Economy* (Princeton: Princeton University Press, 1984).

Kerr, Malcolm, *The Arab Cold War: Gamal 'Abd al-Nasir and His Rivals, 1958–1970* (London: Oxford University Press, 1971).

Kılınç, Ramazan, "İdeoloji ve Dış Politika: Türkiye'de Kemalist (1930–1939) ve İslamcı (2011–2015) Dış Politikaların Karşılaştırmalı Bir Analizi," *Uluslararası İlişkiler*, v. 13, no. 52 (December, 2016), pp. 67–88.

Kısakürek, Necip Fazıl, *İdeolocya Örgüsü* (Istanbul: Büyük Doğu Yayınları, N.D) [originally published in 1959].

Kısakürek, Necip Fazıl, *Son Devrin Din Mazlumları*. (Istanbul: Büyük Doğu Yayınları, 2008).

Kısakürek, Necip Fazıl, *Yahudilik, Masonluk ve Dönmelik*, 2nd ed. (Istanbul: Büyük Doğu Yayınları, 2008).

Kirişçi, Kemal, "The transformation of Turkish foreign policy: The rise of the trading state," *New Perspectives on Turkey*, v. 40 (Spring, 2009), pp. 29–56.

Kirişçi, Kemal, and Gareth M. Winrow, *The Kurdish Question and Turkey: An Example of a Trans-state Ethnic Conflict* (New York; RoutledgeCurzon, 1997).

Kirkpatrick, David D., and May El Sheik, "Morsi Spurned Deals, Seeing Military as Tamed," *New York Times*, July 6, 2013.

Kösebalan, Hasan, *Turkish Foreign Policy: Islam, Nationalism, and Globalization* (New York: Palgrave MacMillan, 2011).

Krasner, Stephen D., *Defending the National Interest: Raw Materials Investments and U.S. Foreign Policy* (Princeton: Princeton University Press, 1978).

Kratochwil, Friedrich V., *Rules, Norms and Decisions: On the Conditions of Practical and Legal Reasoning in International Relations and Domestic Affairs* (New York: Cambridge University Press, 1989).

Kuru, Ahmet, "The Rise and Fall of Military Tutelage in Turkey: Fears of Islamism, Kurdism, and Communism," *Insight Turkey*, Vol. 14, No. 2 (Spring, 2012), pp. 37–57.

Kuru, Ahmet, *Secularism and State Policies toward Religion: The United States, France, and Turkey* (New York: Cambridge University Press, 2012).

Kürkçüoğlu, Ömer, *Turkiye'nin Arap Orta-Doğusuna Karşı Politikası: 1945–1970* (Ankara: Siyasal Bilgiler Fakültesi, 1972).

Lambton, Ann K. S., *State and Government in Medieval Islam* (London: Routledge Curzon, 1981).

Landau, Jacob M., ed. (1984) *Ataturk and the Modernization of Turkey* (Boulder: Westview Press, 1984).

Landau, Jacob M., *The Politics of Pan-Islam: Ideology and Organization* (Oxford: Clarendon Press, 1990).

Lapidus, Ira M., *A History of Islamic Societies*, 2nd ed. (Cambridge: Cambridge University Press, 2002).

Lev, David, "Turkey, Egypt Hold Naval Exercises," *Israel National News*, December 15, 2011.

Lewis, Bernard, *The Emergence of Modern Turkey* (London: Oxford University Press, 1961).

Lewis, Bernard, *The Jews of Islam* (Princeton: Princeton University Press, 1984).

Lewis, Bernard, *Middle East Mosaic: Fragments of Life, Letters and History* (New York: Random House, 2000).

Lister, Charles, "The Free Syrian Army: A decentralized insurgent brand," The Brookings Project on US Relations with the Islamic World, Analysis Paper, No. 26, November 2016.

Lombardi, Ben, "The Return of the Reluctant Generals?," *Political Science Quarterly*, v. 112, no. 2 (Summer, 1997), pp. 191–215.

Lord, Ceren, *Religious Politics in Turkey: From the Birth of the Republic to the AKP* (Cambridge: Cambridge University Press, 2018).

Lowry, Heath, "Betwixt and Between: Turkey's Political Structure on the Cups of the Twenty-First Century," in Morton Abramowitz ed., *Turkey's Transformation and American Policy* (New York: The Century Foundation Press, 2000).

Lüküslü, Demet, "Creating a Pious Generation: Youth and Education Policies of the AKP in Turkey," *Southeast European and Black Sea Studies*, v. 16, no. 4 (October, 2016), pp. 637–649.

Madelung, Wilfred, *The Succession to Muhammad: A Story of the early Caliphate* (Cambridge: Cambridge University Press, 1997).

Maden, Tuğba Evrim and Seyfi Kılıç, "Irak'ta Su Kaynakları Sorunu ve Yönetimi," *Ortadoğu Analiz*, v. 4, no. 43 (July, 2012), pp. 84–97.

Magued, Shaimaa, "Turkey's economic rapprochement towards Syria and the territorial conflict over Hatay," *Mediterranean Politics*, v. 24, no. 1 (2019), pp. 20–39.

Makdisi, Ussama, "Ottoman Orientalism," *American Historical Review*, v. 107, no. 3 (June, 2002), pp. 768–796.

Mango, Andrew, "Turkish Policy in the Middle East" in Clement H. Dodd, ed., *Turkish Foreign Policy: New Prospects* (Huntington: Eothen Press, 1992).

Marcus, Aliza, *Blood and Belief: The PKK and the Kurdish Fight for Independence* (New York: New York University Press, 2007).

Mardin, Serif, "The Nakshibendi Order in Turkish History," in Richard Tapper, ed., *Islam in Modern Turkey: Religion, Politics and Literature in a Secular State*, London: I.B. Tauris, 1991.

Mardin, Şerif, *Bediüzzaman Said Nursi Olayı* (Istanbul: İletişim Yayınları, 1991).

Mardin, Şerif, "Turkish Islamic Exceptionalism Yesterday and Today: Continuity, Rupture and Reconstruction in Operational Codes," *Turkish Studies*, v. 6, no. 2 (June, 2005), pp. 145–165.

Martill, Benjamin, "International Ideologies: paradigms of ideological analysis and world politics," *Journal of Political Ideologies*, v. 23, no. 3 (June, 2017), pp. 236–255.

McDowall, David, *A Modern History of the Kurds* (London: I.B. Tauris, 1996).

McLellan, David, *Ideology*, 2nd ed. (Minneapolis: University of Minnesota Press, 1995).

Mearsheimer, John J., *The Tragedy of Great Power Politics* (New York: W. W. Norton, 2001).

Morgenthau, Hans J., *Politics among Nations: The Struggle for Power and Peace* (New York: Alfred A. Knopf, 1948).

Murinson, Alexander, "The strategic depth doctrine of Turkish foreign policy," *Middle Eastern Studies*, v. 42, no. 6, 2006, pp. 945–964.

Mustafa Sabri [Efendi], *Hilafetin İlgasının Arka Planı* (Istanbul: İnsan Yayınları, 2016).

Nader, Alireza, and Stephen Larrabee, "Turkish-Iranian Relations in a Changing Middle East," Rand Corporation Research Report, 2013.

Narbone, Luigi and Natalie Tocci, "Running in circles? The cyclical relationship between Turkey and the European Union," *Journal of Southern Europe and the Balkans*, v. 9, no. 3 (December, 2007), pp. 233–246.

Nebiler, Halil, *Emperyalizm ve Ilımlı İslam* (Istanbul: Toplumsal Dönüşüm Yayınları, 2010).`

Nirenberg, David, *Anti-Judaism: The Western Tradition* (New York: W.W. Norton, 2013).

Nursi, Said, *Eski Said Dönemi Eserleri* (Istanbul: Yeni Asya Neşriyatı, 2010).

Nursi, Said, *Hakikat Çekirdekleri*: https://sorularlarisale.com/risale-i-nur-kulliyati/mektubat/hakikat-cekirdekleri/663.

Nursi, Said, *Şualar*: http://risaleoku.com/oku/sualar/578.

Nursi, Said, *Sırr-ı İnna A'tayna Risalesi* (Istanbul: Derin Tarih, 2016).

Oğuzlu, Tarık, "The Changing Dynamics of Turkey-Isreal Relations: A Structural Realist Account," *Mediterranean Politics*, v. 15, no. 2 (June, 2010), pp. 273–288.

Okutan, Çağatay, *Tek Parti Döneminde Azınlık Politikaları* (Istanbul, Bilgi Üniversitesi Yayınları, 2004).

Olson, Robert, *The Emergence of Kurdish Nationalism and the Sheikh Said Rebellion (1880–1925),*(Austin: University of Texas Press, 1989).

Onbaşı, Funda Gençoğlu, "Gezi Park Protests in Turkey: From 'Enough is Enough' to Counter-Hegemony?," *Turkish Studies*, v. 17, no. 2 (March, 2016), pp. 272–294.

Öktem, Kerem, *Angry Nation: Turkey since 1989* (London: Zed Books, 2011).

Öktem, Kerem, Ayşe Kadıoğlu and Mehmet Karlı, *Another Empire? A Decade of Turkey's Foreign Policy under the Justice and Development Party* (Istanbul: Istanbul Bilgi University Press, 2012).

Öniş, Ziya, "The Evolution of Privatization in Turkey: The Institutional Context of Public-Enterprise Reform," *International Journal of Middle East Studies*, v. 13, no. 2 (May, 1991), pp. 163–176.

Öniş, Ziya, "The Political Economy of Islamic Resurgence in Turkey: The Rise of the Welfare Party in Perspective," *Third World Quarterly*, v. 18, no. 4 (Sep., 1997), pp. 757–760.

Öniş, Ziya, "Turkey-EU Relations: Beyond the Current Stalemate," *Insight Turkey*, v. 10, no. 4 (Fall, 2008), pp. 35–50.

Öniş, Ziya, "The Triumph of Conservative Globalism: The Political Economy of the AKP Era," *Turkish Studies*, v. 13, no. 2 (June, 2012), pp. 135–152.

Öniş, Ziya, "Turkey and the Arab Spring: Between Ethics and Self-Interest," *Insight Turkey*, v. 14, no. 3 (Summer, 2012), pp. 45–63.

Öniş, Ziya, "Turkey and the Arab Revolutions: Boundaries of Regional Power Influence in a Turbulent Middle East," *Mediterranean Politics*, v. 19, no. 2 (June, 2014), pp. 203–219.

Özbudun, Ergun, "Turkey's Judiciary and the Drift toward Competitive Authoritarianism," *The International Spectator*, v. 50, no. 2 (June, 2015), no. 42–55.

Özcan, Azmi, *Pan-Islamism: Indian Muslims, the Ottomans and Britain, 1877–1924* (Leiden: Brill, 1997).

Özcan, Gencer, "Yalan Dünyaya Sanal Politikalar," in Gencer Özcan ed, *Onbir Aylık Saltanat: Siyaset, Ekonomi ve Dış Politikada Refahyol Dönemi* (Istanbul: Boyut Yayınları, 1998).

Özcan, Gencer, and Şule Kut, *En Uzun Onyıl: Türkiye'nin Ulusal Güvenlik ve Dış Politika Gündeminde Doksanlı Yıllar* (Istanbul: Büke Yayınları, 2000).

Özcan, Gencer, "Rusya'nın Suriye Bunalımına Müdahalesi ve Türkiye," in Gencer Özcan, Evren Balta and Burç Beşgül, eds. *Kuşku ile Komşuluk: Türkiye Rusya İlişkilerinin Değişen Dinamiği* (Istanbul: İletişim, 2017), p. 269–298.

Özcan, Gencer, and Salih Bıçakçı, eds. *Uluslarası İlişkiler*, Special Issue, v. 16, no. 62 (June, 2019).

Özcan, Nihat Ali, and Özgür Özdamar, "Uneasy Neigbors: Turkish-Iranian Relations since the 1979 Islamic Revolution," *Middle East Policy*, v. 17, no. 3 (Fall, 2010), p. 101–117.

Özçelik, Necdet, and Can Acun, "Terörle Mücadelede Yeni Safha: Zeytin Dalı Harekatı," SETA Rapor, 2018.

Özdiş, Hamdi, "Yeni Osmanlıcılıktan İttihatçılığa Bir Portre: 'Esad Efendi' (1842–1901)," *kebikeç*, 26, 2008, p. 7–36.

Özkan, Behlül, "The Cold-War era Origins of Islamism in Turkey and its Rise to Power," *Current Trends in Islamist Ideology*, v. 22 (November, 2017), pp. 41–57.

Özkan, Behlül, "1980 ve 1990'larda Türkiye ve Suriye arasındaki İlişkiler: Siyasi İslam, Müslüman Kardeşler ve İstihbarat Savaşları," *Uluslararası İlişkiler*, v. 16, no. 62 (June, 2019), pp. 5–25.

Özpek, Burak Bilgehan, and Yelda Demirağ, "Turkish foreign policy after the 'Arab Spring': from agenda-setter state to agenda-entrepreneur state," *Israel Affairs*, v. 20, no. 3 (June, 2014), pp. 328–345.

Özyanık, Seçil, "Adalet ve Kalkınma Partisi'nin Doğu-Batı Eksenli Dış Politika Yaklaşımında Din Unsuru," Unpublished Doctoral Dissertation, Hacettepe University, 2015.

Park, Bill, *Modern Turkey: People, State and Foreign Policy in a Globalized World* (London: Routledge, 2012).

Patton, Marcie J., "AKP Reform Fatigue in Turkey: What has Happened to the EU Process?," *Mediterranean Politics*, v. 12, no. 3 (2007), pp. 339–358.

Pope, Hugh, "Pax Ottomana: The Mixed Success of Turkey's New Foreign Policy," *Foreign Affairs*, November/December 2010.

Renan, Ernest, *Islam and Science*, 2nd ed., translated by Sally P. Ragep (Montreal: McGill University, 2011).

Republic of Turkey State Institute of Statistics, *Foreign Trade Statistics* (Ankara: State Institute of Statistics, 1981).

Republic of Turkey State Institute of Statistics, *Statistical Yearbook of Turkey* (Ankara: State Institute of Statistics, 1992).

Reynolds, Gabriel Said, "Divine Mercy in the Qur'an," in Peter Casarella and Mun'im Sirry, eds. *Finding Beauty in the Other: Theological Reflections Across Religious Traditions* (New York: the Crossroad, 2019).

Reynolds, Michael, "Echoes of Empire: Turkey's Crisis of Kemalism and the Search for an Alternative Foreign Policy," Brookings Institute Saban Center Paper No:26, June 2012.

Reynolds, Michael, "The Key to the Future Lies in the Past: The World View of Erdoğan and Davutoğlu," *Current Trends in Islamist Ideology*, v. 19 (September, 2015), pp. 5–38.

Robins, Philip, *Turkey and the Middle East* (New York: Council on Foreign Relations Press, 1991).

Robins, Philip, *Suits and Uniforms: Turkish Foreign Policy Since the Cold War* (London: Hurst & Company, 1991).

Robins, Philip, "Turkish foreign policy since 2002: between a "post-Islamist" government and a Kemalist state," *International Affairs*, v. 83, no. 2 (March, 2007), pp. 289–304.

Robins, Philip, "Turkey's 'double gravity' predicament: the foreign policy of a newly activist power," *International Affairs*, v. 89, no. 2 (March, 2013), pp. 381–397.

Rogin, Josh, "Obama Names His World Leader Best Buddies!," *Foreign Policy*, January 19, 2012.

Rubin, Michael, "Turkey from Ally to Enemy," *Commentary* (July/August, 2010).

Rumsfeld, Donald, *Known and Unknown: A Memoir* (London: Penguin, 2011).

Said Halim [Paşa], *Buhranlarımız* (N.P: Tercüman 1001 Temel Eser, 1970).

Sakallıoglu, Ümit Cizre, "The Anatomy of the Turkish Military's Autonomy," *Comparative Politics*, v. 9, no. 4 (January, 1997), p. 151–166.

Sakallıoğlu, Ümit Cizre, and Menderes Çınar, "Turkey 2002: Kemalism, Islamism, and Politics in the Light of the February 28 Process," The South Atlantic Quarterly, v. 102, nos. 2–3 (Spring/Summer, 2003), pp. 309–322.

Salt, Jeremy, "Turkey's Military Democracy," *Current History*, v. 98, no. 625 (February 1999), pp. 75–76.

Sandal, Nükhet A. and Jonathan Fox, *Religion in International Relations Theory: Interactions and Possibilities* (London: Routledge, 2013).

Saraçoğlu, Cenk, and Özhan Demirkol, "Nationalism and Foreign Policy Discourse in Turkey under the AKP Rule: Geography, History and National Identity," *British Journal of Middle Eastern Studies*, v. 42, no. 3 (2015), pp. 301–319.

Saraçoğlu, Rüştü, "Liberalization of the Turkish Economy," in Metin Heper and Ahmet Evin eds. *Politics in the Third Republic* (Boulder: Westview Press, 1994), pp. 65–78.

Saybaşılı, Kemali, "Siyasal Sistem Bunalımı," in Gencer Özcan ed, *Onbir Aylık Saltanat: Siyaset, Ekonomi ve Dış Politikada Refahyol Dönemi* (Istanbul: Boyut Yayınları, 1998).

Sengupta, Anita, *Myth and Rhetoric of the Turkish Model: Exploring Development Alternatives* (New Delhi: Springer, 2014).

Seyhun, Ahmet, *Islamist Thinkers in the Late Ottoman Empire and Early Turkish Republic* (Leiden: Brill, 2015).

Shadid, Anthony, "Turkey Predicts Alliance with Egypt as Regional Anchors," *New York Times*, September 18, 2011.

Sinjab, Lina, "Syria: How a new rebel unity is making headway against the regime," *BBCNews*, May 1, 2015.

Sinkaya, Bayram, "Rationalization of Turkey-Iran Relations: Prospects and Limits," *Insight Turkey*, v. 14, no. 2 (Spring, 2012), pp. 137–156.

Sinkaya, Bayram, "The Kurdish Question in Iran and its effects on Iran-Turkey Relations," *British Journal of Middle Eastern Studies*, v. 45, no. 5, 2018, pp. 840–859.

Soysal, Coşkun, "The Stillborn Neo-Ottomanist Foreign Policy Aspiration of the Özal Era," Unpublished Doctoral Dissertation, Middle East Technical University, 2020.

Stein, Aaron, *Turkey's New Foreign Policy: Davutoğlu, the AKP, and the Pursuit of Regional Order* (London: Routledge, 2015).

Sunar, Burcu, *Adalet ve Kalkınma Partisi'nin Dış Politika Söyleminin Biçimlenmesinde Bir Etken Olarak Siyasi İlahiyat* (Ankara: İmaj Yayıncılık, 2014).

Sunar, Lütfi, *"İslam'ı Uyandırmak": Meşrutiyet'ten Cumhuriyet'e İslamcı Düşünce ve Dergiler* (two volumes) (Istanbul: İLEM, 2018).

Tapper, Richard, "Introduction" in Richard Tapper ed., *Islam in Modern Turkey* (London: I.B. Tauris, 1991).

Tarhanlı, İştar B., *Müslüman Toplum, "Laik" Devlet: Türkiye'de Diyanet İşleri Başkanlığı* (Istanbul: AFA, 1993).

Taşpınar, Ömer, *Kurdish Nationalism and Political Islam: Kemalist Identity in Transition* (New York: Routledge, 2005).

Taşpınar, Ömer, "The Old Turks' Revolt: When Radical Secularism Endangers Democracy," *Foreign Affairs* (Nov/Dec. 2007), pp. 114–130.

Taşpınar, Ömer, "Turkey's Middle East Policies: Between Neo-Ottomanism and Kemalism," Carnegie Endowment for International Peace Paper, October 2008.

Taşpınar, Ömer, "The Rise of Turkish Gaullism: Getting Turkish-American Relations Right," *Insight Turkey*, v. 13, no. 1 (Winter, 2011), pp. 11–17.

Taşpınar, Ömer, "Turkey's Strategic Vision and Syria," *Washington Quarterly*, Summer 2012.

Taşpınar, Ömer, "Turkey: The New Model?" in Robin Wright, ed. *The Islamists are Coming: Who They Really Are* (Washington DC: Woodrow Wilson Center Press, 2012).

Taşpınar, Ömer, "The Conflict Within Turkey's Islamic Camp," Istituto Affari Internazionali Research Report, November 2014.

Taşpınar, Ömer, "The Sultan and the Tsar: Turkey's Flirtation with Russia has a Long History," *Syndication Bureau*, August 16, 2019.

T.C. Başbakanlık Devlet Planlama Teşkilatı, *Milli Kültür: Özel İhtisas Komisyonu Raporu* (Ankara: Devlet Planlama Teşkilatı, 1983).

TC Dışişleri Bakanlığı, "Bahreyn'de Meydana Gelen Olaylar Hk." Statement No: 72, March 17, 2011.

TC Dışişleri Bakanlığı, "Dışişleri Bakanı Sayın Ahmet Davutoğlu'nun Türk Ocakları'nın Kuruluşunun 100. Yılını Kutlama Etkinlikleri Kapsamında Düzenlenen 'Büyük Türkiye'ye Doğru' Sempozyumunda Yaptığı Konuşma," March 26, 2011.

TC Dışişleri Bakanlığı, "Dışişleri Bakanı Sayın Ahmet Davutoğlu'nun Fas Dışişleri Bakanı Saad Eddine El Othmani ile Birlikte Katıldıkları 'Demokratik Dönüşüm ve Ortak Bölgesel Vizyon' Konulu Seta Panelinde Yaptığı Konuşma," March 19, 2012.

TC Dışişleri Bakanlığı, "Dışişleri Bakanı Ahmet Davutoğlu'nun 'Arap Uyanışı ve Ortadoğu'da Barış: Müslüman ve Hristiyan Perspektifler' Konferansı Kapsamında Yaptıkları Konuşma," September 7, 2012.

TC Dışişleri Bakanlığı, "Dışişleri Bakanı Sayın Ahmet Davutoğlu'nun Diyarbakır Dicle Üniversitesinde Verdiği 'Büyük Restorasyon: Kadim'den Küreselleşmeye Yeni Siyaset Anlayışımız' Konulu Konferans," March 15, 2013.

Tobakov, Igor, "Neo-Ottomanism versus Neo-Eurasianism?: Nationalism and Symbolic Geography in Postimperial Turkey and Russia," *Mediterranean Quarterly*, v. 28, no. 2 (June, 2017), pp. 125–145.

Tol, Gönül, "Turkey's End Game in Syria" *Foreign Affairs*, October 9, 2019.

Tol, Gönül, and Ömer Taşpınar, "Erdoğan's Turn to the Kemalists," *Foreign Affairs*, October 27, 2016.

Tuncel, Mustafa, *163. Madde Hakkinda Kesinleşmiş Kararlar* (Istanbul: Yeni Asya Yayınları, 1983).

Turam, Berna, "The politics of engagement between Islam and the secular state: ambivalences of 'civil society,'" *British Journal of Sociology*, v. 55, no. 2 (June, 2004), pp. 259–281.

Türköne, Mümtaz'er, "Siyasi İdeoloji Olarak İslamcılığın Doğuşu (1867–1873)," Unpublished Doctoral Dissertation, Ankara University, 1990.

Ucer, Murat, "Turkey's Economy: Now for the Hard Part," *Foreign Policy*, August 12, 2014.

Ulus, Özgür Mutlu, *The Army and the Radical Left in Turkey: Military Coups, Socialist Revolution and Kemalism* (London: I.B. Tauris, 2011).

Uzer, Ümit, *Identity and Turkish Foreign Policy* (New York: Palgrave Macmillan, 2011).

Uzgel, İlhan, and Bülent Duru eds., *AKP Kitabı: Bir Dönüşümün Bilançosu* (Ankara: Phoenix, 2009).

Ülgener, Sabri F., *İktisadi İnhitat Tarihimizin Ahlak ve Zihniyet Meseleleri* (Istanbul: Akgün Matbaası, 1951).

Ünal, Mustafa, "Volkan ve Mecmua-yı Ebu'z-Ziya Dergilerindeki Yahudilik ve Masonlukla İlgili Yazıların Dinler tarihi Açısından Değerlendirilmesi," in N.A., *Bütün Yönleriyle Yahudilik Uluslararası Sempozyum* (Ankara: Türkiye Dinler Tarihi Derneği, 2012).

Vali, Abbas, "The Making of the Kurdish Identity in Iran," *Critique: Critical Middle Eastern Studies*, v. 4, no. 7 (Fall, 1995), pp. 1–22.

Van Dijk, Teun A., *Ideology: A Multidisciplinary Approach* (London: Sage Publications, 1998).

Waldman, Simon, and Emre Çalışkan, *The New Turkey and its Discontents* (New York: Oxford University Press, 2017).

Walt, Stephen M, *The Origins of Alliances* (Ithaca: Cornell University Press, 1987).

Walt, Stephen M., *Revolution and War* (Ithaca: Cornell University Press, 1996).

Waltz, Kenneth N., *A Theory of International Politics* (Reading: Addison-Wesley, 1979).

Waltz, Kenneth N., "A Response to My Critics," in Robert Keohane, ed. *Neorealism and Its Critiques* (New York: Columbia University Press, 1986).

Wehrey, Frederic, Theodore W. Karasik, Alireza Nader, Jeremy Ghez, Lydia Hansell and Robert A. Guffey, *Saudi-Iranian Relations Since the Fall of Saddam: Rivalry, Cooperation and Implications for U.S. Policy* (Pittsburgh: RAND Cooperation, 2009).

Weiker, Walter, "Constitution-Making for Turkey's Third Republic," in Sabri M. Akural, ed. *Turkic Culture: Continuity and Change* (Bloomington: Indiana University Press, 1987).

Wendt, Alexander, *Social Theory of International Relations* (New York: Cambridge University Press, 1999).

White, Jenny B., *Islamist Mobilization in Turkey: A Study in Vernacular Politics* (Seattle: University of Washington Press, 2011).

Williams, William A., *The Tragedy of American Diplomacy* (Cleveland: World Publishing Company, 1959).

X [George F. Kennan], "Sources of Soviet Conduct," *Foreign Affairs*, v. 25, no. 4 (July, 1947): 566–582.

Yalvaç, Faruk, "Approaches to Turkish Foreign Policy: A Critical Realist Analysis," *Turkish Studies*, v. 15, no. 1 (March, 2014), pp. 117–138.

Yavuz, Hakan, "Turkish-Israeli Relations Through the Lens of the Turkish Identity Debate," *Journal of Palestine Studies*, v. XXXVII, no. 1 (Autumn, 1997), pp. 22–37.

Yavuz, Hakan, "Turkish Identity and Foreign Policy in Flux: The Rise of Neo-Ottomanism," *Critique: Critical Middle Eastern Studies*, v. 7, no. 12 (Spring, 1998), pp. 19–41.

Yavuz, Hakan, *Islamic Political Identity in Turkey* (New York: Oxford University Press, 2003).

Yavuz, Hakan, *Nostalgia for the Empire: The Politics of Neo-Ottomanism* (New York: Oxford University Press, 2020).

Yeğen, Mesut, "The Kurdish Peace Process in Turkey: Genesis, Evolution, and Prospects," Istituto Affari Internazionali Working Paper no. 11, May 2015.

Yeginsu, Ceylan, "ISIS Draws a Steady Stream of Recruits From Turkey," *The New York Times*, September 15, 2014.

Yeldan, A. Erinç, and Burcu Ünüvar, "An Assessment of the Turkish Economy in the AKP Era," *Research and Policy on Turkey*, v. 1, no. 1 (February, 2016), pp. 11–28.

Yetkin, Murat, *Tezkere: Irak Krizinin Gerçek Öyküsü* (Istanbul: Remzi Kitabevi, 2004).

Yorulmazlar, Emirhan, "The Role of Ideas in Turkish Foreign Policy: The JDP-Davutoğlu Paradigm and Its Role After 2002," Unpublished Doctoral Dissertation, Boğaziçi University, 2015.

Zalewski, Piotr, "How Turkey Went from Zero-Problems to Zero Friends," *Foreign Policy*, August 22, 2013.

Zengin, Gürkan, *Kavga: Arap Baharı'nda Türk Dış Politikası* (Istanbul: İnkilap, 2013).

Zürcher, Erik Jan, "The Vocabulary of Muslim Nationalism," *International Journal of the Sociology of Language*, v. 137 (1999), pp. 81–92.

INDEX

www.ingramcontent.com/pod-product-compliance
Lightning Source LLC
Chambersburg PA
CBHW030328270326
41926CB00010B/1549